VA

37X(12/68) 8/09
38X (4/10) 7/10
40X(12/10)9/11
42X(1/12) 8/12

D0045684

WITHDRAWN

ALSO BY SIMON DOONAN

Confessions of a Window Dresser

WACKY CHICKS

LIFE LESSONS FROM
FEARLESSLY INAPPROPRIATE
AND FABULOUSLY
ECCENTRIC WOMEN

SIMON DOONAN

SIMON & SCHUSTER

NEW YORK   LONDON   TORONTO   SYDNEY   SINGAPORE

SIMON & SCHUSTER
Rockefeller Center
1230 Avenue of the Americas
New York, NY 10020

For information regarding special discounts for bulk purchases,
please contact Simon & Schuster Special Sales at 1-800-456-6798
or business@simonandschuster.com

Designed by Lauren Simonetti

Manufactured in the United States of America

5   7   9   10   8   6   4

Library of Congress Cataloging-in Publication Data
Doonan, Simon.
Wacky chicks : life lessons from fearlessly inappropriate
and fabulously eccentric women / Simon Doonan.
p. cm.
1. Women—Biography. 2. Eccentrics and eccentricities—Biography.
3. Lifestyles. 4. Risk-taking (Psychology) 5. Clothing and dress.
6. Exoticism in fashion. I. Title: Eccentric women. II. Title.
HQ1123.D66   2003
305.4—dc21   2003041620

ISBN-0-7432-4341-2

FOR BETTY DOONAN

AND BETTY BADUM,

SLAG, NARG, GYPSY AND TAN,

LUCIANA AND GERLINDE

AND ROSE

WACKNOWLEDGMENTS

Huge, gushy bouquets of gratitude to all the wacky chicks who patiently endured my endless probing.

Additional effusive thanks to the hordes of behind-the-scenes wacky chicks whose idiosyncratic ways and reckless encouragement fueled my enthusiasm for the subject, including Amy and Cynthia Adler, Nell Campbell, Imogen Claire, Joyce Eliason, Jessy Eliason-Cirolia, Meredith Etherington-Smith, Patricia Field, Henny Garfunkel, Gill Griffiths, Andrea King, Debbie Little, Peggy Moffitt, Ann Ogden, Linda O'Keeffe, Gay Sandler, Deb Schwartz, L'Wren Scott, Isabel Toledo, Jackie Tyrel. Extra thanks to Deborah Hayes.

Everyone at Barneys, especially Howard Socol, Doug Teitelbaum, David Strumwasser, Dawn Brown, Judy Collinson, Tom Kalendarian, Karl Hermans, Suzi Jones, Dave New, Bettina O'Neill, Matt Reed, Mark Vitulano, Philip Johnson and Clara Lopez, and Julie Gilhart (thanks for Isabel).

Thanks to Peter Kaplan and Alexandra Jacobs at the *New York Observer*.

Everyone at Stila, especially Jeanine Lobell—a major wacky chick.

Sincere homage to all the right-on chicks and blokes at Simon & Schuster, especially my editor, Amanda Murray.

Thanks to Tanya McKinnon (gorgeous agent) and James Adams (fab lawyer, also gorgeous).

Lastly, a butch shout-out to wacky blokes Thomas Beeton, Joe Gaffney, Tony Langoria, Todd Oldham, John Pappas, David Rakoff, and very importantly, Danny Evans and Mark Welsh, and most ultra-importantly, Terry Doonan, Jonny Adler and Liberace Adler-Doonan.

If the goal of Women's Liberation was to create a world where the sisters could do whatever the hell they wanted, then the wacky chick *must surely be the screeching apotheosis of feminist achievement.* Non?

CONTENTS

INTRODUCTION

AN UPRISING OF
GLAMOROUS OUTSIDERS

"Life's a banquet, and most poor suckers are starving to death!"

Auntie Mame

We've done something silly.

In our fevered quest to find gurus and role models to admire and look up to, we have not always looked in the best places. In the 1980s, for example, a collective screechy hysteria infected popular culture, and everybody rashly decided that movie actors were really, really, really important. During this recklessly superficial period, they, the movie actors, became the icons of our age. No, we didn't pick useful people like brain surgeons, firemen or coffee shop waitresses. We chose show-biz folk. And then we sat there like puddings and inhaled all this drivel about the supposedly squintingly brilliant glam lives of these celebs, and we actually started to believe the hype. And gradually by the 1990s, we strove to live vicariously through them. If only we could be one-millionth as fabulous as Julia or Nicole or even Linda Hunt!

Movie actors reciprocated this adulation by becoming progressively more self-important. They started to refer to their own bodies as their "instruments." On podiums and red carpets from London to Burbank, they lost no opportunity to share heartfelt, irony-free observations about each other's "interesting choices" and about the "courage" it takes to "build a body of work."

Acting was once thought of as a simpleton's profession. In ancient Rome, actors were held in the same esteem as hookers and shoplifters. At best acting was a grown-up version of "let's pretend": that's why child actors never need acting lessons. By the 1990s acting had become a "craft" and actresses now referred to themselves as "actors."

Though unfortunate, this pretentious buffoonery is all fairly harmless. And thankfully the celebs all look quite delightful in the free drag, which they receive from Giorgio Armani and others. But now, nearly twenty years later, aren't you starting to question the whole notion just a tidgy bit? Shouldn't we expect a bit more from our cultural icons than good looks, the ability to keep their weight down and a talent for showing up on a movie set on time? Shouldn't we, instead, be worshipping people like Isabel Garrett?

If we have this burning desire to deify somebody or other, why didn't we pick Miss Garrett? Busty, coquettish Isabel is so infinitely more worthy of our idolatry than Gwyneth or Halle or even Dame Judi.

Who the hell is Isabel Garrett?

For starters, Isabel is a free bird. She's a skip-along, go-anywhere kind of a gal who is a total dab hand at maneuvering a motor home, which isn't really surprising, since she spends most of the year driving around the U.S. in a rather large one. She stops occasionally and sets up shop at the swinger conventions and biker rallies, where she sells her fetish-wear. This mobile *maison de la mode* is the nerve center of Body Webs, the slashed-and-sexy-spandex business that Ms. Garrett has operated since the early 1990s.

I first became aware of Isabel when an intuitive colleague drew my attention to a piquant write-up about Body Webs in *Women's Wear Daily*. I tracked Isabel down, to a nudist colony.

When not peddling her wares at Dressing for Pleasure or at the Lifestyle Convention in Las Vegas, she parks at the Cypress Cove Nudist Resort in Kissimmee, Florida. She's been a go-go dancer and a follower of Ayn Rand. Oh, and did I mention her white-hot, meteoric rise to prominence in the toy industry, where she gained notoriety as the creator of the acclaimed Whoopsie Doll?

Isabel is a multifaceted, untamed supervixen powered by an uncensored, unfettered creative energy, which could and frequently does blow the toupee/chest-wig off even the most adhesive-conscious swinger. Isabel is one of a new breed of women. Isabel is a wacky chick.

Who are the wacky chicks? And what makes this new breed of insurgent revolutionaries tick? Gird up your loins, stiffen the sinews, paint your wagon and summon the blood, because you're about to find out.

Wacky chicks are a burgeoning and highly entertaining phenomenon. Wacky chicks will change the world. Wacky chicks dare to annoy. Wacky chicks empower themselves and others without acting like blokes. Wacky chicks are having more fun than most regular chicks and all men, except maybe gay men. Wacky chicks are disapproval-immune. Wacky chicks are like grown-up Eloises. Wacky chicks are belligerent, resilient, uninhibited, naughty, creative and hilarious—i.e., wacky chicks are B.R.U.N.C.H.

When I first encountered Isabel, I was bowled over by her reckless individuality. When they made old Izzy, they definitely broke the mold—or did they? Gradually I found I was meeting more and more of these over-the-top broads. Was I witnessing a trend? Almost overnight, I found it was impossible to leave the house without running into obstreperous, fishnet-wearing, nonconformist, often stylish and not infrequently foulmouthed females: Brigid Berlin, the former Warhol muse, who divides her time between scarfing down Key lime pies, cruising round Manhattan in a chauffeured limo with her pugs and making paintings with her ample breasts; abortion activist and vintage-clothing maven Sunny Chapman, who successfully vanquished out swarms of bees from under her dirndl skirt while working as a mead wench at Renaissance fairs; celebrity hypnotist Jessica Porter, who produced and performed in the world's first macrobiotic dinner-theater productions; photographer and Tom Ford–muse Lisa Eisner, who is obsessed with what she has dubbed "geezer chic." This mother of two drives around Bel Air in a ragtop, sleazeball Cadillac dressed in Sammy Davis's old clothes.

Performers too: *Strangers with Candy* star Amy Sedaris, who has decorated her apartment like a woodland glade to appease her pet rabbit, Tattle-tail; Pearl Harbour, the rockabilly queen and former stripper who has always exuded a burlesque 1950s glamour, even when she was living in a storage locker. And women of color like Audrey Smaltz, who fought for her civil rights alongside Martin Luther King. Her weapons? A chinchilla chubby and a mascara wand.

I decided to study this new and terrifyingly fabulous phenomenon.

Locating and interviewing wacky chicks turned out to be relatively easy. Most of these divas have a healthy dose of exhibitionism: for the price of a Kahlúa 'n' cream the average w.c. could usually be prevailed upon to spill her guts and even a few beauty tips. And were they fun, or what!

Wacky chicks are entertainingly diverse—socioeconomically and personality-wise—but they have one thing in common: they are all blowing a giant raspberry at society's expectations. And, most important, they're getting away with it. And there are legions of them: Isabel, as it turned out, had just been the tip of an estrogen-infused, and often quite entrepreneurial, iceberg.

I started to consider the possibility that wacky chicks might not be such a new phenomenon. Since biblical times the critical eyes of conventional folk have forced many a Mary Magdalene type to hide the throbbing disco light of her electric personality under a bushel. History is littered with the corpses of these risk-taking funsters. Burnt at the stake, or eaten by wolves while doing interpretive dancing in the woods, the wacky chicks of yore were often victimized horribly for their kooky ways. If they weren't driven to suicide or absinthe, they were, like disgraced British poofters, sent to live somewhere like Morocco where they took to opiates and inflicted nasty disinhibited adult behaviors on the locals.

Eager to put these girls up where they belong, I profiled a few w.c.'s in my weekly column in the *New York Observer*. The response was dramatic. These strutting eccentrics seemed to have a universal resonance for both my male and female readers. The more deranged they were, the more my readers responded to them. There was only one conclusion to be drawn: it seemed as if the whole female population was ready to support, if not join, this anarchic fringe movement and confront the utter pointlessness of our celebrity-obsessed culture.

Engorged with motivation, I vowed to write a book in celebration of these self-invented tempestuous viragos. I wanted to find out what made these chicks tick. What kind of gasoline were they pumping into their flame-emblazoned tanks? I resolved to learn the magical recipe and share it with the women of the world.

As I truffled and researched, my enthusiasms waxed: in fact I developed a verging-on-inappropriate obsession with these gals. The shriek and yodel of their personalities was a haunting and irresistible siren call for *moi*. I soon found I could spot a wacky chick at fifty paces and invariably tune into her wavelength. My impulse is always to rush toward her and validate the crap out of her wackiness: e.g., "I don't care what they're saying about you—I think you're just great!"

What was fueling this growing obsession? Why did these wacky chicks seem so eerily familiar? It didn't take Sigmund Freud or Ann Landers to figure it out. A cursory survey of my formative years held the answer. You see, dear reader, I was raised by a wacky chick—my arch and hilariously contrarian mother—and I guess I was looking for what caring people like Ricki Lake and Oprah call . . . *Closure.*

Martha Elizabeth Doonan, née Gordon, was born in Northern Ireland in 1918 (the year that British women over thirty got the vote) with a fantastic set of genes. Her mother made hats with birds and fruit on them. Her dad assisted a local interior decorator. But no nelly he: Guinness and off-track betting were his hobbies. From her parents she inherited creativity, joie de vivre and belligerence.

Martha, or Betty as she preferred to be called, left school at fourteen in search of a job that matched her aptitudes, and found it, butchering pigs for a local grocery store chain. By the time war broke out, sassy, quick-witted Betty (it's pronounced "Byaaaatteyh" in Belfast) was second in command. But, determined to "do her bit," she joined the Royal Air Force and became a leading aircraft electrician. Byaaaatteyh, the riveter, was frequently the only woman in a hangar filled with thousands of horny, uncouth males—but she always demanded, and received, respect. Snaps from the time reveal an archetypal 1940s broad: strong, Jewish features (she claimed to be descended from one of the lost tribes of Israel), upswept hair, overpainted Joan Crawford lips, suede platforms and a great pair of legs (which I inherited) encased in sheer seamed stockings.

After the war, she applied for a job at the Huntley & Palmers biscuit factory and was told she would be paid less because she was Irish. Needless to say, she told them where they could shove their chocolate-coated digestives. Undaunted, Betty eventually bluffed her way into the editorial news department of the British Broadcasting Corporation. She held her own for more than twenty years alongside many Oxbridge grads. Like all wacky chicks, she actively cultivated forthright, prejudiced opinions on all subjects and she hosed other people with them, regularly.

Here are a few of the less offensive ones:

- Short people are better balanced emotionally than tall people are.
- Cigarettes are O.K. [she smoked enthusiastically her whole life with no ill effects], but white sugar is white death. Throw it out!
- South-facing rooms must be blue; north-facing rooms must be orange or coral.
- Kittenish behavior will get you pregnant.
- English people are dreary. Jews and Scots are fabulous without exception.
- French and Italians are sleazy.
- Seamed stockings, always.
- Frilly nighties are grotesque and make you look as if you are recovering from a hysterectomy or playing the part of a deranged Tennessee Williams heroine. Pajamas! Pajamas! Pajamas!
- The neighbors are *ordinaire*.
- Not everybody is beautiful—make the best of what you've got and don't get fat.
- Childbirth doesn't hurt unless you are a whiny person.
- Roses are mumsy; gladioli are beautiful.
- Mother's Day is for morons.

On the latter matter, Betty was always very specific: She wanted *nothing!* She found Mother's Day patronizing and demeaning, her theory being that acknowledging her magnificence annually on one paltry day amounted to nothing less than ungenerous tokenism. We always gave in without a fight because Betty was always right. Like all wacky chicks, Betty hated to lose an argument: she would hurl bogus statistics at her opponents and preface her observations with the phrase "California researchers have shown that . . ." Yes, mater was unusual, and that's where the dreaded *Closure* comes in.

At the age of eight I suddenly became aware that Betty was not like the other women on our street: in the 1950s the average British housewife did not ride a white bicycle down the middle of the High Street while smoking a Woodbine and wearing rubber high-heeled galoshes with glitter flecks in them. "Your mum is strange," hectored my fascistic little playmates, igniting a priggish conformist spark in me. I temporarily succumbed to the cringe-inducing censures of my peers and craved a more conventional parent. My mum's splashy dirndls, cleavage-enhancing bustiers and overpainted lip-line became an embarrassment to me.

Then, out of the blue, weird things started happening to me: I found myself staring intently, and longingly, at my scoutmaster's hairy legs and, when my mum was out at work, staring intently at my mum's galoshes . . . on my feet! I was exhibiting—albeit only to myself—all the early signs of an enthusiastic cross-dresser. I fought these disquieting impulses for a few months and then gave up. By the age of ten I knew that I too was different and that my mum and I had more in common than a penchant for Woodbines. We were *Glamorous*

Outsiders whose unconventional tendencies incurred the small-minded censure of the less vivacious folk who surrounded us. My wacky chick obsession results from a deep-seated need to establish that—contrary to popular belief—it's O.K. to be different. In fact, it is positively preferable and really rather fab.

By the time I hit my teens, I decided I wanted be a woman. Not like my mum—that would be too Norman Batesish and creepy. No, I wanted to be a dolly bird. It was during the 1960s. How totally fab it would be—or so thought my cheery, wholesome teenage brain—to iron my hair and wear top 'n' bottom lashes à la Twiggy, and to buy all my clothes at Mary Quant and Biba, and to subjugate myself to a member of the Rolling Stones. How pacey and mod! A gorgeous and stupid knock-kneed fashion model, that's me! Just like Pattie Boyd or Chrissie Shrimpton. I wouldn't eat much. I'd drink Pimm's, giggle a lot and get shagged by Brian Jones. *Pas mal.*

I lost those inclinations when, in the late sixties, the dingbat dolly birds turned into earth-mother hippies. One look at those caftan-wearing, joint-rolling, tofu-stroganoff-baking Mama Cass look-alikes—the female hippies did all the schlepping and housework—and my transgenderish yearnings soured like bong water. Trina and the other Ladies of the Canyon would have to stave off their munchies and thread their wampum beads without my complicity.

In the 1970s I finally became a woman, sort of. And so did every bloke. Glam rock arrived and turned us chaps, both gay and straight, into feather-boa-totin' poseurs. We upstaged any adjacent chicks: remember Angie Bowie? No? I'm not surprised. Nobody was looking at her while Ziggy Stardust was mincing about. *Quel* draggy era for women! And things were about to get a lot worse.

In the 1980s men became men again but so, unfortunately, did women. This era saw the arrival of the pseudo-empowered, having-it-all chick: Alexis Carrington without the estrogen/glamour . . . i.e., a young Hillary Clinton . . . i.e., an all time low. Women with names like Brooke donned Dacron suits and tie-necked blouses and lashed themselves into an overachieving frenzy—all in the name of equality. How naff!

To fulfill herself, Brooke snagged a hubby and kids and a shiny Volvo and she worked like a dog/bitch to optimize her multifaceted, increasingly fraught self. Poor cow. Brooke took on all the really dorkiest aspects of being a bloke—e.g., corporate ambition—and kept all the tragic drudgery of womanhood. Egged on by people like Naomi Wolf, Brooke eschewed feminine allure so as not to be manipulated into buying lots of cosmetics or something like that. And she did it all willingly and with great fervor, while wearing shoulder pads, Reeboks, "scrunch" socks and panty hose!

Now almost two decades later, Brooke's shagged-out Volvo has rusted, and she's driving it, muffler dragging, into the sunset of her exhausted Zoloft-fueled middle age . . . alone, because her turd of a husband has traded her in for some fresh crumpet. She peers through the bug-splattered windshield of her life looking for a welcoming hostelry. There isn't one. The sun is setting: the glare is refracting through a thousand specks of grunge and it's obscuring her vision. Watch out! Oncoming traffic! Ohmygod! There's a big motor home hurtling toward her from the opposite direction. It's Isabel! Look out!!!!! Aaaaaah!!!!

Brooke doesn't know it yet but she has just collided with salvation. It's not too late to tear off that teal, 100 percent Dacron, tie-necked blouse and start living again and Isabel will happily show her how.

Brooke, while you're exchanging driver's licenses, take a long hard look at Isabel. She's totally B.R.U.N.C.H. and she's having a blast. And—*bonjour,* girls!—Isn't that what feminism is supposed to be all about. If the goal of Women's Liberation was to create a world where the sisters could do whatever the hell they wanted, then the *wacky chick* must surely be the screeching apotheosis of feminist achievement. *Non?* Could it be that, after nearly half a century of ridicule and false starts, feminism has, without fanfare, finally achieved its goal? Germaine, Kate, Gloria, Susan, congrats, it was all worth it—unconditional emancipation has arrived at last, and she's barreling down Route 66 in a mobile home on her way to a biker convention. Mazel tov!

Filled with missionary zeal, I reevaluated my concept: this book wasn't just a bunch of kooky case histories. This was a book that would unleash the wacky chick in every woman. This was about *Liberation.*

A fully actualized wacky chick is invincible. She throbs with passion, ambition and creativity. She is, above all, a participant in life, not a spectator, and, just like Auntie Mame, she's grabbing life by the balls. Anyone who tries to rain on her parade will be beaten into submission with her unique brand of chutzpah, bravery and street smarts. Our movie actor gods, upon whose every word we collectively hang, pale in comparison.

Regarding celebs: There is a secret community of wacky chicks in the movie industry. They are extremely closeted and their publicists are making sure they stay that way. These irritating gatekeepers are always poised and waiting with a gag in case their allotted celeb says something revealing or interesting.

In sharp contrast to today's withholding celebs, my girls exhibit a willingness to share the good, the bad and the ugly. The wacky chicks whose lives fill the following pages are fabulously generous and uninhibited when it comes to divulging every aspect of their lives. They give, give, and give. They are compelling and fabulous and entertaining and infinitely more deserving of a private jet than John Travolta.

So study the lives, mores, views and tenets of these, the most insane women in America. Marvel at their kooky ways and their unorthodox lifestyles. Worship at the temple of their irreverence.

Caution! Rule breakers tend to be a tidgy bit narcissistic and w.c.'s are no exception. You will resonate with some more than others, depending on your own hang-ups and inklings. In making my selection of wacky chicks, I tried to gather a democratic cross section. There are no bankers or politicians, though, honesty compels me to admit, I did toy with calling Janet Reno.

Many of my wacky chicks are from the world of fashion, which has always had a high tolerance for loud and proud women. There are, I hasten to add, no fashion victims. All of my girls (sorry if I'm starting to sound like Miss Jean Brodie) are testaments to the ultimate unimportance of dictatorial fashion and the totally raging importance of developing your own unique style. Personal style is the missile defense system of the wacky chick, and all of my chicks have it in bucket-loads.

I have tried to immerse you in their machinations and show you how they live, love and laugh at life: how they earn a living, how they got to be so wacky, how they glue on their lashes in the morning and how they tear them off at night. My hope is that these glamorous outsiders will entertain you and, collectively, they will incite you to unleash all the unorthodox impulses that are no doubt lurking under your blouse. At the very least I hope you get a few laughs, cringe occasionally and acquire a styling tip or two. For those of you who already have a dab of glitter in your galoshes, I hope my w.c.'s will inspire you to greater excesses of strident glamorous originality.

WACKY
CHICKS

CHAPTER 1

THE LADIES WHO ARE OUT TO LUNCH . . . OR B.R.U.N.C.H.

THE BELLIGERENT, RESILIENT, UNINHIBITED, NAUGHTY, CREATIVE AND HILARIOUS SPIDER FAWKE

To say Spider Fawke is a wacky chick is horribly inaccurate. She is *the* wacky chick.

When Barbara Walters latches on to this emerging phenomenon and decides that she is going to devote a *20/20* segment to wacky chicks, old Babs need look no further than Spider. She is the *ne plus ultra* . . . the archetype . . . the paradigwacky chick. The defining elements of wacky chickery are, in Spider Jane Fawke, mixed to perfection. Belligerent, resilient, uninhibited, naughty, creative and hilarious, Spider is the B.R.U.N.C.H.-iest benchmark against which all wacky chicks must be measured.

Miss Fawke lives with a staggering range of lizards—thirty-eight in all—and a four-inch tarantula (*Aphonopelma chalcodes*) in a six-hundred-square-foot one-bedroom apartment in the San Fernando Valley. Her prized possession, Queen Isabella, a five-and-a-half-foot-long iguana (*Iguana iguana*), was peering out of the kitchen window and twitching ominously when I arrived *chez* Spider.

1

"The neighbors don't seem to care. Personally speaking, if I saw a gigantic orange Honduran iguana peering out of the window of my neighbor's house I would have a few questions," says Spider laconically, as we embark upon a tour of her suburban menagerie.

First we visit the smallest of Spider's reptiles, a tiny gecko from Iraq (*Tropiocolotes tripolitanus*) that measures a poignant inch and a half. She has several species of American gecko—*Coleonyx variegatus, Coleonyx bogerti* and *Coleonyx brevis,* to name three—of which she is inordinately fond. "I like them because they have eyelashes and are capable of all kinds of expressions like laughing or scorn, as in 'You dumb cunt, that cricket is far too big for me to eat.'"

Spider's other faves are her *Phelsumas* from Madagascar "because of their intense green, blue, turquoise color variations. They really are living jewels." As we continue our tour, I soon realize that it's not all batting eyelashes and gorgeous iridescent hues here at Spider's reptile house. "Here's my *Phelsuma madagascariensis grandis,*" says Spider warily, "he's a giant day gecko, seven to eight inches long. His name is O.J. because he's killed two females and now has to live alone because I can't stand picking up the shredded bodies."

Forty-eight-year-old Spider's Dr. Dolittle–ish apartment also contains hundreds of insects—mostly crickets and mealworms—that will all eventually find their way into the gizzards of her lizards. Miss Fawke informs me that she herself has partaken of such crunchy fare. It was a few years back. She was designing a range of cashmere sweaters for the Japanese fashion house Hanae Mori and had gone to China to check on production. "I bought them from a street vendor—they were fried and they looked like peanuts. I'll eat anything within reason," chuckles Spider convincingly before continuing her riveting tour. "These two monarch geckos I call the Kray Twins. They're from Asia and these little fuckers can really bite." Their keeper never handles them without keeping her spray bottle of culinary brandy close by: "a couple of squirts and they soon let go."

As I watch her feeding grubs to her peacock day gecko (*Phelsuma quadriocellata*), I cannot help but marvel at the tour de force that is Spider Fawke. This termagant is every bit as striking as her terrifying iguana, and, at six feet two, she's eight inches longer lying down.

If Egon Schiele had painted Jamie Lee Curtis, the result would resemble Spider. If Virginia Woolf had posed for Munch's *Scream*, the result might have recalled our Miss Fawke. Quintessentially *jolie-laide*, Spider has a long striking face, sunken cheeks, a puckery mouth and a regal nose. Despite years in the fashion business, Spider is not prissy about her appearance: Her hair is cut like a choirboy's, her mouth is adorned with "a smidgen of lippie" and her occasionally manicured nails glow with slightly chipped frosted-pink nail varnish. "I throw on a bit of Aveda mascara for special occasions like when the Queen Mother died," concedes Spider as she tosses a strawberry at a haughty, ungrateful Queen Isabella.

Her unusual appearance is not, however, a qualifying component of her wacky-chickery. Though most wacky chicks have tsunamis of idiosyncratic personal style, so does everyone else . . . nowadays. We live in a treacherous world where everyone has incorporated an alternative, exhibitionist esprit into his or her self-presentation. Flip through a few magazines, channel surf for a few moments, walk down your local Main Street and then try to tell me the world hasn't started to resemble the party scene from Russ Meyer's 1970 movie *Beyond the Valley of the Dolls*. In his movies (I also recommend *Beneath the Valley of the Ultra-Vixens* and *Faster Pussycat! Kill! Kill!*), pervy, unsung film director Russ predicted the world we are living in with shocking accuracy: The guys are violent hypermasculine dudes or Mansonesque hippie dirtbags. The women are equally extreme: ghoulish middle-aged swingers, hippie-dippy acidheads and voracious man-pleasers with massive "industry"-sized hooters abound. Freaks, hippies, hoods and strippers—welcome to your World! But are the freaks really freaks?

Time was when alternatively sensibilitied folk could spot one another on the street, salute each other's eccentricities and then flit off somewhere together to perform one of several illegal acts. Now everyone looks like a marginalized freak, and even the dreariest people have misleadingly transgressive trappings: colored hair, piercings and tattoos. How far off is the day when Katie Couric has shrunken heads hanging from her nipple rings?

This democratization of freakiness has made wacky-chick spotting quite tricky. You cannot judge a w.c. by her cover. The visual cues, which formerly signified eccentricity, have been co-opted by the masses who are, incidentally, getting progressively more massive. To put it bluntly, we in the Western world are getting fatter and more groovy. Based on these parallel trends, it is safe to assume that in the future the world will be peopled entirely by gargantuan fashion exhibitionists. Come back to the 5 and Dime, Mama Cass, Mama Cass.

But I digress. Back to the present, and that all-important wacky-chick definition. To understand what it means to be a wacky chick, we must take a long hard look at Spider. To understand Spider, we must dissect the elements that define her wacky-chickery. We must go beyond the valley of her appearance and beneath the ultranarrative of her extraordinary life.

B Is for Belligerent

A streak of feistiness—a soupçon of Genghis Kahn—is as vital to a wacky chick as a good pair of heels. A dab of truculence gives her the wherewithal to deal with the challenging situations and people that come with the wacky territory. It's healthy too: belligerence allows a wacky chick to divest herself of frustrations and aggressions that, if left to fester internally, might turn nasty inside her, like old yogurt. Externalizing the occasional hostility is nothing new: *men have been doing it for centuries—that's why they're less neurotic than women!*

Spider once tried to throttle a woman.

"I was working in Paris for Maison Dorothée Bis—very fem, very girly. Not me at all. We worked in and around a disused swimming pool in the Sixth Arrondissement on Boulevard Raspail. The design rooms were all up with the diving boards—which were still there. The pool was drained. That's where we did shipping and receiving and production."

The attempted throttling of the owner, a Mademoiselle Jacobson, took place after a fashion show. "I had worked like a dog, and she didn't want to pay me for some overtime. I grabbed her by the throat and threatened to toss her into the deep end." Spider's stratagem worked like a dream: she got her check and vamped toward the exit.

Not all wacky chicks have Spider's physical advantage: those who don't are usually adept at dispensing a good old-fashioned don't-fuck-with-me-fellahs tongue-lashing. And why not? Without the ability to stick up for herself in a contretemps, a wacky chick cannot reach maturity, nor can she defend her wacky ways. Without it Spider might not have survived.

Spider was born Jane Fawke, the illegitimate daughter of Dorothy Fawke, in 1954, in the grim carpet-manufacturing town of Kidderminster, England.

Spider and her mother eeked out an existence on nine pounds a week social security. "We were the equivalent of white trash, but we were spotlessly clean," she insists with the guttural accent of the Midlands over a cup of steaming decaf tea. Despite the fastidiousness, Spider's childhood saga is pervaded by a Dickensian aroma. Stench might be a better word.

B Is Also for Bastard

Miss Fawke was never officially notified of her father's identity. "I have a suspicion who he was," she recalls. "One time I wanted money to buy a dress to wear to the annual Kidderminster Whitsun holiday parade—how tragic is that!? And my mum dragged me to some bloke's house to ask for the money and he chased us away with a shotgun. I think that was probably me dad." Being a bastard in 1950s Kidderminster was no Pollyanna picnic.

At age eleven, Spider's burgeoning belligerence was jump-started by some really gnarly bullying. "I was so funny looking—my nickname was Pencil. I really worked hard at school because I knew if I was the best I could get out. I was already six feet tall—I was conspicuous," recalls our heroine without self-pity, "and the didicois on our street used to beat me up."

Didicois, for the uninitiated readers (which would hopefully include as many of you as possible), are gypsies who have ditched their caravans and managed to get themselves into houses. "They had loads of old cars. They were inbred. They had one ear and two fingers, and very mismatched printed clothes—very Comme des Garçons," adds Spider, making an incongruously upbeat reference to the Japanese avant-garde fashion house.

R Is for Resilient

During the course of her lifetime, a wacky chick is subjected to twice as many hideous occurrences and fetid situations as a regular chick. Being a wacky chick—as opposed to a regular chick—is the difference between being strapped to Kermit's head when he floats around Columbus Circle on the morning of the Macy's Thanksgiving Day Parade or being a mere spectator thereof. She's visible, she's out there and if anyone is going to be hit by a rotten tomato, it's the wacky chick. Without bucket-loads of resilience, her wackiness will quickly be eroded by the vicissitudes and decaying veggies of life.

Wacky chicks like our Miss Fawke develop their resilience early on. The typical wacky-chick childhood is often fraught with "character building" challenges, but Spider's was grimmer than most.

Her mother, Dorothy, was a raving hypochondriac. "The doctor gave Mum sugar pills every week to get her out of his office," recalls Spider. Apparently some of Dorothy's hypochondria was justified: she succumbed to heart failure when Spider was fifteen, taking the secret of her only daughter's paternity with her. Spider's dog, Como, died a week after her mother, and then Spider was sent to live with her brother and sister-in-law. "They hated me," recalls Spider undramatically.

Miss Fawke's early years were not entirely hideous: there were a few brightish spots. Before she "popped her clogs,"* Dorothy gave Spider something valuable and life changing. "She sat me down and taught me to read," recalls Spider, sounding genuinely grateful. "I learnt to read from all those kids' books which were filled with darkies and golliwogs— very un-p.c. But it changed my life—I was totally ADD and reading calmed me down. These kids today should learn to read instead of taking Ritalin." Spider takes a gulp of tea and draws a breath as her topic gathers momentum. "But today nobody wants to be the disciplinarian—oh no!—and they're

---

*Regional slang for meeting one's maker; see also "kicked the bucket" and "fell off the perch."

totally scared of their own kids. If they would only take the time to . . ." An impassioned rant on this theme follows.

This is classic wacky-chick behavior. Wacky chicks are always armed with an array of contentious diatribes, which they will unleash upon anyone who will listen. Here's another of Spider's pet peeves: "I hate people who walk round town with lizards on their shoulders. How would you like it if I stuck you on a polar ice cap and surrounded you with polar bears? That would be a bit stressful, wouldn't it?" The assorted hot buttons that polka-dot the w.c. psyche are part and parcel of that vital resilience. They provide healthy therapeutic outlets for the accumulated ire that is as intrinsic to the wacky chick as a good pair of fishnets or a pet iguana.

The rant eventually subsides and Spider returns to her lugubrious childhood. The avid reading cultivated Miss Fawke's mind: she seemed destined for a good, solid English education and with it the possibility of a didicoi-free middle-class future. But it just wasn't in the cards. Fate intervened, or didn't, depending on your perspective. "My mum took one look at the list of stuff we had to buy—uniform, gym-slips and sporting stuff—and saw that we couldn't afford it. So I didn't even take the tests."

Despite the lack of education, Spider's curiosity and enthusiasm thrived, once again thanks to Mum. Egged on by this struggling single parent, Spider became a total animal nut. Her favorite book was Gerald Durrell's *My Family and Other Animals*, in which the author's family trades in the rain and didicois of England for the flora and fauna of sunny Corfu. "I couldn't believe it," recalls Spider, clutching a stack of battered Durrell paperbacks. "They had lizards running through their living room. How fab is that?"

Spider's mum, Dorothy, encouraged her animal fetishisms because it kept her at home and out of trouble. "I had thirty-five pets—dogs, cats, birds—and my brother was a bird nut. He still wins prizes for his canaries. He breeds the ones with the little caps." The pièce de résistance of the Fawke petting zoo was a cockerel, which Spider taught to show-jump round her bedroom over piles of books.

One day Spider spotted a comma butterfly (*Polygonia satyrus*) in a nearby gravel pit. An amateur entomologist at the Kidderminster library excitedly told her it was "a first for Kiddy." Spotting that butterfly is the misty and symbolic part of the Spider movie where everything goes into Technicolor and the Henry Mancini soundtrack soars. Like her comma, Spider was a rare thing of beauty stuck in a wretched gravel pit, but she had the resilience and creativity that is the foundation of all wacky chicks. Just like that butterfly, she was dancing her way up to the rim, and freedom.

(TECHNICOLOR FADES—BUT SOUNDTRACK ADOPTS A MORE SKIP-ALONG TONE)

When it came time to go to technical college, Spider faced a dilemma. "I was a good drawer and gardener so my art teacher, Mrs. Hamblin, and my biology teacher, Jackie Garland, were both pushing me to choose between art and farming colleges." "Would I rather be on a tractor in a snowstorm," thought Spider, "or smoking pot with Mick Jagger?"

Mick won, but art school was "full of brainiacs," so Spider switched to fashion at Hoo Road Technical College, which wasn't exactly the Bauhaus, but here Spider found her second grand passion. "Tailoring was magical to me, it was something that clicked. Fabric and yarn are flat and yet you can create something which moves round the body. You can take an old bit of calico and make something beautiful out of it," recalls Spider, who now found herself the center of attention. Suddenly people weren't calling her names; instead, fellow students were asking her if they could try out their designs on her. "I was a beanpole with no tits. I made friends and soon I was getting shit-faced at the Friday night discos."

U Is for Uninhibited

There are already far too many wonderful, thoughtful, reserved, prissy women in the world and not enough stink-bomb hurlers. Taboo-busting sisters who are capable of rash and impulsive behavior oil the wheels of culture, pop and otherwise. By giving themselves carte blanche to act like jackasses—as men do—and then forgive themselves, they achieve the highest level of emancipation.

It was at technical college that Pencil became Spider: "I was a pioneer of miniskirts. I loved to flaunt me legs. I was six feet two inches and weighed seven stone. I pranced into my art class, all dolled up in thigh boots, red-and-purple-striped sleeveless skinny-rib turtleneck 100-percent acrylic minidress, and this girl, Linda Sheppard, who became, and still is, a great friend, screamed out in her best Kiddy accent: '*Yow looks loike a bleedin' spoider, don't yow?*'" Pencil evaporated and Spider embraced her sassy new identity.

This talented tarantula munched her way up the college food chain and ended up in the Fashion and Textile Department ("the butch printmakers called us 'fascists and reptiles'") of the illustrious Royal College of Art, all courtesy of Her Majesty's Government. Her talent had taken her far away from the didicois to the alma mater of many of British fashion's greats, some of whom have, coincidentally, been known to dress like didicois: Ossie Clark, Celia Birtwell, Zandra Rhodes, Bill Gibb and Jean Muir, to name but a few.

N Is for Naughty

The cheeky charm of a well-timed practical joke or a boob flash leavens the belligerence found in all wacky chicks. Naughtiness can diffuse tensions, both domestic and international: if being naughty were part of every U.N. agenda, it's hard to imagine there being any more global conflicts.

I ask Spider to regale me with tales of the *jeunesse dorée* of her particular year at this internationally known breeding ground for fashion talent. "There was nobody fabulous. I was in the same year as the Emanuels—those two pretentious cunts who made Princess Diana's wedding dress," responds Spider with the charming bluntness so intrinsic to the wacky-chick persona. "When we had our final-year show," recalls Spider with a disdainful lip curl, "they rented furs and dogs and jewels and God knows what to upstage everyone else."

(Regarding the c word: I am saddened by the American prohibition against the use of this centuries-old conversation-spicer-upper. The best thing about visiting England is hearing the word "cunt" thrown around with jolly Chaucerian abandon. In fact "cunt" is so commonly used in the U.K. as to make it comparable to such innocuous American expressions as "dipshit" or "dickwad."

When I immigrated to the U.S. in the late 1970s, my expletives were often met with astonished faces. It took me several years of living here to moderate "cunt" out of my vocabulary, and I must confess to missing it terribly. Like every other normal English person, I most often used it to refer to myself, usually when I had done something silly or forgetful: e.g., "What a silly cunt I am, I left my umbrella in a taxi!"

I wasn't trying to be vile. Like many happy, well-adjusted U.K. youngsters, I grew up on "cunt." Walking to school as a child one often heard truck drivers and construction workers happily calling one another "fucking cunts." Male-to-male working-class use of the majestic c word is the most common, and was brilliantly parodied, on the record *Derek and Clive* by Peter Cook and Dudley Moore, in a skit called "This Bloke Come Up to Me" [unofficially known as "You Calling Me a Fucking Cunt, You Fucking Cunt?"].

Use of the c word in the U.K. is not, however, class-specific. Mrs. Crowther, my very posh high school English teacher, missed no opportunity to highlight the "cunts" and the "shits" and the "farts" that make Chaucer such a pleasure. She knew how to keep our attention from wandering.)

Back to 1977. So what did outsider Spider do to compete with the well-connected but cunty Emanuels? "It was the

Queen's Jubilee—the height of punk," says Spider, as if recalling a major offensive in the Second World War. "I had no money so I bought red, white and blue dishcloths from Woolworth's and sports gear. I made the models into glamorous punk footballers with long scarves which I knitted myself." The teachers at the Royal perceived Spider as "a troublemaker with no talent." In accordance with tradition, Spider, the lowest-ranked student of her year, had the shameful distinction of being allocated the first spot on the runway. "Those poncy Emanuels with their Pekinese dogs were last," recalls Spider with a guffaw, her punk sensibility still utterly intact.

The Emanuels' showboating did not eclipse Spider who, as a result of her cheeky footballers, landed a plumb job designing for the sporty house of Daniel Hechter in Paris. Armed with cinematic Godardesque fantasies of *la vie bohème*, Spider excitedly prepared for her new life, even learning the language in record time at six A.M. Berlitz classes. Louche Paris would surely be the antithesis of uptight, unsophisticated Kidderminster. Spider was ready to morph into an oversized Papillon: she stormed up the Champs-Elysees, with her mouth shaped to shriek out a giant *bonjour Paris!* But she didn't quite get the *willkommen, bienvenue* or welcome that she anticipated. All she got was abuse.

For risk-takers like Spider, there always seems to be a tall dark stranger waiting in the wings to piddle on her parade and curtail that naughty exhibitionism. "Every day, people would come up to me on the metro and say . . . things." At first Spider didn't understand what was being said to her; as her

French got better, she found she was deciphering phrases like "Is the circus in town?" As Spider dusted the Buddhist shrine in her living room, she described for me a typical outfit from her early days in Paris: "Leatherette trousers, an old men's pinstriped suit jacket, all nipped in and tailored—by me—and really high porno heels from the Pigalle, the ones the glam cross-dressers wear, because I had big feet." I quickly calculate that, with the addition of the aforementioned heels, Spider would now measure a shocking two meters—i.e., about six and a half feet. Her hair was dyed bright red, "and it stuck out, and my makeup was like Papua New Guinea tribal markings."

The hostile reception that greeted her look surprised even Spider. Clearly Paris wasn't going to be quite the laissez-faire whirligig that it was cracked up to be. The experience has left her less than Francophilic: "I hate the fuckin' French."

Spider's out 'n' proud Francophobia is refreshing and not without justification. Who amongst us has not fallen victim— on some random occasion or other—to that snotty bourgeois French superiority? Is there anything less fun than a frog blathering on about the finer things in life and asserting his cultural preeminence? *Rien!* It's really the antithesis of wacky chickery. *Non?* And, it's just a smoke screen. Clichéd montages of Paris—a romantic city peopled by the glamorous Proustian intellectuals and accordion-wielding Maurice Chevalier types—are just a *fromagey* façade. *Les grenouilles* are intent on concealing their darker side from us right-thinkin' tourists.

If you think Spider and I have lost our petits fours, and that the French are really O.K., then you probably haven't read much about the French Revolution. Before they cut off her head, the revolutionary rabble subjected Marie Antoinette, one of history's femmiest wacky chicks, to countless well-documented horreurs. To alleviate the boredom of her incarceration, the crazed mob waved the dismembered genitalia of her best friend, the Princesse de Lamballe, on a stick in front of Marie Antoinette's cell window. There's that French charm at work again—you turn your back for a minute and they've got your vulva on a stick!

Despite the lack of *entente cordiale* between Mademoiselle Fawke and *les grenouilles,* she eventually found kindred spirits. "I became a big fag hag. The poofs accepted me and thought I was beautiful and mental and a good laugh. Straight people wouldn't take the time to find out what I was like."

There is, it should be noted, a universal rapport between wacky chicks and gay men: I have yet to meet a wacky chick who didn't have at least one of her Pigalle heels plonked firmly down in the gay world. The reason is simple: both groups , if they are not ballsy, run the risk of being relegated to the dusty margins of society. They fight for their rights with the same weapons: passion, creativity and the occasional pair of false eyelashes. And, most important, both gay men and wacky chicks understand the power and beauty of H-U-M-O-R.

C Is for Creativity . . . and Claude

Wacky chicks are unencumbered by stodgy preconceived ideas about their place in the universe. Their mission in life is to eradicate the quotidian. Whether needlepointing or primal screaming, they will find a new and more creative way to do it.

* * *

For the next ten years Spider, egged on by her nelly friends, cut a jagged swath through the *maisons* and *ateliers* of Paris. She recalls each work experience with a blizzard of enthusiastic sound bites: "I designed for Jean-Charles de Castelbajac . . . fringed blanket coats . . . kimono sleeves . . . leather boots . . . very gaucho"; "Marcel Lassance . . . men's clothes . . . very straight . . . very preppy . . . a French Paul Smith . . . classic proper tailoring . . . loved, loved, loved."

By this point Spider had worked just about everywhere in Paris except the Folies Bergères: she was running out of *ateliers* in which to stage her legendary contretemps. More important, the *bon chic/bon genre* (good looks/good class) of Parisian style was starting to "bore the tits off" her, and she looked utterly dreadful whenever she tried to wear it. As Spider so eloquently puts it, "Classic French dressing on a six-foot-two girl with Bugs Bunny's teeth and red hair—you do the math!" This tormented style crisis, which caused her to seriously contemplate alternative careers, ended when she was hired by Claude Montana in 1983. Here Spider had found not just a groovy house with international visibility, but her spiritual home. Her statuesque bearing conformed to the sleek extraterrestrial Montana ideal. "Claude's woman was an Amazon with broad shoulders . . . very sculpted . . . very sci-fi and tailored to perfection . . . very *moi*."

Spider's responsibility was to design the men's knitwear for Maison Montana and she loved it. "Claude is a genius—it's quite nice to be touched by one. He was fabulous."

Spider was not, it should be pointed out, M. Montana's muse: that honor went to another eccentric beauty, Wallace Franken. "Wallace eventually married Claude—even though

he was gay—and later she jumped out of a window and died."
Spider catches the look of concern on my face and adds
hastily, "No, I didn't push her—it was a few years after I left."

Her own departure from Montana was much less dramatic
than that of poor Mademoiselle Franken: "Claude's look was
very specific. Fashion moved on and it just started going out
of style and I had decided I wanted to move to America to become a park ranger." What brought on this professional
about-face? "Hey! I'm a Gemini, what can I tell you!"

Ten years later, Spider has now fulfilled her dream, albeit
as a weekend volunteer. Every Saturday she leaves her lizardry
at eight A.M. to drive to the national park in Thousand Oaks.
"I wear army pants and big socks and a little polo shirt. I have
a walkie-talkie. I can do first aid, bee stings, CPR, that sort of
thing." On reaching the park, Spider hikes down to open the
bogs (Brit schoolboy vernacular for toilets). She then begins
her three- to five-mile hike around the park, "picking up trash,
making sure no one is smoking and telling people to put their
dogs back on the leash." As Spider talks about her work, an
unbelievable aura of contentment envelops her. Wacky though
it is, she has crafted exactly the life she wants.

H IS FOR HILARITY . . .
AND HOWARD STERN

Without a fabulous sense of humor a wacky chick is not a
wacky chick, she's a strident, narcissistic headache inducer.
It's just that simple.

Spider's typical day starts at six o'clock with what she calls
a P.T.A.: "I wash my pussy, tits and armpits—why waste water

in the shower every day?" Then she tends to her lizards while guffawing to Howard Stern, paying special attention to the Madagascan geckos, which she is breeding with passion and care. "They are on the list of endangered species, but smugglers manage to get them out. People want them because they are so beautiful—emerald green and pink and blue . . . spots and stripes . . . with Pee-wee Herman's face. I've bred about forty. I thought it would help the hemorrhaging—but it hasn't." Undeterred, Spider continues to breed the colorful critters. "You have to have the right conditions," purrs Spider, who has seen the slapstick courtship but never the shag itself. "The male shudders his head and then waves his tail slowly back and forth saying, 'Come on baby.'"

Once "the kids have had their brekkie," Spider—a Buddhist since 1991—chants her *nam myoho renge kyo*s in front of her birch-wood shrine. Yes, it's a tad Ab Fab, but then so—as you will by now have gathered—are wacky chicks. Once she has prayed for world peace, Spider focuses on running her small business. "I sell vintage textile swatches to fashion companies. It's my main source of income and it keeps me connected to the fashion world," says Spider who maintains a *W.W.D.* subscription and still delights in the foibles and excesses of La Mode.

In the afternoon she takes a break from phone *hondling* to chuckle at the irate participants of *People's Court* and *Judge Judy.* On the first Wednesday of every month Spider attends the Southwestern Herpetological Society. Her fun-filled life is totally extraordinary and yet incredibly ordinary. And Spider does it all on a natural high.

The skip-along spontaneous hilarity is a relatively new

thing for Spider. She kicked booze and dope back on November 11, 1987. "I woke up with a total blackout and my apartment had been trashed. I knew I had been fucked but I knew not by whom. I had friends dying of AIDS. I realized if I kept going I was going to get murdered or die of the plague." Spider had, like many wacky chicks, been a total *bon viveuse*—i.e., a substance abuser. "I was an 'orrible mean drunk. I don't know how I ever had any friends. I threw up on so many people's feet." In the eighties she added cocaine to her list of preferred stimulants: "Those days were about working all day and playing all night. How were you supposed to do that without a bit of help?" Spider enjoyed the burst of energy that cocaine gives and the instant self-esteem high. "You talk for hours and you feel totally scintillating. The only problem is, you're not."

Her only addiction now is collecting Desert Sands pottery. "It was made in Barstow in the 1950s. I've got over five hundred pieces." On Sundays Spider can be found scouring the L.A. flea markets for the signature marbled glazes of Desert Sands, like a crack addict looking for a fix.

And what, you are no doubt asking yourself by now, does this drug-free B.R.U.N.C.H.-y babe do for sex?

Is sex even important to wacky chicks? Though they love a bit of nooky as much as the next girl, wacky chicks invariably fill their lives with such passionate consuming interests that they are not generally to be found waiting around for men to fill any voids.

However, back in the 1990s, while living in New York, Spider made a concerted earnest effort to snag Mr. Right: she joined the Tall Club, an organization that brings together larger-than-life folk like Spider. "We giants would meet once a month, do dinner and a movie, or ice-skating—it was really a laugh." The laughter stopped when she met a six-foot-three goth electrician whom she now refers to disturbingly as "the Mong," and upon whom she is reluctant to elaborate.

So what about now? The Madagascan geckoes are copulating like crazy, but what about their flamboyant keeper? Basketball-player-sized eccentrics like Spider are not exactly hit on every time they go to the corner market. Assuming Spider might well be single, I ask tentatively if there might not be a few eligible gentlemen in the lizard community. "You've got to be joking!" responds Spider with genuine horror. "I was just at the International Reptile Breeders Association get-together. Let me tell you, reptile people are unfriendly— mostly big beer-drinking jerks who are in it for the money. But I don't care," continues Spider, getting ever so slightly coy and kittenish, "because I've got . . . Alan."

Alan, Spider's boyfriend since 1998, is a sixty-five-year-old collection officer. "He's a total barracuda. I met him through my Buddhists." Apparently, Alan had done some highly effective debt collecting for Spider's Buddhist group. In fact, the leader was so happy with the outcome that he decided to throw a bit of instant karma Alan's way. "What can I do for you?" he apparently said, to which Alan replied, "get me a date with a skinny thirty-five-year-old." *Et voilà!* Spider the reptile freak and Alan the collection officer.

"We're in love but we don't live together," says Spider, trying hard not to sound gooey. Fortunately Alan is a snappy dresser with a preexisting interest in fashion, which "gives us something to talk about." Dapper Alan takes good care of Spider: he even found her an apartment. The day she moved in, he helped her bring in all her reptiles, concealed in nylon totes. Next year he is accompanying Spider on an important mission: she is going back to Kidderminster to try to extract the secret of her paternity from her unforthcoming brother.

"I'm not doing a Sally Jesse—I just want to know the facts," says Spider of this trip. Like all wacky chicks she is more likely to respond to the vicissitudes of life with humor or belligerence rather than victimy self-pity. She prefers a good shriek or a belly laugh to any navel-gazing self-analysis. What's to analyze when you are comfortable with yourself? To be a wacky chick of Spider's caliber means you have come to terms with your wackidom—warts and all—and reached a peace accord with your own idiosyncrasies.

That said, it should be noted that a good wacky chick never sits on her laurels. Complacency is simply not part of the job description. Wacky chicks are reckless pioneers, always biting off more than they can chew, and then somehow managing to masticate their lives back into a digestible mouthful, and swallow it.

As we hug good-bye, Spider announces, apropos of nothing, "I'm dying to go to Papua New Guinea. Oooh lovely! Bugs up your dick and down your nails—and cannibals! Oooh! I would love it."

CHAPTER 2

ORIGINS

NATURE OR NURTURE . . . OR TORTURE

A re you next? The wacky-quake is reverberating throughout America. The fault lines are crisscrossing the land,
leaving fishnetlike marks across field and valley, and leg. Have
you heard the call? Are you ready to trade in a life of normalcy
for the life of Spider? Is it even possible to choose the wacky-
chick lifestyle, as in, for example, converting to Judaism,
learning the macarena or joining an exciting gang like the
Crips? Are these hordes of outré and vivacious gals con-
sciously jumping on a trend bandwagon or were they geneti-
cally predisposed to become wacky chicks? What role does
mothering play? Nature or nurture? Is it time to stop asking
questions and answer a few? I think so.

Unfortunately, there is a dearth of hard sociological research on wacky chicks. As of yet, no population studies or
doctoral theses exist. The ideal way to test a nature/nurture
hypothesis would be to undertake a twin study. Interrogating
and probing pairs of identical and fraternal twins might yield
some epoch-making revelations. At the very least it would
provide a few chuckles.

There are currently no wacky twin studies in the pipeline, though I myself have been keeping a watchful eye on the Barbi twins. Celebrity bulimics Shane and Sia Barbi seem to have wacky potential: if those overscaled assets and pouty lips aren't wacky, I don't know what is. But self-obsessed, humor-impaired Shane and Sia show no signs of developing the requisite hilarity that would qualify them as wacky chicks. One wonders if they lost their *joie de vivre* when they lost their lunch.

Re the Olsen twins: I'm optimistic. They have the kind of massive wealth that often goes hand in hand with an isolationist Michael Jackson–ish wackiness.

In the absence of any legitimate research, how about some semi-illegitimate research?

In this chapter I will compare and contrast two case studies—Brigid and Sunny. Both have clawed their way into the Wacky Chick Hall of Fame, but one was traveling on the Concorde and the other was on Trailways.

Brigid Berlin, daughter of Hearst muckety-muck Richard Berlin, was born with a silver spoon in her mouth, while Sunny Chapman, daughter of Ed Seymour, unemployed steelworker of Freeport, Illinois, grew up in grinding poverty. Though they hail from opposite ends of the economic spectrum, both have attained stratospheric levels of wacky-chickery. Clearly, material wealth is not a determinant of wackiness.

So what were the common denominators, if any, that propelled these two hilarious, multifaceted and endearingly abrasive women into the Wacky Chick Hall of Fame? Did they fall down the rabbit hole, or were they pushed?

BRIGID BERLIN—THE WARHOL FACTORY GIRL

Brigid Berlin is fondly remembered by many as the plump, Fifth Avenue–bred Warhol superstar who lolled around shooting whipped cream into her mouth and amphetamines into her ass through her jeans in the 1966 movie *The Chelsea Girls*. In the 1960s Warhol milieu, she found the perfect platform for her grandiose exhibitionism and monumentally obsessive-compulsive personality. Within the confines of the Factory, Warhol's legendary tinfoil-lined studio, she was a fully functional creative freak who actually made a significant contribution to twentieth-century art. Brigid's mania for recording conversations, Polaroiding anything that moved, making paintings with her breasts and general hell-raising informed and shaped large chunks of the Warhol canon.

We meet in Brigid's surprisingly un-Warhol-ish Manhattan apartment. Where are the Reynolds-covered walls, the stained couches and the lolling degenerates? Where is the track-marked scrunge of yore?

Brigid, it would appear at first glance, has become the Park Avenue Wasp her mother always wanted her to be. Well-groomed, gray-haired and classically featured, Miss Berlin gives the initial impression of having reverted to type. Her archetypal, szhooshy Park Avenue décor suggests that the occupant might have a keen interest in pugs and gardening: blazing floral chintzes are juxtaposed with needlepoint pillows and leopard carpet. At first glance it all looks very Upper East Side. Then I take a closer look at those needlepoint pillows.

The first one to catch my eye is a portrait of Yasir Arafat with the words THEY'RE OUR COUSINS provocatively needle-pointed across the face. Then I see a Chandra Levy pillow nestling next to a Michael Jackson pillow into which are needlepointed the words I'M NO FREAK—YES YOU ARE! Then Brigid plonks herself down in a squishy armchair, opens her mouth and all is revealed. She is crazier than ever.

"I'm doing a Martha Stewart pillow right now," crows Brigid, lighting a cigarette and muting the TV, which blares CNN all day long into her spotlessly clean, camera-ready abode. "There are prison bars in front of her face and it says, THIS IS NOT A GOOD THING."

I find to my delight that the uncensored, outré Warhol muse is utterly intact. More voluble than ever, Brigid is only too happy to free-associate about needlepoint, what makes her tick and especially about her highly strung mom.

"At our apartment, at 834 Fifth Avenue, my mother had needlepoint thrones, not toilets—very French. Her name was Honey. She was a New York society girl—twenty-two years younger than my father. She smoked. She didn't read books—only W and Town & Country, Harper's Bazaar, blah, blah. 'The last book I read was Raggedy Ann,' she used to say, proudly." Upscale Honey Berlin wanted her daughter Brigid to wear white gloves and marry Prince Charles, but her anal expecta-tions got derailed by the freight train of Brigid's oral impulses, et voila! The resulting operatic disappointments were the leaded gasoline that fueled their tortured relationship and upped the stakes on their mother/daughter wackodrama.

At sixty-one, Brigid the brilliant raconteuse (see The Philos-

ophy of Andy Warhol: From A to B and Back Again) has lost none of her ranting piquancy—especially when her late mother is the topic. "She slept with her makeup on. When I was ten years old I found her Tampax, and she told me they were for removing makeup. So every night I cleansed my face with cold cream and wiped it off with a Tampax. She had plastic vibrators, and she told us they were for her neck. I cannot picture her having sex. She wore heels at home—in the house, for chrissakes!" Brigid lights another ciggie and inhales Tallulah-ishly. "My mother didn't work," she continues with borderline vehemence. "She got her hair done every day, over at the House of Charm on Mad. and 61st Street. When I was eleven, she gave me a permanent. She went to every fashion show because Daddy was the big cheese at Hearst." Ms. Berlin is referring to Richard Berlin's fifty-two-year stewardship of the media giant. "He got the company out of debt; he sold off newspapers to buy television stations. When Patty Hearst was kidnapped, he held the purse strings, and he was reluctant to give up the ransom money to get her back."

Brigid's tale of privilege ping-pongs back and forth, managing to cover every seminal event and place in twentieth-century history. "I would pick up the phone and it would be Richard Nixon. My parents entertained Lyndon Johnson, J. Edgar Hoover, and there were lots of Hollywood people because of San Simeon—Clark Gable, Joan Crawford, Dorothy Kilgallen."

European royalty also dined *chez* Berlin. "I have a box full of letters, written to my parents in the late 1940s and 1950s, from the Duke and Duchess of Windsor." Ms. Berlin proceeds to read me a few of these fascinatingly doltish missives; the main topics are communism ("the war of nerves being conducted by the Kremlin") and upcoming golf games.

In the 1950s, Ms. Berlin made a life-altering discovery about Honey and her glitterati friends. "My mother would go to Pavillon and the Colony and have three asparagus spears. She was a one-spoonful gal. Not me! She used to take us to Paris, but she spent her whole time in couture fittings, so my sister and I ran around Paris eating. They all ate like birds, so I started to sneak the uneaten food in the middle of the night."

As a result, Brigid did the unforgivable, at least in Honey's eyes: she got chubby. "I was sent to the family doctor to get amphetamines. I was eleven. Dexedrine, too—little orange hearts. Mother would take Preludin. Then diuretics became popular—my sister wouldn't drink water. Everyone was doing it, even Jack and Jackie Kennedy." Despite the modish doses of speed, the weight piled on.

Honey's attempts to rein in Brigid's wackiness and reduce her heft took on an international flavor. "When I was sixteen, my mother sent me to a school in Switzerland called St.-Blaise to lose fifty pounds—and I would pilfer the other girls' money and go on pastry binges."

In Switzerland, teen Brigid launched into an addiction-fueled rebellion, and the results were much more impressive than anything Robert Downey Jr. has so far come up with. "My roommate and I decided to get drunk. I got so fucking wasted I was doing Indian dances. I woke up the next day, and there was shit on the floor next to my bed. One of the mademoiselles entered the room and demanded, *'Qu'est-ce que c'est que ça?'* I said, *'C'est le chien,'* " blaming it on the dog. "She said, *'C'est trop grand!'* Then they wrote home to my parents and told them I was using my bedroom as a toilet."

Feeling grossed out and less than empathetic toward the gnarly excesses of Brigid's gilded youth? Cut a wacky chick some slack and keep in mind the following: If a guy did stuff like that you wouldn't be nearly as grossed out. And wait till she meets Warhol—it gets wackier. Also keep in mind that Brigid was coming of age at a really freaky time. Bombarded with mixed messages and changing expectations, a nice up-town girl like Brig wasn't sure whether to don white gloves and head for the cotillion or become a fetid beatnik. Lastly, Brigid's stories—even the foul ones—are *très amusant.* Now, let's continue in a less judgmental frame of mind.

During her school holidays, Brigid's parents sent her to work at *Harper's Bazaar.* "All the women wore hats—so I wore one too. My job was to detach the dollar bills from the letters people sent in requesting the *Harper's Bazaar* Beauty Box. The editor then, Carmel Snow, took me out to lunch. 'Get that thing off your head,' she said. How was I to know that only editors wore hats? Daddy was Carmel's boss, so I just thought I was an editor and that I was entitled to a hat. Vreeland was on the second floor wearing a snood."

Brigid pauses to admonish one of her pugs and fast-forwards her rollicking riches-to-riches epic. At eighteen, she finished her schooling at the Convent of the Sacred Heart Eden Hall in Pennsylvania and returned to New York just in time for her coming-out party—and a fresh assault on her mother's nerve endings. "I was a debutante, so I needed two escorts. I invited the electrician who was working on our TV wires at our house in Westchester. . . . I can't remember the other one. My mother went crazy."

Are you like Brigid and Honey? Does every interaction between you and your mother degenerate into a rage-filled psychodrama? Are you experiencing matricidal impulses? On Mother's Day, instead of feeling grateful—washing her feet with your hair, etc.—all you can think about is what kind of sentence you'd be handed down if you strangled that hypercritical bitch during your mother-and-daughter day of beauty at Elizabeth Arden. During brunch with Mom, you are in constant danger of using the c word.

If this is you, try remembering that it takes two to tango, and that you are doubtless playing Veda to your mom's Mildred (see: Mildred Pierce, *the 1945 noir epic starring Joan Crawford). Don't bother dragging her to your therapist—you need a far stronger remedy. I'm talking radical cathartic therapy, e.g., a mother-and-daughter rental of* Pie in the Sky, *the brilliant documentary about Brigid directed by Vincent and Shelly Dunn Fremont. I guarantee that, no matter how painfully baroque the psychodynamic between you and Mom, you will both come away from this hilariously poignant shock-doc feeling relatively normal. And loving each other . . . and Brigid.*

La Berlin lights another Marlboro and recalls the swanky milieu of her young adulthood. Eschewing college, Brigid hung around the city with the likes of Wendy Vanderbilt and George Hamilton. "I think I spent the night with him—I'm not sure. Anyway, we used to go to Michael the II's on 70th,

Malachy McCourt's—Frank's brother's—bar on Third Avenue and Clavin's, opposite the first Serendipity."

These skip-along years were enhanced by an escalating speed intake. "Dr. Freiman—we called him Dr. Feelgood—gave me my first injection in my arm. He blindfolded me with my Hermès scarf and said, 'I'm going to make you feel better than any man has made you feel.' His shots were amphetamine, diuretic and B_{12}. By then I was nineteen and very high, and my sister and I would go straight to Bloomie's and start charging."

Honey Berlin was not, according to Brigid, unduly phased by Brigid's escalating amphetamine use. "It was legal. Her issues with me were weight and lifestyle." However, when Brigid started hanging out with poofters, she really touched a brand-new nelly nerve. "Mother called them 'pansies.' She was on the phone to Bill Blass every day, but for some reason that was different—my friends were mere pansies!" scoffs Brigid, who enjoyed the company of homosexuals so much she decided to marry one. "I knew all the window dressers up and down the Avenue—Joel Schumacher, Gene Moore. When I was twenty-one, I married John Parker. He dressed the windows at a store on 57th and Fifth called the Tailored Woman. He had the deepest windows in town."

Brigid and her new husband embraced a flamboyant, grifter lifestyle. "We stole Daddy's Cadillac and ran off. I rented a house in Cherry Grove [on Fire Island]. We renamed it Brigidune. I used to come into the city on the seaplane just to get checks. I hung out with all these piss-elegant queens . . . Jimmy Donohue—have you heard of him? I was insane, but also very grand. I went through $100,000, and my mother went berserk." Had she known what was about to happen, Honey Berlin might have saved her energy.

Brigid can't quite remember how she met Andy Warhol. "I think it was 1964. Henry Geldzahler took me to the old Factory, but I already knew about Andy through all the staple-gun queens." To say they hit it off is an understatement. She inspired Andy Warhol, and he in turn encouraged her entertainingly degenerate antics, much to the horror of Honey. The Berlin-Warhol symbiosis produced a filthy and fabulous avalanche of creative collaborations, including movie appearances—*The Chelsea Girls, Bike Boy, Imitation of Christ* and more. Brigid, who now went by the name Brigid Polk—"because I poked myself in the heinie with speed"—even recorded her mother's telephonic reproaches and turned them into an off-Broadway play.

According to Brigid, her job at the Factory was "to come to work every day." Though she transcribed tapes and conducted her own interviews, she is mostly remembered as the stern gatekeeper who interrogated would-be visitors with rottweilerish commitment. *Pie in the Sky* interviewee writer Bob Colacello remembers arriving at the Factory for the first time: "Brigid gave me a dirty look which lasted about five years."

The Factory years flew by in a blur of drugs, booze, food and general grooviness, with the occasional random attempt to modify her behavior. "In the early seventies, I went to Woolworth's and bought a jigger so I could have just one getting-dressed drink. By the time I left the house, I'd had twenty. One time, I was in a hairdresser under the dryer getting bored. I went to the bar across the street in my rollers and had a glass of white wine. Then another glass of wine and another. I can't remember anything else until I woke up in a Howard Johnson near La Guardia Airport. And there were pancakes and maple syrup. There was a cute boy in the room watching *Kids Are People, Too.* I think I thought that Andy would put him on the cover of *Interview.* He didn't."

I am starting to wonder how come a wacky chick like Brigid is not a household name. Compared to the cautious image-conscious celebs of today, Brigid's penchant for hilarious and brilliantly detailed self-disclosure is like a gust of exhilarating, though occasionally fetid, wind. What kind of world deifies uptight unifaceted, boring celebrities and allows fascinatingly indiscreet and ultracreative freaks like Brigid to slide into obscurity? It's simply not fair.

I attempt to bring our time together to a lachrymose crescendo with a few Barbara Walters–ish questions. Did Brigid ever buy her mother a gift on Mother's Day? "Daddy would always give us a couple of $100 bills," she replies, and then skips away, dry-eyed, on another free-association bender. "Daddy's Alzheimer's was really fun. He denied everything— 'You're not my children!'—and gave my gay sister's girlfriend a cigar when she came over. He thought she was a guy. There are four of us; I was first. Then Richie—she was named after my father. Then my brother, Richard, and my sister Christina, who arranged the defection of Baryshnikov. I remember Daddy went nuts: 'If she marries that commie bastard. . . .!' He sent us to Catholic schools. He'd say, 'At least you're not going to get communism from the nuns!'"

Brigid returns to the subject of Honey and, with the clock ticking, she goes in for the kill. "When *Mommie Dearest* came out, I told my mother it was the best movie I'd ever seen. She was a friend of Joan's. She said, 'How could Christina do that to her mother?' I told her Joan was just like her. She used to go through our closets and throw it all on the floor, looking for wire hangers pointing the wrong way. 'These beautiful clothes I buy you! . . . You can't fit into them because you're getting fat!' The clothes itched. I used to cut the sleeves."

Feeling just a tad Oprahish, I take a deep breath and ask Brigid if she loved her mother. "I'm not sure if I loved her. I don't have much experience with love. I love my sister Richie, and I love my pugs. When Honey [the pug] died recently, I went out and got another one. But you can't do that with people. Death is weird . . . it's too abstract. Andy said it's as if somebody went off to Bloomingdale's and never came back. When my mother died, I went upstairs with two pocketfuls of Toll-House cookies and started going through her jewelry."

This haunting image leaves us both at a loss for words. Having dragged Brigid through the doll-filled valley that is her life, I feel obliged to restore her former ebullience. How about a jolly word-association/acrostics game using the word M-O-T-H-E-R? Anything-for-a-laugh Brigid rallies enthusiastically.

M: "Maids! My mother had tons of them—always women. No butlers, because they drank. She didn't like couples, because they conspired. Irish maids. One was called Minnie Curtain."

O: "Obsessional. In 1986, my mother was lying in her bed, dying of cancer, and she was still calling the saleswomen to get new Adolfo's at the Saks in White Plains. She had them hung on her door so she could look at them. She died four months after Andy."

T: "Tweezers! Her French tweezers! I have to have a tweezer in my night table to pull out stray hairs, and the highest-magnifying mirror—an X5. They sell them in Bergdorf Goodman. She was hooked on them."

H: "Hair. And so much Spray Net. And H is for Honey—I named a pug after her. I've turned into her. It's scary. She was right to be disgusted by so many things I did. I'm a mother now, to my pugs—India and Africa. I don't like it when they call them 'dogs'—they are my children. I have to have a car and a driver; I want them with me. Every day we go buy their dinner—chicken breasts from Grace's Market."

E: "Esther, another maid. She was obsessional and she drank, with a thousand hairpins. On her day off, she would stay home and polish our doorknobs; that was her idea of fun."

R: "Rigaud scented candles. The original green ones. The Cypress—Mother bought them in Paris before you could get them here."

Brigid does not appear to regret those years of driving her mother bonkers. "I enjoyed it, but I didn't do it on purpose.

Growing up, I was really scared of my parents; they were strict. I just rebelled. Then one day I just got sick of waking up in the plants."

These days Brigid's life is much simpler. Her oral compulsions are confined to binging on Key lime pies, hence the title of that therapeutic documentary, and valiant efforts to keep her weight down. "I'm on this program—sort of like Overeaters Anonymous. Lots of lettuce, and I'm allowed one apple a day, so I bribed everyone at the Union Square green market to put aside the really gigantic ones." On a recent trip to pick up her special order, a horrified Brigid saw a lady from her program rummaging in her box of oversized apples. Brigid reacted violently: "I slapped her hand. So she started calling for the cops claiming I had assaulted her." Brigid fled in her town car and has not been back to the program: "I'm terrified to run into her."

I ask the naughty Brigid how it feels to be an enduring symbol of counterculture rebellion. "I couldn't care less," she replies with a derisive snort. "I voted for Nixon for chrissakes! I'm a total Republican."

SUNNY CHAPMAN—THE GLUE FACTORY GIRL

Like Brigid, Sunny Chapman also let it all hang out in the 1960s. But, unlike Brigid, she still looks the part. While Brigid's personal style has morphed into one of urban, Wasp, chic anonymity, Sunny's still reeks of Janis Joplin. When Sunny holds court at her 26th Street flea-market booth in

Sunny enthusiastically when we kick off our interview at her three-story Brooklyn town house. Sandwiched between rails of vintage clothes on the first floor, Sunny and I attempt to figure out the origins of her wackiness.

She was born Patricia Kay Seymour in Woodstock, Illinois, a town famous for its metal and rubber casting. "My father, Ed, was a sheet metal worker, but he couldn't keep a job. He was a terrible boozer. When he was a kid he was dumped off at Boys Town. Later he used to write enraged letters to the Pope complaining about his experiences and asking to be excommunicated." Sunny's perky, petite mother, Betty, brought in a few bucks waitressing at family-style restaurants.

Despite the less than sparkling socioeconomic milieu, Sunny's eccentricities blossomed. At age six she was sent home from school with a recommendation for counseling because she drew pictures of people wearing evening gowns and tuxedos but gave them animal heads. When she was eleven, Sunny, her parents and her four sisters, moved to Oshkosh, Wisconsin, in search of work for Ed. "This was way before the Oshkosh kids' clothes," recalls Sunny, kneading Punky Boy, one of four cats, with her long fingers. "The factories made work clothes and plywood glue. Sheeesh! The smell!"

One night she made an announcement to her entire family during supper, "When I grow up, I'm going to move to New York and become famous." Sunny's parents greeted this announcement as if it was just one more evil-smelling blast of hot air from the glue factory. "We were always told we were stupid and useless. Any show of self-esteem was squashed." By the time she was a teenager and the family had moved

Manhattan she cuts a stately, bohemian figure: in her loud floral dresses—a mink stole and a mukluk boot if it's chilly—
fifty-two-year-old Mrs. Chapman is both compelling and
stylishly intimidating.

Regardless of their personal style, height or poundage,
wacky chicks are invariably blessed with a congenital, impos-
ing physicality. Sunny and Brigid are no exceptions—both
women, though vastly different in so many aspects, have what
can only be described as *Magnetic Presence*. When they deign to
mingle with the rest of us, we lumpen masses are scythed in
two by their progress. Like the resilient show-offs that they
are, they excite and enthrall us just by showing up.

Regal Sunny's shoulder length dyed black hair frames the
perfect face. Yes, her skin is good—she doesn't smoke drink or
do drugs, and she eats vegan—but when I say perfect, I don't
mean perfect in the dewy, cosmetics industry sense. I mean
perfect, as in the perfect visual medium for expressing the torrent of emotions that accompany her hilarious river of caustic
asides and pungent observations about "organized religion,
the corporate elite, pedophiles not already included in the organized religion category, corrupt governments, rapists, people who are cruel to others and to animals, terrorists of all
stripes." It's an un-Botoxed ever-changing face that would
give any Picasso ceramic jug a run for its money. In Sunny's ir-
regular kinetic features, the music of her anarchic invective
has found the perfect instrument.

Cubist-faced Sunny's childhood was every bit as extreme
as Brigid's. "Most people who had my sort of childhood have
Multiple Personality Disorder, or they're serial killers," says

again, to Freeport, Illinois, things between Sunny and Ed and Betty had gone from chilly to hideous, culminating in a visit to "some fruitcake psychiatrist" who diagnosed Sunny as a sociopath.

It was during her increasingly rocky teens that Sunny first became aware that she possessed strange Hitchcockian powers. "Wild birds would fly into our house when the windows were open and stay, but only in the rooms I spent time in, like my bedroom and the living room. Friends would come over and there would be birds lined up, just sitting along the chair backs." I ask Sunny if she has any idea what this means. An expression of resigned incomprehension hopscotches across her cantilevered features and she responds by topping this story with a couple of even stranger ones: "When I lived in New York on 38th Street, I put plants out and clouds of butterflies appeared. It was strange. Nobody could explain it. I wasn't religious so I didn't think I was Saint Francis. One time I was walking down Astor Place and the street cracked open and burst into flames. It wasn't Satan. But I couldn't tell you what it was."

From an early age Sunny's vivid imagination was stoked by voracious reading. As with many of my underprivileged wacky chicks, developing an enthusiasm for books was the first leg of the escape route from the drizzle of the underclass into a sunlight-dappled world of wacky optimism and curiosity. "My father taught me to read when I was very young. He walked me to the library and demanded they give me an adult card," recalls Sunny with gratitude. A sickly child, Sunny had ample time for books. "I was an unhealthy sprout, with bad allergies and a flaky immune system. I stayed home and read. *Lawrence of Arabia* made me want to be heroic. When I was fifteen I hitchhiked forty miles to Rockford to get J. D. Salinger because they were banned in Freeport." When Sunny read *The Diary of Anne Frank* she had an epiphany: "I realized there were bad people in the world and that I need to do something about it." Mrs. Chapman's activist sensibilities were already gurgling.

At age sixteen, book-smart Sunny became part of a Lyndon B. Johnson program for poor kids called Project Upward Bound at Northern Illinois University. One of her field trips became a life-changing event: she and her co-Upward Bounders went to Chicago to hear Martin Luther King speak. "This was amazing. Hearing him speak was magic. My parents were working-class right-wingers, very racist. Suddenly I found out that everything I had been told was false."

Just like Brigid, Sunny dedicated her late teens to a stink-bomb-hurling, baroque rebellion against her family and their cherished values. "At seventeen I had myself declared an emancipated juvenile by the court. I told everyone to piss off, and headed for Chicago. I had been removed from my family's home and made a ward of the state. They couldn't find a home, so they sent me back to my parents and gave them temporary custody. I kept running away from home because I was being physically abused by my dad when he was drunk." In 1967, Sunny finally made it back to Chicago and snagged a totally happening girl Friday job working for an underground newspaper, *The Chicago Seed*.

This was the real beginning of what Sunny calls her "life-

time commitment to social justice activism . . . civil rights . . .
the Vietnam War." As a *Seed* staffer, Sunny was involved in
planning the demonstrations at the infamous 1968 Chicago
Democratic National Convention. But she ended up quitting,
"in disgust at the way I was treated by New York sexist hippie
assholes."

Sunny encountered yet more of these wolves-in-hippie-
clothing when she moved to California. While Brigid was ex-
ploring and helping create the underbelly of Manhattan
bohemia, Sunny was in San Francisco living the hippie life.
She supported herself working as a mead wench at various
northern California Renaissance fairs. "Fucking bees! Stinging
me! Up my dirndl! Bees just looooove mead," recalls Sunny,
getting instantly in touch with her thirty-year-old Renaissance
rage. "It's the damn honey. You see, the mead booth would be
full of bees, O.K.? and the bees would fly up our skirts. The
only way to get rid of those little bastards was to hold out our
skirts till they flew out. If you tried to chase them out by flap-
ping your skirt they would sting you."

As if the sugar-lovin' bees weren't enough, Sunny was also
tortured by horny hippies. "Pouring mead means using both
hands—an earthenware jug in one hand and a tankard in the
other. The drunk hippie guys would take advantage of the situation and grab my tits while I was pouring their stupid
mead."

When she wasn't fighting off hippie gropers and bees,
Sunny was designing and making groovy gear—"macramé
necklaces and belts, and custom groovy embroidery on denim
clothing"—and selling it on the sidewalk in the Haight and on

the Embarcadero: "It wasn't lucrative, but there were no jobs. This was San Francisco before there were yuppies. Everyone was on welfare." Alfresco street vending and mead-wenching gave a tawny hue to this flower child's complexion, earning her the nickname Sunny.

The unenlightened, patchouli-wearing slobs who plagued Sunny and her sisters in the late 1960s actually did the girls a favor. By relegating counterculture chicks to a subservient role (rolling joints, preparing vegetarian food and ignoring their boyfriends' multiple infidelities) and totally pissing them off, these mead-guzzlin' hippies created the Women's Liberation Movement and the irate feminist persona that still burns brightly to this day in many chicks of Sunny's generation.

Meanwhile, over in England a highly politicized feminist debate was taking place, *chez moi*. My mum and my sister, Shelagh, were the key dramatis personae in this brief but explosive drama. It all started when Betty, in a Honey Berlin–esque gesture, did what any right-thinkin' woman of her generation would have done when her daughter started "filling out": she bought my sister a long-line girdle. The drama reached a crescendo when Shelagh did what any Joan Baez–lovin' teenager at the time would have done when presented with this symbol of oppression: she tossed it down the hall at a retreating Betty and fled to her room to listen to her doleful Buffy Sainte-Marie albums.

Back in Chicago, a girdleless and braless Sunny embraced the feminist cause and its related issues. She had finally escaped the long shadow of that glue factory and found an identity.

Over the years, Mrs. Chapman's feminism and activism found its most energetic focused arena in her pro-choice work. To date she has made two documentary films on the subject, *In Bad Faith* and *Misguidance*. The high point of Sunny's feminist trajectory came when she was asked to show her films and speak at Princeton. "Not bad for a high school dropout," says Sunny as she finishes sewing the button back on a 1960s Pauline Trigère duster coat in readiness for the Saturday flea market.

Over the years Sunny's agitations have become progressively more creative and demented. In 1996 she started what must surely be the most perverse anti-abortion campaign in herstory. She calls it Satanists 4 Life. Purporting to be Satan worshippers, she and collaborators Karen Elliot and Monika LaVey stage *demon*-strations at abortion clinics where, alongside horrified Christian pro-lifers, they rail enthusiastically against the evils of abortion. Wearing horns and devil masks and holding placards that say "Don't abort your fetus . . . it could be the Anti-Christ!" and "Pro-Life is Pro-Satan," they invariably send their crucifix-wielding adversaries scurrying to the other side of the street.

Sunny's other feminist platform is a long-term project that she calls I Hate You! This literary work-in-progress debuted in 1963 as a handwritten book of poems about "my drunken father," one of which was a parody of the Lord's Prayer:

> *Our father, who art in the living room,*
> *Ed be his name,*
> *He will be drunk, on earth and probably in heaven. . . .*

I Hate You! was resurrected as a series of photocopied magazines starting in the late 1970s. "I ranted about all the stuff I hated," recalls Sunny, sounding quite unvehement. "Nazi skinheads, boring people, stupid people, frat boys who beat up my friends, incredibly jerky guys I went out with." The last issue came out in 1995. Sunny admits she has mellowed since then: "If I were to put out a 'zine now, it would more likely be called something like *You Vaguely Annoy Me But You Don't Matter So I'll Ignore You.*"

The I Hate You! leitmotif, which has perfumed most of Sunny's adult life, did not stop her marrying . . . five times: Said Boromand ("a handsome Iranian lunatic"), Thomas O'Hara, ("a used office furniture salesman and father of my daughter"), George B. Chapman IV ("a handsome Wasp architect and lunatic punk rocker—this is when I got tired of changing my name"), Jonathan Formula Plenn ("an utterly brilliant punk rock lunatic"), and her current spouse.

Vintage diva Ms. Chapman is currently on a roll: her tumultuous life seems to have reached an eerily comfortable plateau. Her current union with husband number five might well be her last. "He's a deeply private man who prefers to remain anonymous. He teaches at a midwestern university, loves to cook and garden, and is good to his mother, his kids and his grandkids." Sunny lives mostly in New York while he lives a few states away. "It's a commuter marriage," explains Sunny, adding roguishly, "I'm a girl who rules, rather than plays by the rules."

Despite her comfy ménage, Sunny continues to carry the irate torch of feminism. Anyone who swings by her booth at the flea market is likely to get a Camille Paglia–esque earful. Though Sunny's feminism is a tad more old school and reductive than Camille's,* they share a common disenchantment with media-friendly feminist writer Naomi Wolf. "It's unfair for Naomi Wolf to say we shouldn't wear makeup. It's O.K. for her—she's good-looking," says Sunny with faultless logic.

Activism doesn't pay the rent and Sunny was never dumb enough to think that it would. She has always supported herself with her other passion—no, not mead-wenching; I'm talking about fashion.

In the late 1970s Sunny moved back from California to Chicago, where she opened a series of vintage-clothing stores with names like Sage and Butterfly or Chinoiserie ("nobody could pronounce the name—Jewish women called it chiazerie, like matzo-brie, and black women called it the chinisery, as in misery").

Sunny's kookily monikered boutiques take me back to the glory days of seventies retailing, when stores had names like Granny Takes a Trip, The Marquis de Suede and I Was Lord Kitchener's Valet. I vividly remember my first trip to Stop the Shop I Want to Get Off, a revolving shoe store on London's King's Road.

Now we have grim one-word boutiques—Gap, Prada, Costco, Armani, Gucci. Lazy consumers have even abbreviated

---

*La Paglia is the B.R.U.N.C.H.-iest broad in academia and also, given the magnificence of her output, the most inappropriately underrecognized. While Naomi Wolf has infiltrated the system, becoming the Diane Sawyer of feminism, Camille is still a scrappy outsider. Unsurprisingly, Camille has an explanation, for this inequity: "I'm a scholar, O.K.?, and she's a twit!"

Banana Republic to Banana, and Ralph Lauren to Ralph: I've even heard a languid plus-sizer refer to a recent purchase from Lane, as in Bryant.

The tide may, however, be turning. On a recent trip to London's trendy Hoxton, I was happy to note that some fun-lover had named a boutique Eat My Handbag, Bitch!

Back to Sunny. In the 1980s, she started making jewelry again: she moved to New York and by the early 1990s our heroine was enjoying a modicum of success: "I sold to better stores and I was in all magazines, *Vogue, Bazaar, Elle, New York,* etc." Sunny's creativity found an outlet in jewelry designing and wholesaling, as did her belligerence. Once a slow-paying, hostile retailer pushed an infuriated Sunny to extreme measures. "This guy had a store over by Tower Records—an English cunt with a massive personality problem. I was a single mother with a small child. I got twenty-five bucks a week child support. I went into the store and politely asked for my money. He went berserk and threw me against the wall and called me a cunt in front of customers. He dragged me to the door and shoved me onto the street."

Hell hath no fury like a wacky chick shoved. "I got into a rage and decided to take out his window," recalls Sunny with a mixture of pride and remorse. This fracas took place during the Gulf War. "All the peace demonstrations seemed to end up near his store. I did it in front of mounted police. I took a brick and made a sling out of an old T-shirt and smashed his window. Nobody saw me do it because I have a cloak of invisibility. I got away with it."

During this period, friends recall being recruited by Sunny

to help her restore the balance of justice. Sunny vehemently denies any violent acts, but admits to "joking about tossing a jewelry designer who knocked off my entire line under a train at the Astor Place subway station."

During this period Sunny was taking back the night, but she was also attracting disaster. "One night the back wall of the building where I lived and worked fell off in the middle of the night." The building was condemned and padlocked on the spot and Sunny and daughter Emily, who was in elementary school at the time, found themselves in the street, with no possessions and nowhere to go. What follows is a story of wacky resilience and maternal chutzpah that I will let Sunny tell in her own words.

"There I was on the sidewalk with two suitcases, a child and a cat. I think I had about thirty bucks. First I convinced my landlord that even though I was illegally living in the building, he should give me another space and replace all the stuff I had built in my space. Amazingly, he went for this. He gave me a raw space in the building next door and agreed to have his workers build walls and put in a kitchen and bath. Then I convinced my jewelry caster to set up a workshop for me in a corner of his factory in Queens, which he gladly did, so I could keep working. The next thing I did was bribe one of my landlord's workers to give me a key to the padlock. The building was being watched by the cops, so we couldn't move my stuff out of the building by the front door. The way we moved my stuff out of the condemned building was pretty amazing. We would go in a group of three. One person would stay downstairs and put the padlock back on the door. The new space was next door but one floor up. I set up a ladder going from the roof deck in front of my space through the window of the new space and we secretly moved everything up the ladder, at night so no one would see us. Everyone helped. I got all of my stuff out of that building."

As one door closes, another door closes. Sunny's resilience was further tested when, in 1993, the building that contained her new studio was burned to the ground. "I lost a lifetime of drawings, photographs and films." More doors banged shut when Sunny developed chronic fatigue syndrome in 1997 and couldn't work for two years. "I lost my business entirely, everything went down the tubes." Instead of watching daytime television, Sunny used her two-year convalescence to edit her documentaries.

By 1999 Sunny was back on her feet, supporting herself with her old standby—the purveying of vintage garments. During the last three years she has become something of a legend at the 26th Street flea market and the other vintage shows around Manhattan, where her knowledge of fashion history and her acerbic witty diatribes make her a popular destination. She keeps *au fait* with fashion and cleverly markets her clothes based on current trends. Equestrian? Victorian? Rich hippie? You want it, Sunny's got it.

Buying vintage clothing has never made more sense than it does now. Fashion continues to be driven by a retro sensibility, which is a polite way of saying fashion designers are not designing anymore: they are just knocking off old tat from the flea market, much of it no doubt purchased from Sunny. This is great news for you, the ordinary woman in the street. Get there early, i.e., when all the designers are jostling for the best pickings. Don't toady up to them—use it as an opportunity to vent any lingering fashion rages and settle old scores—e.g., "Hey, Donna, what the hell am I supposed to do with all those old blouses you sold me which snap in under the crotch?" And remember, all you have to do to be totally *au courant* is watch what Tom Ford's or Marc Jacob's assistants are buying from Sunny and her ilk and snag similar garments. And you'll save a fortune!

Exactly how much money you save will also be contingent on your bargaining skills. Here are some tips on *hondling* that will serve you well. They come directly from the horse's mouth.

Here is the Chapman guide to flea-market haggling:

First and foremost, asking retarded questions will be rewarded with epic public humiliation: a German couple recently made the mistake of waving a bracelet bearing a forty-eight dollar price tag in Sunny's face and asking, "This number is *not* the price, is it?" "No, it's just a random number," replied Sunny with arty sincerity. "This entire booth is a conceptual art piece I created. I like to assign random numbers to objects." According to Sunny, the humorless couple then asked, "So what is the price?" "Forty-eight dollars," said Sunny, to which the stone-faced Germans replied, "But that is what the tag says." "Yes," explained Sunny, "my art piece is also about . . . coincidence." By this time everyone within a fifteen-yard radius of Sunny was screeching with mirth.

Second, never offer insultingly low prices. "What's the best you can do?" is Sunny's preferred approach, though she cautions "there is no way to bargain with me without pissing me off—it's just a matter of degree. And only people I'm married to and fierce drag queens are allowed to call me 'honey.'" The biggest crime in Sunny's book? "If you want something and you can't afford it, then for chrissakes don't tell me, 'There is a tiny, nearly microscopic mend on this fabulous Victorian dress that's 120 years old, can you give me a discount?' Instead say something nice about it, or me. Tell me how young I look."

So exactly what were the common denominators that propelled these two w.c.'s into the Wacky Chick Hall of Fame?

Sunny was poor and Brigid was "top drawer." Sunny was passionate about social issues. Brigid could not have cared less about such things—as she told me during our interview. "I never cared about abortion. I had a couple, of course. I went to the Theresa Hotel in Harlem. Oh! And once I got an abortion in exchange for getting this doctor a ticket to the New York Debutante Cotillion."

A penchant for creative rebellion and a big mouth are their common denominators. Brigid found her identity by rebelling against the expectations that came with her privileged upbringing, whereas Sunny's equally pungent identity came from rebelling against the equally restrictive working-class ignorance and oppression that would have suffocated her like plywood glue fumes if she hadn't bolted. Though differing wildly in their priorities, somehow they both ended up frolicking, ranting and wallowing in the same marginal territory, with the same feisty lack of gentility.

Both made their break with normalcy against the backdrop

of counterculture tumult and turned their lives into a plangent but totally engaging piece of performance art. The global 1960s freak-out enabled Brigid and Sunny to take their individual revolutions to a more extreme and fabulous place. Who is going to care that your undies are on your head if everyone else in the room has lemon-yellow ostrich feathers stuck up their bums? It's a bit like Sunny, with her "cloak of invisibility," breaking that window during a massive peace demonstration. She got away with far more than she would have done had she been the only bohemian agitator on the street.

The wacky-chick kryptonite that gave Sunny and Brigid the ability to survive is found at the crossroads of convention, rebellion and social upheaval.

Here's the good news: they're actually becoming even wackier. Brigid and Sunny, like so many of the baby boomer kooks I spoke with, have reached that couldn't-give-a-shit age. Though they may have found familial coziness with their pugs, mensches and assorted reptiles, they no longer have anything invested in inhibiting their wackiness. During the 1980s the Brigids and Sunnys of the world made sincere attempts to mainstream their lives. Now as the laissez-faire of middle age digests their B.R.U.N.C.H., their wackiness, and that of so many w.c.'s of their generation, is going into high gear. Hence the current phenomenal eruption of wacky chicks onto the scene, and hence the groundbreaking exposé that you are currently enjoying.

My girls can no longer sit on their emotions—or anyone else's—even if they tried.

CHAPTER 3

STYLE

The Missile Defense System
of the Wacky Chick

Fashion is deemed by many "sensitive," politically correct types to be little more than a source of oppression and exploitation, a decadent and conspiratorial force propelled by evil queen-y designers and food-disordered, fag-smoking hags who have collectively dedicated their tragic and fetid lives to inflicting their warped, carcinogenic view of femininity on a gigantic segment of a defenseless populace—i.e., you—while faceless men in gray suits wait to catch the resulting cash in large buckets.

The root causes of all contemporary malaises—so say these caring folk—are traceable to fashion and the marketing thereof. Anorexia, mood swings, booze and dope addiction, fallen arches, excessive bloat, delicate cutting and bunions are all, so they say, catastrophic by-products of the horrid fashion machine.

As with all hysterical p.c. rants, there is some truth to these accusations: fashion has indeed taken a gruesome toll on many devotees. Interpretive dancing queen Isadora Duncan for example, was throttled by her own stylishly trailing scarf after it got snarled up in the wheel of her sports car, and—as if that wasn't bad enough—a friend of my mother's once dislocated her thumb while packing herself into her long-line girdle. Yes, there's no question about it, fashion is no place for sissies.

Be that as it may, the negative influence of fashion is more than canceled out by the positive role it has played in herstory. Yes, I said positive. The great screaming, raging truth of the matter is that, paradoxically, the world of fashion, far from victimizing women, has, in many cases, provided them with what social workers love to call a "safe space."

How ironic! At the very epicenter of this despicable hell-hole is a nurturing romper-room for unorthodox creative types. And it's been that way for centuries. The welcoming forgiving arms of La Mode have been embracing society's mis-fits since fifty-foot powdered wigs and twelve-inch waists—and that was just the men!

Some notable wacky chicks have found far more than just safe haven inside the great cosmic fashion *atelier*: many clever girls found creative fulfillment, material success, fame and in-famy. Pauline Trigère, Jean Muir, Zandra Rhodes, Betsey John-son, Madame Gres, Madeleine Vionnet—these chicks found a noncritical arena where they could shriek and declaim and de-sign their boobs off.

Some went beyond mere creativity and became icons of their age. Visionary broads like Coco Chanel who freed women from the busty, gussied-up, Christmas-tree chic of the Belle Epoque. This former nightclub singer and demi-mondaine also liberated women from the oppression of corsetry—an oppression that women wisely reembraced a decade or two later.

The rule-breaking Coco, known around Maison Chanel simply as "Mademoiselle," knew instinctively that twentieth-century women were ready for change. For whatever reason, they were now totally desperate to start striding about in a modern butch kind of way, voting and smoking fags and what-not, so she introduced the idea of sportswear and casual suits. To prevent her thoroughly modern Mimis from looking too dykey, Coco festooned them with gobs of costume jewelry. *Et voilà!* Twentieth-century fashion was born.

By the early 1980s women's career clothing had become altogether too butch. In their preppie suits and broadcloth button-down blouses, women had started to resemble hormonally challenged men in skirts. Enter another great visionary, Donna Karan. She freed women from this terrifyingly sexless world of Dacron, masculine power dressing and gave them ways to look sassy and glamorous in the workplace. Day-to-evening Donna—an inveterate wacky chick who believes she was an Egyptian princess in a past life and has been known to indulge in the occasional bout of therapeutic primal screaming—showed women that their real power lay in their allure. She replaced the Margaret Thatcher–ish overly practical stringency of the early eighties with a wrappy, stretchy siren glamour, complete with Dietrich turbans, dark hose, high heels and jangly bracelets. This don't-fuck-with-me-fellahs sexy, total look gave women power in the workplace that was based on their allure, not on their ability to behave like pushy blokes. Donna's style helped propell many careerist chicks into the boardroom and—in some instances—in under the boardroom table.

Not every female fashion designer uses her creativity to solve women's problems like Donna and Coco. Some are provocateurs who delight in inciting women to look totally extraordinary and even deranged. These women are invariably wacky chicks: the experimental outré nature of the high fashion arena relies on the cage-rattling creativity and originality that only a wacky chick possesses.

Elsa Schiaparelli, a prewar wacky chick who hung out with the Surrealists, made hats that looked like shoes and pork chops, and invented "shocking pink," was one such enfant terrible. In 1937, Schiap, as she was known to her chums, collaborated with Dalí on a proto-punk frock printed with trompe l'oeil tears and another with a giant lobster. Excitable, attention-crazed Dalí is alleged to have leapt from his front-row seat and spattered the latter frock with mayonnaise as it came down the runway.

Vivienne Westwood wasn't born posh like Schiap: she was a working-class girl who became a schoolteacher and then stopped being a schoolteacher in order to invent punk. By marrying sleazy fifties style with porno/bondage and a nebulous desire to be obnoxious, Vivienne (aided by Malcolm McLaren) gave birth to one of the most influential movements in the history of fashion. Punk neutralized the smelly vestiges of the counterculture hippie aesthetic and pumped a tough urban gasoline into the world of style that kept it going for the next two decades—until the hippie thing got revived again. Oy veh!

History-obsessed Viv went on to spearhead the insane Boy Georgey New Romantic style: she brought back pirates and gave women a postfeminist thumbs-up on the controversial issue of corsetry. Ultrawacky Viv, who, aged fifty-six, received her OBE from the Queen *sans* panties, believes that there is nothing more powerful than an alluring courtesan brimming over her basque. Far from being a potential rape victim, the bosomy odalisque holds all the cards.

Vivienne believes in courtly formality, even at home. In 2002 she told *W.W.D.*, "I have no recreational clothing. When I get home, I take off my dress, get down to my stockings and bra and put on an apron to do the cooking. That is how I sit down to eat with my husband."

Wackiest of all, and infinitely more enigmatic than Donna or Vivienne, is Rei Kawakubo, the female designer for the most respected and successful avant-garde fashion house in history—Comme des Garçons. During her twenty-plus-year career, Miss Kawakubo has accomplished the supreme feat of being so insanely prescient that nothing she has done has ever gone out of style. Her innovations are endless: she turned the fashion flock into a bunch of black-clad crows; she built brutalist stores that looked like concrete bunkers, because they were; bored with the organic movement, she created a fragrance that was made from the smell of granite, electricity and aluminum.

Once in a while, wacky Rei's much anticipated, experimental collections have caused frissons of incomprehension, even amongst the most hard-core fashion followers. In 1997 she sent out models wearing randomly placed, massive funguslike humps and bumps. Her intent was to challenge our preconceived notions about which parts of the body should be exaggerated and which should be reduced. The thought-provoking results put the mode back in Quasimodo—or vice versa.

Enough about fashion designers! They are no longer important. The tyranny of the fashion designer—male or female, talented or untalented—is over. That tight-assed elitist world where a woman wore clothes to express her allegiance to a particular designer is gone. You no longer need fashion designers to create a style for you—you can do it yourself. The decks are cleared; the way is paved for you to develop your very own unique *je ne sais quoi.*

Style, it must be emphasized, is very different from fashion: style is democratic; style is free (almost). There are no rules. Fashion is dead! Long live style!

What's the point, you may well ask? Why invest time and effort in developing a unique style? Why not just wear functional sweats and shower shoes? There are a myriad of non-fashiony reasons that you should put effort into developing a look.

First, style = protection. An unusual ensemble can provide a gal with her very own scuds. Since Flintstone times, one's chosen raiment has provided crucial nonverbal information about one's tribe and about one's self. Wacky style provides extra protection because it is, by nature, indecipherable. If strangers cannot unscramble your code, they become distracted and disoriented. A sidetracked adversary is a vulnerable adversary.

Style is philanthropic. It's a way of giving back to your community: onlookers are entertained and amused by your various looks, and it gives them something about which to kvetch. Their humdrum lives are forever enhanced.

Style is democratic: you don't need money to have style.

The following three chicks, Susanne, Janet and Lisa, have each—on a low-ish budget—successfully evolved their own unique style. Utilize this upcoming peek into their fabulous and occasionally unwholesome closets to inspire you. If you allow them to, they can be the wind beneath your bat-wing sleeves.

So go for it, and remember, there's nobody keeping score. The hamster's wheel of trends is spinning so fast that the taste Nazis could not possibly keep track of your successes and failures. They are all too busy working on their own looks.

SUSANNE BARTSCH—SHOWGIRL CHIC

Susanne Bartsch gets paid by large corporations to squeeze her body into pancreas-mangling Folies Bergère corsets and paint her face like a Vegas Barbarella. This is the way she would dress anyway, but the men in gray suits don't know that, so they happily pay her. And do they get their money's worth or what? Susanne infuses and electrifies their otherwise dreary promotional *affaires* with her unprecedented, transcendent, transgender, Mardi Gras spirit. She pours her sequined grooviness and spangled exhibitionism—and that of her gang of trannies and freaks—onto people who have neither. She's a trailblazing, glitter-throwing gang leader whose meticulously crafted personal style has paid her rent for more than twenty-five years.

Re gangs: Susanne was once arrested in a sting and accused of being the leader of a gang whose main aim in life was stealing sewing machines. One wet Saturday in the early 1970s, Susanne had gone to the Peter Jones department store on Sloane Square to shop for a sewing machine. Like many style-obsessed chicks, she couldn't always afford to buy the trendy duds she wanted, so she had taught herself to make clothes, thereby creating an original and provocative wardrobe for herself without breaking the bank. And, like many w.c.'s, she has always been a magnet for suspicion and drama.

Charming, chatty Ms. Bartsch had, as was her wont when dealing with any service person, engaged the saleslady in several minutes of enchanting persiflage.*

Meanwhile, the aforementioned gangsters were shoving sewing machines up their coats and down their knickers, unobserved by the distracted saleslady. A police investigation followed: it was not long before the coppers put two and two together and concluded that the vivacious European girl with the penchant for home stitchery was not an enthusiastic potential customer. *Au contraire!* She was a wicked woman whose role was to distract the saleslady while the rest of the gang made off with the booty. A dramatic police raid followed: six

---

*Persiflage: flattering banter, from *per*, thoroughly, and *siffler*, to whistle, hiss or boo. Wacky chicks are big deployers of persiflage and if that doesn't work they will happily resort to persiflage's butch sister, badinage—i.e., persuasive banter. Bartsch has even been known to use both at the same time.

uniformed men blasted into Susanne's apartment and arrested her.

Zeliglike appearances at major and minor international dramas and tragedies are part of wacky-chickery. And Susanne is no exception: like so many w.c.'s, she really puts herself out there and reaps both the rewards and the dog poo. Also like her sisters-in-wacky-high-chickdom, Bartsch, always manages to walk away in one piece—usually wearing metallic thigh-high boots with seven-inch heels. For examples, when Susanne bought a little shack on the island of Vieques, it was only a matter of time before the worst hurricane in recorded meteorological history would hit. Bartsch survived, but the shack was never seen again.

Back to the sewing machine debacle: Susanne was subsequently cleared of all charges. Little did the police know as they apologetically bid this Swiss Miss *adieu* how accurate they had been in identifying Susanne's type. She is an instigator and a catalyst—she's as honest as the day is long, but if circumstances forced her into a life of crime, a creatively coordinated sewing machine heist would be right up her *strasse*.

Fast-forward a quarter of a century.

Our interview location is the gaudy, mural-covered apartment in the Chelsea Hotel, where Miss Bartsch has lived, worked, fornicated, cooked and gotten tarted up since she came from Switzerland via London twenty years ago. Susanne lounges on her overscaled red-lacquered Chinese bed and, looking a bit like a shagged-out Rainbow Brite, she regales me with her life story. "I was born in Bern sometime in the last half century. I'm postwar. That's all I'm telling you, bitch! Oh, and I'm a Virgo." She pronounces it "Wirgo": Ms. Bartsch does to v's and w's what the Japanese do to l's and r's. I once heard her telling a costume maker, "I vant something wery showgirl—something viz a vig inwolved." During her late-1980s-and-early-1990s reign as Queen of the Night, there was inwariably a vig inwolved.

But Susanne did not start out as a wig-wielding nightclub promoter. "It was 1981, girlfriend, during the New Romantic scene when everyone was dressing like a bloody pirate," recalls Bartsch mistily in her Swiss/Cockney/Harlem Ball Queen lilt. "London street fashion, Bodymap, John Galliano and that whole gang of lunatics. They were all so fokking creative but nobody was helping them and you couldn't buy their clothes in New York. I became their big sister." Like a tarty, latter-day Maria von Trapp, Bartsch protected and promoted her prancing protégés, and she wore their clothes. Encouraged by the mostly positive reaction to her wacky outfits, fashion evangelist Bartsch opened her own eponymous, unforgettably kooky boutique on Thompson Street: she commissioned designer Michael Costiff to decorate it like a Dalíesque funeral parlor and filled it with the wares of her design visionaries.

In the 1980s, elitist, recherché fashion emporiums like Browns in London, Charivari in New York and Maxfield in Los Angeles were patronized solely by chichi folk with oodles of cash and buckets of savoir faire. Susanne was different: her innate goofiness coupled with her complete inability to recognize iconic celebs always prevented her from being overly sophisticated. In her Thompson Street boutique, the snotty intimidating vibe of high fashion was totally absent. In its place was a new brand of bawdy, creative hilarity. It was the beginnings of the democratization of hip and bohemiana that we now see, twenty years later, in Diesel, Anthropologie and Banana Republic.

In 1983, spurred on by the success of her boutique, Bartsch attempted to take her unruly *kinder* to a wider audience and wholesale their wares. "I did a fashion show at the Roxy with Leigh Bowery and a whole bunch of freaks modeling—New London in New York, it was called. I hadn't a clue about fashion-show politics." This Swiss neutrality is a leitmotif: I remember Susanne meeting legendary fashion-editing royalty Polly Mellon and saying, "Molly, Dolly, Polly, whatever yer name is. You look fantastic! Have a seat!"

Despite the lack of protocol, this show blew the vigs off the fashion establishment, in a good way. "Every store uptown bought the clothes. Half a million dollars' worth." Then the reality of wholesaling these unorthodox designers hit. "Basically, I love them all but they drove me fokking bonkers—so I went back to retail." In 1985, Bartsch opened a much larger designer shop in SoHo, on West Broadway next to Artwear. "It was doing well, but I walked away in 1987 because I wasn't happy with my partner's visions" (pronounced "wisions").

One day, while shaking out her piggy bank, Susanne noticed that downstairs from the Chelsea Hotel, busy beavers were putting the finishing touches to a disco called Sauvage. "I had all these flamboyant clothes and nowhere to wear them, so I thought, 'Why not?'" Bartsch took her unwaveringly irreverent sense of style, aimed it at the whirling discoball of New York nightlife and scored a bull's-eye.

Tuesday nights at the Sauvage—choreographed and overseen by ringmistress Bartsch in a black-rubber cat-suit, pornoheeled thigh-high boots (purchased in Paris from a Pigalle store owner who gave Susanne a discount because she helped him "translate his bloody dildo catalogue from German") and a black lacquered ultravixen vig—were "high-energy, very mixed: straight, gay, uptown, pier queens to trust fund. My mission was to get people to mix and dress up." Bartsch's freak-friendly approach created a unique vibe where humor and attitude and a willingness "to make a total nitvit out of yourself" were the keys to admittance.

Within weeks, the now insanely popular Susanne had outgrown the Sauvage and moved to Bentleys—"a black secretaries' dive"—in the forties near Madison Avenue. "Drag queens downstairs and Sister Dimension spinning, and upstairs we had house music with fabulous strippers," recalls Ms. Bartsch with a huge grin.

Bartsch is not what you'd call a rocket scientist, and she doesn't spend hours—or even minutes—in heavy-duty introspection. However, she does possess a zeitgeisty knack for giving people exactly what they need. Just when the AIDS epidemic had made sex virtually synonymous with death and most New Yorkers were wondering how they could possibly have a shag without donning an asbestos suit, Bartsch served up a fabulous safe alternative: voyeuristic porno-chic.

The weekly quest for new and unusual "industry" acts became Susanne's focus: "I had Chi Chi the Smoking Pussy, and Honeydew—her tits were more like watermelons, actually— lots of beefy guys in sequined jockstraps and, of course, Lady Hennessy Brown." Those who attended Bentleys will never forget the great Lady Hennessy Brown, a six-foot-two Amazon whose jaw-dropping act inwolved not just vigs, but seventy- six pairs of knotted stockings.

Miss Bartsch's own personal style was reaching an ex- treme apotheosis. Inspired by a trip to the Rio Carnival with her pal Gerlinde Costiff—a highly influential wacky chick who is, alas, no longer with us—Susanne added garish sequins and feathers to her corseted porno-chic. British corset-maker Pearl—a wacky bloke with a sixteen-inch waist—was now working round the clock to create her looks. Her showgirl style had become so exaggerated that the arch excesses of de- signers Jean Paul Gaultier and Thierry Mugler had now be- come her popping-out-to-the-Korean-market daywear.

Susanne's rollicking life story—told in that gorgeously idiosyncratic accent—is starting to give me vertigo. I decide to hit the pause button, take a breather and ask Ms. Bartsch to disclose the secrets of her ageless beauty. She obliges with a surprisingly idiosyncratic list of products. Deaf to the persi- flage of luxury skin-care marketers, Bartsch has traveled her own hippieish route and, if her own radiance is anything to go by, come up with a winning regimen.

Nivea cream: "can you believe it?" gurgles Bartsch when asked to disclose the secret of her milkmaid's complexion. "I love Nivea. Sometimes Bailey," continues the birdlike, beauti- ful Ms. Bartsch, referring to her eight-year-old son by husband, David Barton, "he takes it and hides it as a joke. He knows I can't live without my Nivea cream."

Apricot kernel oil: "there nothing like it for cleaning heavy drag makeup. I buy gallons of it at the health food shop on my block." Witch hazel and rose water: "I mix it myself, as an astringent, half and half." Baking soda: "I bathe in it. I do! Bubble baths are dead glamorous but they make my skin dry. Baking soda is ph balancing or whatever the fok they call it." M.A.C. Russian Red: "I put it on with a brrrrush," continues Bartsch, rolling her r's, "putting on lipstick without a brush is like eating dinner without having any food on the plate . . . or something like that." Angel perfume by Thierry Mugler: "I can't live without it. I drink it." A no-surgery instant face-lift: "sometimes when I feel tired, I pull my hair back with these rubber bands from Europe, and, I make a really tight ponytail to look more alive."

Now back to the Bartsch bio. After inventing stripper chic at Bentleys, Bartsch moved on up to the Copacabana on 60th Street. Here she ratcheted up the majesty of her Coney Island ambience by adding Harlem voguers* ("the same bloody kids from Harlem who used to come and steal things from my bloody shop") to her three-ring circus.

As captivating as the voguers were, it was Susanne's much anticipated arrival each week that created the major fracas: she was invariably greeted with a collective thundering whoop. After a quick curtsey, Ms. Bartsch would then make

---

*The defining treatment of this subject is Jennie Livingston's sublime 1991 documentary entitled *Paris Is Burning*.

her way through the crowd goosing and tweaking whoever she felt might benefit from a little frottage. The Copa—Ms. Bartsch's Sistine Chapel—had all the high-low, countesses-to-rent-boys democracy of Studio 54, without the polyester pretension. Less druggy and dark than the Michael Alig club-kid scene,* Ms. Bartsch's Copa—like the Swiss Miss herself—was cheeky, sexy, unsnobby and fun.

It was during her Copa phase that Suzanne developed the really annoying habit of sprinkling glitter onto the revelers from the stage. Glitter—as you may be aware—is *forever*: it will never biodegrade and it will never leave the planet. And it sticks: deglittering your scalp after a night at the Copa was pointless. You had to wait weeks for it to fall off your head and into your clothes, or onto your face, and thence into the shag-pile where it will stay for the rest of eternity. I still find specks of Bartsch glitter—circa 1989—on the snout of my Norwich terrier, Liberace.

Susanne's next incarnation occurred when she extrapolated her sense of style into the hitherto frumpy world of New York philanthropy. "By 1988, AIDS had taken half of my Rolodex," says a teary Bartsch as she recalls this hellish period and starts to list the names of deceased friends and collaborators, "Gary, Julio, Peter and Mark. . . . I survived this period by becoming a fundraiser." Bartsch donned the mantle of this then unpopular cause: for inspiration, Susanne retapped the world of vogueing balls.

With swishily Swiss anal retention, Ms. Bartsch set about organizing a seminal event called the Love Ball. In addition to

*See wacky chicklette P5, page 208.

Harlem gangs competing, Susanne enlisted corporations from Armani to Sara Lee. Held at Roseland in 1989, this event was the apotheosis of Uptown-Downtown crossover: "There were ball queens serving champagne to CEOs."

And there was Madonna. Her attendance contributed hugely to the success of the Love Ball, and vice versa. Though the eagle-eyed pop icon was unquestionably having a blast that evening, she was also, as it turned out, doing homework for her next incarnation. There was much nudging and wink-ing—and applauding—among the trannies and ball queens when, a few months later, Miss Ciccone reinvented herself à la vogue and even recruited her chorus boys from the House of Extravaganza. Bartsch had unearthed a bit of obscure urban fabulousness and Madonna took it mainstream.

The pragmatic, creative, image-controlling Madonna dis-qualifies herself from joining the Wacky Chick Hall of Fame because she is simply too organized and goal oriented. She, along with Oprah, Margaret Thatcher and Martha Stewart, is a classic example of a parallel awe-inspiring phenomenon: the Godzillionairettes. But that's a whole other book entirely.

After a sequel—the Crowning Glory in 1991—and a couple of smaller events, the Swiss Miss had raised over $2 million for DIFFA (the Design Industries Foundation Fighting AIDS) and APLA (AIDS Project Los Angeles) at almost no expense. "I even got the bloody union to work for free," chuckles Ms. Bartsch, with the pride of a chick who used her wackiness to make a difference.

Her next incarnation—her personal fave—was motherhood. "In 1992, I met David Barton. He opened his gym, and I helped him make it trendy. We're a good combo—nightlife and health life—and then along came Bailey. David and I are separated now, but Bailey knows how much we both love him. He was one year old when we got married so he doesn't remember the ceremony."

Wacky chicks invariably have wacky weddings, and Bartsch's ballsy nuptials—part runway show, part cross-promotional event—were no exception. This might sound cheesy until you remember that c.p.e.'s (cross-promotional events) are second nature to Susanne (e.g., "I'm doing a party in Miami and I'm gonna get Absolut to pay for the invites and liquor, etc.").

The Barton/Bartsch wedding was sponsored by *Playboy*.* Susanne reminisces fondly, "Our marriage was the finale. It wasn't to save money; we just didn't want a conventional wedding. It was very camp. I came out of an egg. RuPaul and Thierry Mugler were David's best men." Susanne had forty-three bridesmaids, including loads of wacky chicks, e.g., Roxanne Lowitt, Polly Mellon, Beth De Woody and Betsey Johnson. (Note: wacky chicks are not solitary creatures. Whether in the wild or captivity, their impulse is to congregate. Their distinctive shriek allows them to identify other members of their species over considerable distances.)

---

*Cash-poor brides craving an opulent wedding might—à la Bartsch—try finding a strategic partner to help offset production costs. If your dad can't pay for your wedding, maybe Budweiser can! Warning: without celebrity wattage, your cold calls to liquor and fashion companies may be met with indifference or even derision. Don't give up! *Badinez* and *persiflez!*

Though they separated in 1999, Mr. Barton and Ms. Bartsch remain tight, connected by a surprisingly conventional commitment to parenting. On the morning of September 11, 2001, the Barton-Bartsches were on their way, by town car, to Bailey's school in Brooklyn when the first plane hit the World Trade Center. "We drove right past the Towers two minutes before it happened. When we got to Brooklyn, we felt the ground shake. Fokking hell! I thought it was a bloody gas explosion," remembers Ms. Bartsch, who then watched the Towers come down from across the East River. "Oh, girlfriend, it was 'orrible. We were right in the path of the cloud of debris. Bailey picked up burned memos from people's desks. I explained that it wasn't an accident, but when we got home I didn't let him watch TV."

Though mama Susanne still works regularly—she is hired to create events by corporations like Chiquita, the Grammys, Dewar's, Ian Schrager and Sony—her son, Bailey, is her current raison d'être and mental stabilizer. "When you have a child, you can't go fokking bonkers—you have to set a good example." Bossy Bartsch considers herself an authority on stress management and will spew helpful tips at anyone who looks even remotely ragged out.

How not to go "fokking bonkers"—the Bartsch way:

Yoga: Ms. Bartsch is a Sivananda devotee. "It's not Prada-handbag-trendy yoga. It's about looking good inside."

Homeopathy: "Get yourself a vitch doctor," advocates Ms. Bartsch, whose insides are tended to by a woo-woo-but-fabulous alternative wacky chick named Linda Lancaster. Dr. L. specializes, according to Bartsch, in "nature treatments for mental balancing and homeopathy and hippieish stuff and it vorks vonders."

Philanthropy: "Open your handbags, girls!" advocates Ms. Bartsch, who has a knack for inserting the word "handbag" into every other sentence. "You're helping yourself as well as other people."

Escape: "I have a little house near Montreal," explains Bartsch with a twinkle in her eye, suggesting that her Canadian retreat might be quite bijoux, "no trannies, no parties and no vigs. It's a total escape."

For somebody who has subjected herself to New York nightlife (and vice versa) for over twenty years, La Bartsch has an enviable, Piafesque lack of regret, lots of verve and more than a dash of Clicquot. "I'm an innovator," boasts Bartsch, "I got copied a lot, but I'm not bitter. All the celebrities and Warhols and Malcolm Forbeses, Liz Taylors, they all came to my clubs—but I didn't really care about them. I always want to bring the freaks from the outside, and shove them into the limelight." Pied Piper Bartsch continues, "I took the tacky drag queens out of the shadows; now they do fancy bar mitzvahs! That's all thanks to me! What a contribution to society!"

Despite the fact that she is clearly no *poulet de printemps*, Bartsch insists she is ready and eager for her postmaternal incarnation: "I'm a tvitchy bitch who has to keep vorking." One thing is for sure: there will somehow be a vig inwolwed.

JANET CHARLTON—SABOTEUR CHIC

You could be forgiven for thinking Janet Charlton's hair is a wig. But it's not. Like the rest of her personal style, it's really more of an assault weapon. "I love this color because everyone hates it," says the defiant, lemon-yellow-haired Janet. Where Bartsch uses her personal style to attract, allure and entrance, Miss Charlton uses hers to subdue, repel and intimidate.

"Dressing aggressively helps you get the job done and it makes you memorable, two very important things in my profession," continues Janet, looking and sounding like she might be a glamorous hired assassin or an haute-couture hooker. As she strides confidently through the parking lot of Fred Segal, the West Hollywood fashion mecca, she calls to mind the hypergymnastic Daryl Hannah character in *Blade Runner.*

While Janet orders two $4 lemonades at the adjacent café, I check out her ensemble at close quarters. Miss Charlton is fashionably attired in a rumpled, black cotton, multizippered paratrooper jumpsuit by Martin Margiela. Under the jumpsuit she wears a vintage Clash punk T-shirt. Despite the trendy vintage T, Miss Charlton is not a fan of the ubiquitous dirt-bag look, i.e., hagged-out faded T-shirts teamed with impossibly low-slung, butt-crack jeans, vintage trucker belts and Jesus sandals.

The sleazy, druggy dirt-bag look is peaking in popularity at the time of our interview. This Mansonesque style is typically topped off with the dirt-bag coiffure, a rat's nest of dusty unwashed worms. All around us very rich Mulholland Drive–dwelling dirt-baggers are emerging from Porsches looking as if they have just crawled up an embankment after a train derailment.

Janet's look has more military precision. Besides, she would never drive a Porsche: she prefers her burgundy ragtop 1984 El Dorado. "When I grew up in Chicago, this was the dream car. Style has always been way too important to me," admits Janet as she pauses to give a cheery *hola* to the parking valet, adding, "I care more about a man's shoes than his face." Re her own footwear: Janet favors black thick-soled Doc Martens, black-and-white classic saddle shoes, penny loafers and Martin Margiela flats. Six-foot Janet does not need high heels, but she wouldn't wear them even if she did: "I like to be able to run fast if necessary.

"My goals when dressing? I usually like to surprise people or make them laugh," adds Miss Charlton, sounding more like an inspirational speaker than a hired assassin. She tells me proudly that she has a closet full of Hawaiian tropical outfits for lounging around the pool: "You never know when you might feel the need to dress up like Marlo Thomas or Barbara Feldon. Or Sandra Dee, for that matter."

What could possibly be the métier that necessitates these quick exits and nifty disguises? Private dick? Some Hollywood publicists might say ultrastylish Janet Charlton was indeed a hired assassin. But her legions of fans know her as a kick-ass gossip columnist: a tough-talkin' tattle-monger who loves the steamy, seamy side of Tinsel Town. In her Martin Margiela, she haunts the Hollywood entertainment scene like a Ramboed Louella Parsons, always on the lookout for hot, cheesy dish with which to fill her weekly column in the *Star*.

Her unrelenting quest for gossip is every bit as uncompromising as her radical personal style. To say she's fascinated with the sleazy underbelly of celebrity is a total understatement. "I always have the best dirt: I had the scoop on the Madonna and Sean Penn breakup," twinkles Janet gleefully as she unzips her jumpsuit. She sighs with satisfaction and recalls more of her tabloid triumphs. "I blew the whistle on Ricky Martin's butt pads. He had a flat butt so he was wearing pads and then shaking his ass at the audience. My story went around the world." Miss Charlton claims that Ricky read her story and he started working out like a maniac. "On his next tour he wore a thong to prove it was real."

Janet finds the men of Hollywood to be just as skewerworthy as the women and a good deal more sensitive. "I prefer to pick on men, especially obnoxious male movie stars. There is more to write about because they're always cheating." Stallone called Janet one day and implored her to stop writing about his trysts. "You're breaking my girlfriend's heart," he said. To which an equally impassioned Janet replied, "No I'm not. *You are!*"

Does Janet have qualms about her muckraking métier? *Au contraire!* She feels she is doing a huge favor to the celebs she so often pillories. "I'm writing about them and keeping their name out there. It's not my fault if they behave badly. If people misbehave they deserve to be written about. I'm an old-fashioned kind of a gal," continues Janet with a cavalier toss of her yellow tresses, "good manners are important to me."

Janet's joyful commitment to gossip-mongering has made her something of a Hollywood *bête noire*. "I envy my friends who go to parties and are not kicked out." Her height and her penchant for outré fashion have always made gossip-harvesting more of a challenge, one that she always meets with stylish enthusiasm. "I love transforming myself," says Janet, who wore loads of wigs in the 1970s for kicks but now wears them to disguise herself.

A bewigged Janet hit pay dirt one night when, undetected, she successfully crashed Shannon Doherty's birthday party. According to Janet, the *90210* star was "out of her mind and screaming at everyone, 'Who invited you to my party?'—very Neely O'Hara—but she never guessed who I was. She ran out into the street—I don't know if she was plastered—but she started screaming, 'I hate you!' at everyone." Janet's photographer was hiding in bushes across the street. "We got some great shots. It was a fabulous story."

At the height of Roseanne's tabloid fame Janet tried to crash her birthday party and was thrown back onto the sidewalk. Undeterred, she regained her composure and hatched a plan. "I was going to get into that party if it killed me, so I sneaked up her fire escape, and I walked right into *her*. I just said 'Hi!' and kept walking. She didn't seem phased—maybe people did that all the time at her house."

Janet has now, thanks to regular TV appearances, become something of a stalkable celebrity herself. She can no longer sidle up to celebs in Safeway and count the gin bottles in their shopping carts, or lip-read via her compact the conversation taking place in the next booth at Musso and Frank. No amount of wigs will give her the requisite incognito to elude the protective publicists who are the bane of her existence.

This new notoriety does, however, have its benefits. "People recognize me in shopping malls and come running after offering major dish," laughs Janet, slapping the side of her vintage gold-vinyl 1960s Las Vegas souvenir purse. "Word has gotten out that I pay. One hundred and fifty dollars for a good tidbit, five hundred if it becomes a lead piece and a thousand if it becomes a bigger story."

Janet's weekly spread eats up large quantities of dish: to feed the supply she relies heavily on a somewhat creepy tactic that she calls "befriending the innocents." This involves getting friendly with those individuals—children, nannies, relatives— who are in the orbit of celebrities but who are insufficiently savvy to recognize the perils of sharing info with the friendly lady with the combat boots and the yellow hair. "I managed to get to Eddie Murphy's gardener. He told me that he was forbidden to look at Eddie's wife. He felt dissed. Befriending the innocents is gratifying on two levels: I get good dish and the innocents themselves enjoy attention which they don't normally get because they are treated badly or neglected by some egomaniac."

As well as her "innocents," Janet has her "regular sources." These include kitchen workers, catering staff, Beverly Hills shop assistants and, naturally, her coiffeurs. "I have two hairdressers: a more conservative one, Terrence, who gives me gossip, and Tina, a goth, who does the yellow."

Janet's lemon-hued shoulder-length tresses are her trademark. "I love this color because nobody else does. It livens up a dull outfit and it's great on TV." Unlike Dame Edna, who always claims to have been born sporting a violet rinse, Janet Charlton is quite open about the fact that she was born a brunette. She is less forthcoming about her age. A "Not on your life" greets my request for Janet's exact date of birth.

She is, however, willing to divulge the location. "Riverside Chicago—there were Frank Lloyd Wright houses in the neighborhood." Janet grew up middle class. "My mom was a housewife and my dad was in tobacco distribution so we did O.K., but we were poor compared to the neighbors. I walked to school but there were kids being dropped off in limousines." Herein, one would naturally posit, lie the origins of Janet's desire to deconstruct the spoilt limo-riding celebs of Hollywood. Janet denies this. She believes that this early proximity to wealth, far from making her resentful, instead simply made her "want to work hard to get more stuff."

The first thing Janet recalls wanting really badly was a pair of black tights because of the whole "beatnik thing." Her tights did more than show off her fabulous legs. "I was tall and extraordinarily thin. My mom didn't cook much. I ate less. The worst day of my year was always the weigh-in in gym class. I would wear three pairs of underwear. But the boys chased me anyway."

Janet, a conservative teenager who was still playing with dolls when she was fifteen, was not at all sure what to do with these horny boys. But she was starting to figure out which ones she preferred. Despite her wholesome, all-American childhood with its barefoot summers, style-driven Janet found she was attracted to "the big stupid cute boys with pompadour hairdos. I appreciate that whole greaser thing."

By the time Janet was studying art and psychology at Bradley College in Peoria, her taste in boys had become more Catholic, and also more Hebrew. "I became the sweetheart of the Jewish fraternity and met my first black people. They taught me things—how to dance and speak—and suddenly I felt life was fabulous and anything could happen."

Her stylish impulses now went way beyond black tights. "I was voted best-dressed girl. I had no money but I was already going to thrift stores and inventing my own looks." Janet's sources of inspiration came from across the pond. "I was fascinated by European weirdness, Marianne Faithfull in particular. The more excessive the better."

To fund her burgeoning clothes addiction Janet started modeling, in catalogues. "Sears and Marshall Field's, back when they hung big weights on our hems to get rid of the creases and there were marks on the floor where you had to stand." When Janet found out she could get time and a half for modeling slips and double time for undies, she went for it. "The money was great and there was nothing sleazy about it because the panties were lined in flesh fabric to eliminate show-through."

Fashion-crazed Janet decided to ditch graduate school and—with her modeling money—open a clothing store.* "I

---

*It's hard to find a wacky chick who has not, at some point in her life, opened her own store. Paradoxically, retail per se is of little interest to wacky chicks: my girls are motivated to set up shop because of the boundless opportunities for creative expression and social shenanigans. They also, bless their evangelical little hearts, see themselves as missionaries of sorts, duty-bound to enrobe and enhance the lives of the less fortunate with their radical style.

took every modeling job which came along—I even posed with ironing boards and barbecues."

In the early 1970s Janet opened a store called The Garment District on Wells Street in Chicago, selling vintage and army surplus and her own designs. With her extreme personal style, Janet the retailer/designer made a big impact. "I started wearing the most insane outfits: extreme mod, giant plaids, huge lapels. Anything to intimidate a little." Janet's outré appearance caught the eye of another raving fashion exhibitionist. "I was going out with this English guy who was in a band called The Soft Machine. They opened for Jimi Hendrix. He brought Jimi to my shop." When Janet met Jimi she was blown away by his creative personal style. "He was so out there—military jackets, feather boas, scarves round his jeans and ruffled shirts." Meanwhile Jimi was checking out Janet and looking slightly uneasy. Janet felt a tingle of satisfaction when the soft-spoken musical legend admitted he was scared of Janet because of the way she looked.

Business boomed, but Janet had a falling out with her two partners. Drawn inexorably to her spiritual home, Janet moved to L.A. and, using the same store name, set up shop on Sunset Boulevard, just a few blocks east of Schwab's, the legendary drugstore where Lana Turner—a Charlton fave—was discovered years before.

Janet was by now a seasoned retailer who ran her business like a battleship. Those foolish enough to be caught shoplifting in her store lived to regret it. "I would drag the scum back to my office and hand-cuff them to my desk." Vigilante Charlton would then demand twice the price of the garment that they were attempting to steal. If the shoplifter did not have the money, magnanimous

Janet would allow him or her one phone call to summon a cohort bearing the requisite shekels. "If they couldn't come up with the dough, I would call the police and when they were being thrown in the paddy wagon I would go out on the street and scream, 'Crime doesn't pay,'" recalls Janet triumphantly.

The apotheosis of Janet's retail career was the legendary MGM sale in the late 1970s. "This was the highlight of my shopping life—scratch that!—it was the highlight of my entire life," kvells Janet as she recalls the miles of historic garments, which were sold off for a song. "This is when I bought Lana Turner, for twenty bucks." Miss Charlton is referring to her most prized possession, the original saucy white shorts and halter that Miss Turner wore in *The Postman Always Rings Twice*, a gorgeous piece of scandal-bespattered memorabilia if ever there was one.

L.T. was indeed tabloid royalty: she's the movie star whose daughter Cheryl did time for stabbing Johnny Stompanato, mommy's stylish, sleazeball boyfriend, to death. Speculation has always been rife that it was Lana who did the deed, and that the underage Cheryl did time to keep Mommy out of the big house and possibly even the electric chair.

Lana, like Janet, had a very distinct personal style, albeit of a more tight-assed genre—literally. Lana's chic, tailored, studio-groomed image was complimented by a unique way of walking that she self-consciously developed by imagining she was clenching a nickel between her butt cheeks.*

Lana's hot shorts and halter hang framed in Janet's bath-

---

*Try Lana's technique: it really does give a purposeful wiggle to an otherwise featureless gait. Remember Lana had the small tight butt of a cellulite-conscious movie star: voluptuous girls might need to imagine something larger, like a quarter or even a hockey puck.

room, where their class A tabloid provenance always elicits shrieks of delight from visitors. As Janet removes a piece of lint from the Plexiglas case, she recalls her own contretemps with the late Lana: "She was upset because I reported that she was very high-maintenance on the set of a TV movie she was shooting. She said nobody would employ her because of what I said. I tried to sidetrack her by telling her I had her *Postman* outfit. She wasn't interested." Janet then switched tactics, telling Miss Turner that people would think she was glamorous and special because of what Janet had written. "I don't think she bought it," recalls Janet with an all's-fair-in-love-and-war type sigh.

The focus on Lana has taken Janet right back to the hysteria of that bargain-filled MGM sale. "Even now I get chills when I think about how much stuff they were selling and I can still remember the prices: Adrian dresses for twenty dollars, Clark Gable's trench went for twenty-five dollars. Judy Garland's shoes, fifteen dollars." Sweating, feint and with an empty bank account, Janet packed every square inch of her El Dorado with vintage booty and drove it straight to her store, where she sold it at appropriately inflated prices to the likes of Barbra Streisand and Julie Christie.

"I always had loads of celebrity customers and I was always interested in them—but not in a sycophantic way. I collected juicy tidbits about them. I guess I was always a tabloid person," says Janet, opening the page on what was to become her next career. When celebs came to Janet's store she would always take note of their foibles and obnoxiosities; she would then regale her less illustrious customers with this accumulated material, thereby enhancing their shopping experience.

These dish-lovin' customers always came back for more. Gossip was good for business.

Encouraged by legendary editor William Royce, Janet decided to see if she had what it takes to become a pro. "Bill worked for Rona Barrett—he got me freelance work writing for her magazines. I was still a total amateur."

Re Rona: it's impossible to gloss over the name Rona Barrett without pausing to savor the majesty and wackiness thereof.

RONA BARRETT GAVE GOOD HEDDA

Rona and Janet—along with Louella Parsons and Hedda Hopper—are part of a long dynasty of wacky gossip-mongers, all of whom used an arch personal style to intimidate detractors and adversaries. Their jobs might have been easier had they worn anonymous twinsets and gray flannel skirts, but they were determined to shine, even when surrounded by the great gowned beauties of Hollywood. At the end of the day it was their stylish excesses—Hedda's hats, Louella's corsages—that made them into Hollywood icons.

Rona probably made more bucks than all of these gals put together. She started young. At the age of thirteen, Queens-born Rona walked (with difficulty, due to arrested muscular dystrophy) into the Milton Blackstone Agency in New York and told them she would need a space to work, since she would be starting the Eddie Fisher fan club. According to her gripping 1974 autobiography, *Miss Rona*, she switched from Eddie to Steve Lawrence when, at fifteen, she found out that "Eddie Fisher was as much into apple-cheeked, fat-bodied chicks as Hitler was into B'nai B'rith."

The whip-smart adenoidal dynamo quickly morphed from drooling fan into self-appointed champion of young postwar Hollywood—James Dean, Natalie Wood, etc.—pumping out syndicated columns and eventually editing her own tattle mags. By that point, she had developed quite a reputation.

Johnny Carson once said of the probing, scoop-crazed Ms. Barrett, "She doesn't need a steak knife. Rona cuts her food with her tongue." Rona's the broad to whom Ryan O'Neal once mailed a live tarantula, and Mae West sent an enema bag with a note reading, "Stay pretty. Love, Mae." Rona was tough, with a drive and a creative output that makes Madge Ciccone look like Fran Lebowitz.

By the 1970s, she was defining and monopolizing TV celeb reportage, paving the way for the careers—and hairdos—of people like Janet and E!'s Steve Kmetko. (No offense, Steve, but I often think of Rona's fluffy blonde tornado when I'm watching your show.)

Rona's style was grounded, like Janet's, in an extreme hairdo. In Rona's case, it wasn't so much about the color as the shape. Rona's courageous coiffure rose several inches off the top of her head, giving her a glamorous and distinctive coneheadlike presence on the TV screens of America.

I called La Barrett at her Santa Barbara ranch and asked her if she was still sporting that signature do. "Yes—but it's a variation," replied Rona, with that unmistakable nasal monotone that had nightly filled the living rooms of America for so many years. "It's not as wiggy as before. In those days, I used to be five inches taller with hair spray."

Rona's current personal style? "Right now, I'm wearing chinos from Target, shoes by Ecco from Nordstrom, socks

from Costco and a shirt from Ralph Lauren via Nordstrom."
Rona's wardrobe is a bit of a comedown for the gal who once
splurged on Puccis and Scaasis from Giorgio Beverly Hills, but
perfectly consonant with her new Barbara Stanwyck–ian role
as ranch boss. Ranch boss??

In the 1980s Rona disappeared from the Hollywood landscape in a puff of hair spray . . . but now she's back! Yes, the
celebrity pooper-scooper with the frosted and feathered Mount
Etna coiffure *est revenu*! And she's channeling her wacky-chickery into a new arena: the cutthroat world of celebrity foods.
Paul Newman, watch your back!

Rona's latest venture, entitled Lavender by Rona Barrett
and cunningly subtitled "aRONAtherapy," is headquartered
amid ten acres of pesticide-free lavender in Santa Ynez, near
Santa Barbara. Impelled by her belief in the "magical healing
qualities" of lavender, Rona has begun producing skin creams
and mood-enhancing sachets.

But wacky, creative Rona is also chucking fistfuls of lavender into food! Yes, despite the fact that she was "born without
the K gene, as in kitchen," and the fact that most people are
mildly appalled by the idea of ingesting lavender, Rona has
given birth to the first-ever line of lavender-based food products: lavender ginger sauce, lavender honey mustard, lavender
chocolate sauce, lavender mayo.

Her ability to creatively reinvent herself and think of ever
more deranged ways to make a living—and style her hair—has
earned Rona a place in the W.C. Hall of Fame.

It was while writing for Rona's mags that Janet realized she
had found her calling. "I was getting paid for doing what I had

done for years. So, I closed my shop and went full-time at the *Enquirer.*" She soon realized that dish gathering was very competitive: if she didn't get there first somebody else would.

Dressed like a fluorescent Femme Nikita, Janet embarked on her stop-at-nothing dish-quest. "I would talk to dry cleaners, pharmacy managers. I wanted to know who was loading up on prescription drugs. Who was pumping their own gas because they were too stingy to pay the extra. I would use a makeup compact at the supermarket to see how much liquor Dick Van Dyke or Lucy was buying."

She ping-ponged back and forth between the *Enquirer* and the *Star,* finally settling in the mid-1980s at the *Star,* where she has reigned ever since.

By this time Janet's personal style was evolving and maturing, "In the early eighties I discovered Cholo culture—those fabulous Mexican gang boys who drive low-riders. They started the whole oversized thing. I would see them hanging out on Hollywood Boulevard, wearing hairnets and oversized Dickies belted tight." Janet got more than her fair share of attention from these unlikely lads, because of not just her looks, but her car. "I had a pink 1968 Ford Excel convertible. I copied the Cholos and put crucifixes—pre-Madonna—dangling from the rearview mirror."

For a while Janet dated her very own Cholo: "He was so sweet and *cute!* He drove a delivery truck for a kosher bakery. He used to drop off kosher cheesecakes at my apartment to win me over. If I wouldn't let him in, he would sleep overnight in his truck outside my apartment."

Janet's fearlessly empowered attitude toward men is totally consonant with her tough, assaultive personal style. It started at an early age. "I knew when I was very young that I did not want to get married. I wanted to make my own decisions and be master of my own life," says Janet, recalling the proud words of another Hollywood heroine, Myra Breckinridge.

The opening of Gore Vidal's mistresspiece resonates with Charltonesque empowerment:

I am Myra Breckinridge whom no Man shall ever possess. Clad only in a garter belt and one dress shield, I held off the entire elite of the Trobriand Islanders, a race who possess no words for "why" or "because." Wielding a stone axe, I broke the arms, the limbs, the balls of their finest warriors, my beauty blinding them, as it does all men, unmanning them in the way that King Kong was reduced to a mere simian whimper by beauteous Fay Wray whom I resemble left three-quarter profile if the key light is no more than five feet high during the close shot.

Janet lives right down the street from the Ravenswood, a Hancock Park apartment building that once sheltered *Breckinridge* star Mae West. "She was so liberated and ahead of her time. I loved the way she had these muscle guys in little trunks at her beck and call—very me." Janet's 1961 sprawling cement-block compound is the antithesis of Mae's satin-covered rococo bower and yet there is a parallel emphasis on stylish hedonism. Janet's Palm Springs–style pad makes one feel that, at any moment, an obedient leopard bikini-clad manservant might appear and give Janet a foot rub. As I mull over Janet's ball-breaking philosophy, a framed *Confidential* magazine cover on the wall of Janet's office catches my eye: "Kim Novak won't marry—one man can't satisfy her."

Janet attributes her Breckinridgesque view of men and marriage to watching her parents: "Men have all the fun. My dad was an independent spirit, if you know what I mean. I didn't want to marry and end up with the passive victim role."

This uniquely empowered attitude has resulted in neither celibacy, lesbianism nor a predilection for effeminate types. Like ultravirago Brigitte Nielsen, Janet has dated some of the butchest, if not *the* butchest, men in Hollywood. "For a year and a half I dated Arnold Schwarzenegger," says Janet, smiling broadly. "He was great—and single at the time, I might add." Herr Schwarzenegger shared Janet's irreverence and fondness for goofy practical jokes: "We used to go to parties and go into another room and make slapping and screaming noises and pretend he was beating me up to freak everyone out." The relationship fizzled when the gossip diva and the muscle dude realized they had different long-term expectations. "He wanted to have eight kids. I didn't want any. And dating him was also annoying because wherever we went, he got all the attention."

As Janet hops back into her El Dorado, she checks out a dashing Lenny Kravitz look-alike swaggering toward the store entrance in full Funkadelic 1970s regalia. "Gorgeous!" says Janet with a wackily predatory leer. The apparition sends her down memory lane and then causes her to qualify her initial approval rating: "I have to admit my favorite style of all times was the slick fashion of black men in Chicago in the 1950s. Unbelievable pimp style! Conked glossy hair and drapey pastel suits. So much better than that cheesy Superfly look." Miss Charlton throws her car into reverse and squeals out of the parking lot.

LISA EISNER—CRITTER CHIC AND GEEZER CHIC

"I'm always just a pussy hair from going over the edge. I walk a fine line," says Lisa Eisner, whose raunchy, entertaining dia-tribes are often peppered with cheeky expressions involving pussy hair, or even salty bumper-sticker slogans like "If it's got tires or tits it's gonna give you trouble." Despite her dainty, clotheshorsey femininity, Lisa often talks like a Cadil-lac-driving, toupee-wearing, secondhand car salesman, and she occasionally dresses like one too. Unlike Susanne or Janet, who ground their wacky-chickery with a signature look, Lisa bounces between several style identities. To say she has multi-ple personality disorder is a bit harsh, but there is more than a pussy hair of truth to the accusation.

Forty-four-year-old Los Angeles–based book publisher and photographer Lisa is a raving fashion exhibitionist with a very special gift. Part Millicent Rogers, part Lucille Ball, with a dash of Tina Chow* and lots of Sammy Davis, Lisa has the unique

---

*If you aren't familiar with these two twentieth-century style titans, then you are prob-ably at least familiar with the trends that they pioneered. Midcentury bohemian Milli-cent Rogers popularized the wearing of humungous gobs of American Indian turquoise jewelry with nonethnic attire. The unbelievably chic Mrs. Chow—restaurateuse and jewelry designer—was the first broad to wear vintage drag and not look like a homeless person or a refugee from a suburban production of *Guys and Dolls*.

ability to flirt with the grotesque while remaining unimpeach-ably chic. An Indian headdress; a Bob Mackie/Shirley Bassey frock; a cowboy hat with a tiara on top; a full-length, A-line, trapunto, floral kaftan found in a Palm Springs thrift store and resembling a giant oven mitt—these are a few of her favorite things and they just happen to look great on her.

Illustrious devotees regularly throng the temple of La Eisner to drink of the perversely inspiring waters therein. "I would like to be reborn as her child," says collaborator and friend Tom Ford. "She would let me dye my hair pink, wear turquoise jewelry and high heels and bathe naked with the other children in the neighborhood." He is one of many who hang on her every word, and accessory. "She's a touchstone," says Isaac Mizrahi. "If she likes it, I know it's good." How the hell did this hick chick get to be so darn groovy and know so many fancy people?

Lisa blames the rodeo girls of Wyoming. "They're my idols. Sometimes I think they even stopped me becoming a lesbian," says Lisa referring to the bronco-riding glamour-pusses who would compete at the Cheyenne Rodeo during her teen years. "I was such a tomboy. They introduced me to *Dynasty* glamour, nails, frosted hair, suntan panty hose and glitter. Oh! And kitchen-sink accessorizing—baubles, bangles, spangles and neckerchiefs à la Glen Campbell." When she started her bou-tique publishing house, Greybull, with Roman Alonso in 1999, she wasted no time in paying homage to her teen muses: *Rodeo Girl*—a collection of Lisa's photos—was Greybull's first and most successful book so far. But what about her freaky side? She didn't learn that from the rodeo girls.

When did she first realize she was a bit strange? "I remember exactly—I was in home ec. class and I was the only one making Siamese-cat-print corduroy hot pants. The other girls were making dirndl skirts. I realized I was a freak." In many American schools an unorthodox attitude such as Lisa's would have resulted in ostracism and bullying, but not in Wyoming. "Cheyenne was full of very sweet accepting people, plus I was a cheerleader—any excuse to dress up—so I was accepted."

While in high school Mrs. Eisner produced fashion shows at Fowler's, the local department store. Her entrepreneurial, modish ways continued to blossom at the University of Wyoming, where she wrote a monthly fashion column in the school newspaper. "My look at that time was gauchos, Frye boots and head wraps—very Mica Ertegun," recalls Lisa. The cheerleading also went to the next level: "We had a white Shetland pony for a mascot. Every time the team had a touchdown we would scream round the field with that pony. It was insane!"

Lisa dropped out of college, found her way to New York and an internship at *Mademoiselle*. A three-year stint at American *Vogue*'s office in Paris followed. She came back to New York—"I missed supermarkets and drugstores"—and took a design job at Ralph Lauren. In 1983 she met and married Eric Eisner and moved to Beverly Hills, where she has lived ever since, just down the street from Elvis's old pad.

"I have always felt totally at home here. For a while I was the West Coast editor of *Vogue*, which meant nothing because in the mid-eighties everyone hated L.A.—but I loved it." Lisa finds L.A. totally hilarious and embraces its absurdities, even the new age stuff: "I love the Sikhs in their do-rags. I have a holistic dentist, Dr. Shukard; he gives you a giant ruby to hold to get rid of pain. I have a shitload of jewels in my teeth. He puts these Barbie jewels under your gold fillings—for good energy. Los Angeles is a cartoon," says Lisa, describing what would appear to be a bigger, glossier version of her hokey Cheyenne childhood.

It was on the smoggy, broken-dream-strewn boulevards of Los Angeles that Lisa discovered a hitherto undocumented indigenous species—the geezer—and found her true calling. "I saw these old guys driving their Cadillacs with their custom clothes and eyewear. I felt like I had unearthed a whole secret geezer scene." Her passion for upscale, customized sleazy style gathered momentum. "I was at the Sammy Davis estate sale about ten years ago, and I just went bonkers. I bought a ton of his jackets and shirts—he was tiny—and I wear them with pride."

Luckily for Lisa, the well-buffed fingernails of what she calls geezer chic had yet to loosen their grip on the 90210 zip code. "I found all these great stores in Beverly Hills and became a drag king. Then I bought a Cadillac. My two kids, Louie and Charley, were embarrassed. But now they think it's cool 'cuz it's sort of hip-hop. I just got my third Caddie. A ragtop—I got the 'gold package.' Can you believe?" said Mrs. Eisner, her voice filled with unabashed passion for the geezer lifestyle.

Geezer chic, once you have the basic tchotchkes, is a low-maintenance lifestyle. Which works for Lisa at this point in her life: since founding Greybull Press, she doesn't have the time "to be quite as fabulous as I used to be." But she's not complaining—*au contraire.* "Book publishing rocks! We didn't know any of the rules so we went into it like Elly May and Jed Clampett." This hasn't stopped Lisa and Roman from being successful. Collections of photography by geezer documentarian/paparazzo Ron Galella and actor Dennis Hopper have sold well.

The latter book, *1712 North Crescent Heights: Dennis Hopper Photographs, 1962–1968,* is a unique window into the life of Dennis Hopper and his then wife Brooke Hayward, and their groovy existence in early 1960s L.A., the bohemian pre-Manson, pre–Joan Didion, pre-Wonderland murders, pre-riots L.A. These previously unpublished photos show an enviably wacky, creative existence not dissimilar from the one that Lisa has created for herself. It's a world of unencumbered frontier silliness.

"This is a totally L.A. wardrobe," says Lisa, sporting the biggest silver fox hat I've ever seen and making a sweeping gesture across the racks in the massive closet* of her szhooshy Bel Air hacienda. The overriding impression given by Mrs. Eisner's extensive clothing and accessory collection is one of wildlife, as in Museum of Natural History, as in fur, hair, horns, and feather, feathers, feathers. Total critter chic. "These shoes are made from the undersides of turtles," says Mrs. Eisner, proffering a pair of fascinatingly butch, Miss Marple shoes.

As we chat La Eisner throws on various fur hats and makes endless moues in the mirror: after the oversized, two-feet-wide silver fox comes a series of fetching chinchilla berets, fol-

---

*The oversized closet is, regardless of socioeconomic milieu, a w.c. trademark. My girls are chronic hoarders; they often suffer from delusions as to the posterity potential of their old clothes, e.g., "This skort is part of fashion history—one day I'll donate it to the Smithsonian!"

lowed by a white fox hat that resembles an electrified afro.
The entertaining Mrs. Eisner has a well-rehearsed series of
hammy routines involving her fur hats: "Look! Michael Jackson. Wow! Carol Channing!" A fuchsia fur hat with matching
boa becomes a giant, saucy French beret or a big 1950s pompadour. Still wearing her fuchsia beret, Lisa models a series of
vintage critter couture coats: ocelot, rabbit and a mink vest
with python strips: "I sort of love the whole idea, like a
python eating a mink. This is food-chain chic.

"It's all vintage. I could never buy new fur." To illustrate
her point she grabs a 1960s white chiffon pleated wedding
dress with a white rabbit-fur bodice. Around her shoulders
she throws a fox fur complete with head, legs and rhinestone-
button eyes. "Because I really love Nature and, you know, this
critter was shot fifty years ago."

We move from fur to feathers: we're talking grouse, pheasant, ostrich, even crow feathers. "I talk to birds in my head
and I understand them. I know what they're saying," says
Mrs. Eisner, looking like a total nut in a navy-feathered cloche.
"Isn't that the first sign that you've got to check yourself in?
Anyway, I guess I've always been aware of birds and hawks because they've always sort of communicated to me."

Looking even more deranged, Lisa pulls out the Indian
headdress that she wore on her book tour and plops it on her
head, transforming herself into a giant feather duster. She
chuckles at herself in the mirror. "It totally works if you wear
it with a conservative blouse and skirt. But after a while I get
a raging headache, and it leaves a huge lobotomy line on my
forehead so I can never take it off."

Via feathers we access Mrs. Eisner's more femmy side. "I

used to do this thing where I'd go to Palm Springs. I wouldn't bring anything and I would just wear what I found in the consignment shops—sixties hostess gowns: Bob Mackie, Scaasi, Galanos, Ethel of Tel Aviv." Before I can ask Lisa to elaborate on Ethel, she is enthusiastically screeching, "This one belonged to Vikki Carr!" and wafting a pink sleeveless jumpsuit with matching beaded bolero. With Vikki Carr tossed nonchalantly over her left arm, Lisa takes me on a tour of her drawers of accessories: a tiara; a custom fez that says "Eisner Photographer"; mounds of raw cavemanish turquoise jewelry, saber teeth and a Shriner tiger claw. "It's all about scale," says Lisa, her fez tassel swinging in her eyes. Her accessories and her clothing all seem to fall into the "conversation piece" category. I ask her if this is important to her. "No, not really because I don't really give a shit about talking to anybody about what I'm wearing. That takes the fun away."

Having now decimated her closet, Lisa heads for the geezer section, which she recently moved into her husband's allotted space. "I mostly feel really girly, but sometimes I feel like, I got to get some shit done and so I put on a Jack Taylor," says Lisa, gesturing toward a row of meticulously hung suits. Mr. Taylor is Mrs. Eisner's curmudgeonly and utterly fabulous tailor. A brilliant raconteur and an unbelievable craftsman, Mr. Taylor is geezer royalty. With his store of geezer anecdotes and his devotion to an elegant seventies silhouette, he has, despite the cost attendant with his bespoke skills, attracted a new generation of Hollywood bucks and buckesses: Jason Schwartzman, Justin and David Murdock, Roman Alonso, Stephanie and Dewey Nicks, Peter Getty and modish costume designer Susan Becker are all flocking to have their inside legs measured by Jack. His famous former clients include *über-*

geezers Danny Thomas, Sid Caesar, John Wayne, Charles Bronson, Hal Roach, Jack Lemmon and Monty Hall.

In one hand Mrs. Eisner holds a black tuxedo in waffle velvet with polka-dot lining, in the other, the ultimate in customized geezer chic, a suit with Mrs. Eisner's name woven as a pinstripe. Lisa accessorizes her suits with shirts by Anto—Formerly Nat Wise, the maker of Sammy's shirts. Mrs. Eisner tracked this company down after seeing the name in the shirts, which she had purchased at the Sammy estate sale. Owner Anto Sepetjian and his sons, Jack and Ken, have the entire rat-pack archive: she can order custom shirts where Frank Sinatra used to—and Jerry Lewis and Frankie Avalon still do! "I just got a Jerry Lewis shirt made—six-inch cuffs. How cool is that?" screeches Lisa.

The house specialty is a style called the Lady's Man. This particular shirt was Sammy Davis's fave: It's an unbelievably groovy, fitted eveningish number with a giant, four-inch, rolled button-down collar, lace-trimmed placket and cuffs and pearl buttons. It is cut without tails; two cheeky slits adorn each hip. Mrs. Eisner wears hers, just as S.D. did—outside the pants.

Lisa is an authority on the ever-diminishing L.A. geezer hangouts. After an exhausting shirt-buying spree, Lisa often staggers up the street to Nate 'n Al; this beneath-the-valley-of-the-ultra-geezers deli, at 414 North Beverly Drive, has everything a hungry guy might enjoy, including caramel-colored booths. Other Eisner favorites: the Polo Lounge ("I always have the McCarthy salad") and La Scala.

Looking as if she might be suffering from a mild case of multiple-personality-related exhaustion, Lisa rummages in her geezer accessory drawer and extracts her prize possession: a pair of cheesy gold "face furniture" sunglasses bearing a light-ning bolt and the initials TCB. "Taking Care of Business! Elvis used to give these to his people," she explains with a shriek.

L.A. wacky chicks like Lisa and Janet are drawn to the fetishistic sizzle of celebrity relics, and they incorporate them into their personal style. They revel in the camp of celebrity culture. It's their way of disarming and debunking a sytem that has no room for chicks of their ilk. Nonetheless, Lisa gets all misty and philosophical when she talks about her idols.

"The thing about Elvis that's always so great is that he looks exactly like his personality. It's not like he's trying to look dif-ferent or pretend to be somebody else. His personality and his look are so perfect together—same with Robert Evans."* Lisa and I both lament this dying breed of hairy chested, man-tan-smeared gold-chain-wearers.

"The pancake, the mancake, the virility. It's the Vegas in-fluence," says Lisa perceptively. "That whole Duke of Windsor uptight Wasp thing. *Who cares!* It means nothing here in L.A. Whenever I do my man thing it's always Vegas inspired, it's always Elvis inspired or Bob Evans inspired. Your collar is way too big and you wear lots of gold jewelry and you wear these

*The stylish, charismatic, movie-producing Mr. Robert Evans (*Chinatown, Rosemary's Baby, The Godfather,* etc.) defined 1970s Hollywood, that intelligent era when directors and producers (and Sue Mengers) were all much more important than the movie stars. Medallion-wearing Bob, the patron saint of custom life styling, has one pant and one shirt, and he orders them in a million colors. According to Mr. Evans, whose must-see docu-bio, *The Kid Stays in the Picture,* was released in 2002, this is not a uniform, "it's a silhouette." Mr. Evans's style connoisseurship is rigorously egocentric. What does loner Evans do if somebody compliments him on his tie? "I go home and I'll shred that tie. I don't want to make the tie look good; I want the tie to make me look good."

Elvis sunglasses. It's about making money and spending money. Forget about the Wasp thing."

As Lisa rants, I think of those drearily attired English aristos with their worn-out shoes. They shop at Marks & Spencer once every ten years and go to snotty emporiums like Trumper on Jermyn Street where they can actually get their toothbrushes rebristled. The flashy geezer thing may not be very highbrow, but it is utterly devoid of snobbery.

Before leaving Mrs. Eisner to the mayhem of her closet cleanup, I ask her if there was ever a period in her life when she had one personality. Lisa scratches her head through a chinchilla beret and replies thoughtfully, "People said to me, 'You are never going to find a man dressed like that.' And I was like, O.K., you've just got to look hot or something. So I tried to go that way, and I actually attracted a lot more men. It worked, but then I thought, 'Oh please.' It was just not for me. I felt like I tried rehab and it just didn't work." Lisa puts Vikki Carr back under plastic and bids me farewell.

The above chicks have all successfully developed a signature style, but they have something else in common, a little indefinable extra *quelque chose*, without which they would not have left the starting gate.

Pulling off a unique style requires something the French call *"le chien."* No, I'm not suggesting you buy yourself a corgi. I wish it were that simple. Permit me to explain.

Du chien is an elusive quality, but in her sensational novel *Scruples,* Judith Krantz takes a good shot at defining it: "When a woman has *du chien* she has something that is not chic nor elegance nor even glamour," she writes. *"Chien* is spicy, tart,

amusing, pungent, tempting." But not tarty. "Catherine
Deneuve has glamour, but Cher has *chien*."

Susanne, Janet and Lisa have each propelled their individual styles with gallons of Cher-like *chien*. It's that ballsy, air-
biting confidence that neutralizes all critics and allows any
chick—regardless of how wacky—to soar. When you have *le
chien*, there is no such thing as a *faux pas*.

So cultivate your *chien*, and let rip. And remember, developing
and adopting a signature style requires masses of uninhibited
experimentation. So, go ahead, smother your lids in cerise-
colored eye shadow, hot-glue a glazed cock-feather to your
chapeau and overload your lobes with turquoise-encrusted
shoulder-sweeping earrings.

Let Susanne and Janet and Lisa be your inspiration: ape
their *chien*, but don't copy their individual styles, or they will
get really mad and set their *chiens* on you.

CHAPTER 4

HOME

SAFE SPACES FOR SPACE CASES

They say the Marchesa Casati kept a gorilla in her living room. In the early part of the twentieth century, this vampy show-off funneled all her cash and creativity into the decoration of her brazier-lit Venetian *palazzo*. She filled her decadent Aubrey Beardsley–esque hellhole with appalling and fascinating artifacts from the ancient world, thereby creating the sound stage for the ongoing one-woman narcissi-fest that was her life. Late at night, the Marchesa, dressed in high-priestess drag, could be seen strutting from room to room throwing fistfuls of rotting meat to her bored pet panthers. On casual Fridays she wore tweed pajamas with gold cowboy boots, and if one of her braziers went out, they say she shrieked like a peacock until it was relit. Just a simple girl with a dream!

Though clearly a tad pretentious, the Marchesa was a trendsetting kind of gal: it wasn't long before every woman in Europe was festooning her bedroom à la Scheherazade and screeching for a Nubian to come and light her brazier. The Marchesa popularized the residential exoticism that eventually

brought camel saddles and peacock chairs into the naffest*
reaches of suburbia. The influence of her szhooshy crib-style
on twentieth-century residential design lives on today in the
evergreen fondness among campier folk for leopard print.

"Little" Edie and "Big" Edith Bouvier Beale, though infinitely less exotic than the Marchesa, were no less influential,
and a hell of a lot more silly. The codependent spiral of this
mother and daughter—cousins of the late Jackie Kennedy—
was immortalized in the 1975 Maysles brothers documentary
Grey Gardens. The setting for this shockumentary is the fabulously dilapidated Beale East Hampton house. The tick- and
vermin-infested yard and the weed-strangled house are so
overgrown with creepers that they are indistinguishable from
one another. The unemployed Beales, long since inured to the
decay around them, putz around their stinky manse while the
rain pours in through the roof and raccoons munch playfully
on the banisters.

Narrow-minded cinéastes have blasted this film for its exploitative intrusions: to me it just looks like objective docu-
mentation of two wacky chicks letting rip. This theatrically
inclined mother and daughter keep boredom at bay by
singing, tying blouses on their heads and hurling accusations
and "family truths" at each other. The edgy radical neglect of

---

*The origin of the word "naff:" now widely used in the U.K. to mean "a depressing lack
of style," "naff" was originally a gay slang acronym for "Not Available for Fucking"—
i.e., straight, i.e., nowhere near as fabulous as a gay person or thing. "Naff" is a great
word with no American translation. Remember, "tacky," means "cheap or glitzy,"
whereas "naff" is about stylistic shortcomings that are horrifyingly average and pathetically ungroovy. Use the word "naff" and become a connoisseur of naff.

their crib recalls that of the late Quentin Crisp, who once said, "Cleaning is a waste of time—after the first four years it doesn't get any worse."

Now, twenty-five years later, the esprit of *Grey Gardens* has morphed and evolved and reincarnated itself into the annoying "shabby chic" movement. Happy well-adjusted middle-class people around the world now pay good money to have their banisters racooned. Sadly, Little Edie and Big Edie are not around to share in the proceeds of the lifestyle, which they clearly originated.

Jackie O.'s cousins may not have possessed the entrepreneurial moxie necessary to brand their wackiness, but that's not to say that other wacky chickoraters have not managed to alchemize their kooky residential style. Some have even made a bloody fortune.

Elsie De Wolfe, aristocrat, exercise freak and decorator *par excellence,* lived a life of chauffeur-driven Churchillian grandeur, and she funded it with the proceeds of her interior design company. Say the words "interior decorator" and most people will imagine a bow-tie-wearing, pasty-faced fop skipping around town toting a man-bag full of swatches and a pocket full of dreams. Elsie De Wolfe was anything but nelly. In fact, she was a dynamic lesbian with a huge ego: when she saw the Parthenon she is reputed to have screamed, "It's beige! My color!"

A prominent society broad who married an aristocrat and became Lady Mendl, La Wolfe (Le Wolfe to her friends) hid her sexual inversion under the hydrangea-colored blue rinse that she invented and shared with a series of dyed poodles called "Blue-blue." Go-getting Elsie was the antithesis of those suicidal *Well of Loneliness** dykes who also inhabited the early part of the twentieth century.

Miss De Wolfe was a self-invented woman when nobody was double-checking the facts: she grabbed life by the balls and decorated it. She was driven by a proto-Martha-Stewart-ian desire to impose her aesthetic on the world. When she was in hospital at the end of her life, she was so appalled by the décor she redecorated everything and then sent the hospital a bill.

Sister Parrish, another deranged and deceased doyenne of interior decoration, was also a tad fascistic about inflicting her highly evolved aesthetics on others. When she took on a job she would wheel a little red cart through the prospective house ruthlessly editing, tossing sentimental keepsakes and offensive souvenirs into it—oblivious to the teary protestations of her paying clients. For extremist Sister, everything was either utterly fatal or wildly fabulous. "If you don't do something about your hair you will be ruined," she once advised an innocent bystander.

Eccentric though they were, it is important to remember that the twentieth century was festooned by these archly wacky creative women. Dorothy Draper vanquished the postwar blues with gigantic cabbage rose chintzes and monstrous birdcages, while Syrie Maugham filled huge urns with bleached pheasant feathers and sloshed gallons of white paint

---

*The Well of Loneliness, by Radclyffe Hall, is a lugubriously poetic 1928 wrist-slasher of a lesbian novel about "a soul that finds itself wandering, unwanted, between the spheres." Memo to you: triple your Zoloft before reading.

on everything, including priceless French escritoires and Renaissance tallboys. These w.c.'s, like their sisters in fashion, found a milieu in which their provocative originality was a plus, and they went for it, inflicting their own unique tastes on other people over and over again and then billing them for it over and over again. Eccentrics have always perpetrated their greatest excesses behind closed doors, but these gals were smart enough to open their doors and turn their own homes into cash-producing portfolios.

You certainly don't have to hire a crazed pseudo-aristocratic lesbian interior decorator in order to create an atmosphere of bohemian wackiness *chez vous.*

In the early 1970s, pink-haired British fashion designer Zandra Rhodes got a great deal on a rambling pad in London's trendy Notting Hill Gate. The kicker? There were sitting tenants who had lived in this old house for years. "A lovely old couple and a fabulous spinster called Miss Hunter," recalls landlady Zandra. "They didn't have any idea what they were in for when I moved in."

Like all genuine wacky chicks, Zandra was incapable of moderating her extreme approach to life. Despite living cheek-by-jowl with her straitlaced tenants, she blithely pursued her unorthodox lifestyle to the hilt. Her home became an art installation, and her sitting tenants became the rent-paying George Segal sculptures who haunted her hallways.

An inveterate interior design extremist, ultragroovy Miss Rhodes filled her pad with fluorescent hues, chiffon drapes, provocative art and cacti made from pleated satin. She daubed the walls with her signature squiggles and built a womblike alcove bathroom in the hall and lined it with pleated red plastic. The sitting tenants bore witness to the daily hilarity and excesses of Zandra's zany life. Miss Hunter et al. would wave amiably to Zandra as she quaffed champagne and took her hallway bubble baths, surrounded by urns of gaudy plastic flowers.

Gradually, the sitting tenants fell under Zandra's wacky-chick spell: they enjoyed the spectacle and embraced Zandra's friends who included media maven Janet Street-Porter (*Ab Fab*'s Patsy is based on her) and massive gender-bending thespian Divine. "Miss Hunter loved him," recalls Zandra of the deceased *Pink Flamingos* and *Hairspray* star. "She always left out a tray of jam tarts or fairy cakes for him whenever he stayed, even after she found him in a compromising position with a rent boy."

Miss Hunter outlasted the others, eventually becoming Zandra's housekeeper. A meticulous laundress, she flagellated herself for hours by tentatively trying to iron Zandra's Frederick's of Hollywood trashy nylon undies without scorching or shriveling them. She was found dead one morning with her cold legs sticking out of the red rubber bathroom by one of Zandra's houseboys.

Creative Zandra "tarted up" her crib on a tight budget, using store display materials, her own printed chiffons, plastic flowers and gallons of paint. When w.c.'s have more cash, they can really take their décor Auntie Mame*-ing over the top.

---

*If you do not understand this reference, then you have my deepest sympathies. Rent the Rosalind Russell version of *Auntie Mame* and rectify this contemptible gap in your knowledge.

For example, when British wactress Hermione Gingold moved to New York, she found herself pining for the cottagey comfort of rural England. The solution? She added a thatched roof to her Park Avenue penthouse. After comedic legend Joan Rivers made a few bucks, she turned her New York apartment into a fantasia of such baroque gorgeousness that it makes Versailles look like the Unabomber shack. Meanwhile in Chicago, socialite and wacky tour de force Sugar Rautbord ditched her Lake Shore Drive apartment and moved into the three-story hotel ballroom in the wildly ornate Blackstone Hotel. "I'm doing minimalist opulence. Very haunted. Very Dostoyevsky. Very Zhivago, like when the Communists have moved into the Palace."

One of the most thrilling aspects of writing this book was gaining special access to the inner sanctums of the wackiest women in America and witnessing the creativity therein. I can honestly say I was never disappointed. Whether filled with live reptiles or daubed obscenities on the wall, every wacky-chick abode held tons of decorating tips and endless surprises. Whether rich or poor, extremism is the principle that guides a wacky chick as she decorates her lair.

PEARL HARBOUR—HOME IS WHERE THE TART IS

At one point in her life, Pearl Harbour, former front-gal for 1970s new wavers Pearl Harbour and the Explosions, lived in a storage locker. "It was in Mill Valley, Marin County," recalls Pearl, who was thus named because her parents married on

Pearl Harbor Day 1947. "I lived there for three years. It had a
sink with cold water and a kitty litter box, which was another
sink, with a hole cut in it, and a hot plate. I just put rugs on
the dirt floor and there was a hole in the window." As we sit
and drink tea in Pearl's unbelievably gussied-up Hollywood
music-box house, it's hard for me to visualize my hostess in
the grim, eco-lesbo, survivalist surroundings she is describing. As her story unfolds, I start to understand how this
makeshift abode might well have been the perfect backdrop
for Pearl's gypsy years.

In early 1973, this cheeky seventeen-year-old high school
dropout arrived in San Francisco, the wacky Mecca, with a
song in her heart. "I always knew I wanted to be a singer," recalls Pearl, momentarily holding an imaginary mike in her
right hand, "so my family let me drop out of high school and
head to Frisco. I told my dad I wanted to be a country singer
because that was his favorite. He didn't realize that to be a
country singer Nashville might have made more sense."

Pearl, whose real name is Pearl Gates, twinkles at her own
teenage duplicity while simultaneously trying to detach herself
from the pink-vinyl couch to which her bare thigh has adhered.
"I like this cheap sixties furniture," says Pearl, accompanied by
that distinctive drawn-out unsticking sound that flesh makes
when separating from vinyl, "but it's not good if you like to
wear minis, which I do, to show off me legs."

Me legs? American-born Pearl has a strange accent: it vac-
illates between genteel California and Cockney sparrow.
Pearl's intonation is legitimized by the fact that, during the
1980s, she was married to the gorgeous Paul Simonon, bass

guitarist for punk-rock legends the Clash. "He was voted one of the top ten most attractive blokes, and he was all mine!" recalls Pearl of their eight-year London-based marriage.

Pearl, who looks a bit like a redheaded Bette Midler/Dolly Parton hybrid, isn't chopped liver either. For a broad of forty-seven, she has remarkably flashable legs. Today they are clearly visible because she is wearing a sleeveless minishift emblazoned, front and back, with a giant photo-portrait of Bobby Kennedy. "It's a vintage campaign dress," explains this radical songbird while toying coyly with the torrent of suspiciously thick, silky, auburn tresses that cascade from the crown of her head. "I bought it at the Marin County flea market for only a dollar from a woman who actually campaigned for him." Pearl's overall look is that of a politically aware burlesque queen gussied up for a night at the Grand Ole Opry, circa 1965. Her cat-eyes are accentuated with Maria Callas tadpole-shaped slashes of black eyeliner and her lips are stained red with a drugstore product called Deadly Darling. Those fake auburn tresses—"me add-ons"—are expertly pinned in under her own russet locks.

Pearl's feet and legs are adorned with a pair of very Maria Montez–ish snake-themed sandals. The beady eye of each reptile starts at the big-toe cleavage; the long, wired, metallic gray body of each snake winds its way up to the knees à la a Cecil B. De Mille slave girl.

Burlesque has been a bouncy leitmotif in Pearl's life, dating back to her storage-locker days. Her first gig in S.F. was tap-dancing with legendary art-rock band the Tubes. Wearing satin shorts, boxing gloves, an eye patch and fake bruises,

Pearl had entered a Tubes-sponsored talent competition. The prize? "Three weeks performing onstage with them at Bimbo's, this really cool club." Pearl and the boys hit it off and the gig became permanent. Through her alliance with the Tubes, Pearl made her first forays into the world of burlesque. "We had these crazy show-biz gals who danced onstage with us. When they weren't dancing with the band they were stripping." This close encounter would have a lasting impact on Pearl's highly individual interior decorating aesthetic.

Hypnotized by the whirl of sequined pasties and the snap of garter belts, Pearl was drawn inexorably into the tawdry netherworld of adult entertainment, becoming a topless dancer at the El Cid on Broadway. "I didn't turn tricks so I wasn't a threat to anybody. Everybody lent me all their incredible costumes. This was the beginning of my glamour girl obsession: I got to wear rhinestone bikinis with rhinestone tiaras and matching rhinestone shoes and white rabbit-fur bikinis. It was like . . . the ultimate."

Stripping and tapping paid the rent and then some. "I always had loads of dough in the bank 'cuz my storage locker was only seventy-five dollars a month. But I always had dirt and leaves in my stilettos, because it was at the bottom of this muddy ravine."

Through the Tubes, mud-spattered Pearl made an important career connection, "There was a comedian named Jane Dornacker, pronounced "door knocker"—she was married to guy called Bob Knickerbocker, which made her Jane Door-knocker-Knickerbocker. She had written the Tubes song 'Don't Touch Me There.'" Miss Dornacker recruited Pearl for her all-girl band, Lela and the Snakes. "She covered all genres, so I changed costumes. I hula-hooped and tapped and sang in German."

In 1977, Miss Gates left the Snakes and formed the now legendary Pearl Harbour and the Explosions. "Three guys and me. We weren't punk—we were early new wave. We did really well and got a record deal with Warner Brothers." The record company put a lot money and time into Pearl's band but after two years the lead singer was disenchanted with her genre. "I was becoming obsessed with rockabilly music, way before the Stray Cats. Warner Brothers got really angry, because they spent all this money on this new wave band and I wanted to go to England and play rockabilly."

Pearl explains the enduring power of this blue-collar musical genre. "Rockabilly is very wacky. I mean, 'ave you ever heard the 'Castro Rock' or the 'Ubangi Stomp'—that's another one." Pearl's stirring a cappella renditions of these rockabilly classics, which she performs from her sticky couch, are accompanied by hilariously goofy hand gestures.

Though clearly adoring the rockabilly style—which, is the second biggest influence on her interior decorating aesthetic—Pearl has her reservations about the philosophy. "The scene is a little too narrow-minded for me. A lot of rockabilly fans are racists and homophobic. They're Republican and right-wing."

For Pearl the biggest stars in the rockabilly firmament are Elvis ("he started out being rockabilly"), Gene Vincent ("one of the most popular coolest cats") and Eddie Cochran. Chicks have also made their mark in this male-dominated musical niche, Janice Martin and Wanda Jackson being the most important. Pearl is realistic about the limitations of the rockabilly sociology. "The only way for a girl to hold her own in rockabilly culture is to look good all the time. She has to have her hair done, full makeup and her frock has to be perfectly fluffed and starched, which I find annoying." Pearl's approach to the music itself has always been to speed it up, "but not too fast—that's called 'psychobilly.'" Her enthusiasm and creativity brought this genre to a whole new audience. Pearl's most popular successful rockabilly recording was "Fujiyama Mama," made famous and written by her idol Wanda Jackson. She entertains me with a few incendiary stanzas, belted out in double-quick time.

At the time she embraced rockabilly Pearl was dating a guy named Cosmo Vinyl, the personal manager of the Clash and of the groundbreakingly deranged Ian Dury and the Blockheads of "Hit Me with Your Rhythm Stick" and "Sex and Drugs and Rock and Roll" fame.

Pearl gets teary as she tells me about the influence upon her life of the great Ian Dury. A childhood polio victim who died in 2000, Mr. Dury adored Pearl and encouraged the lyricist in her: "He bought me me first thesaurus and rhyming dictionary. He was more wacky than any chick I ever knew. All the punks, even the Sex Pistols, they were scared of him. If you pissed him off, he would hit you with his leg iron."

Cosmo and Pearl headed across the pond. In 1980 Pearl made a rockabilly punk album with the Clash and the Blockheads called *Don't Follow Me, I'm Lost Too.* With stardom—or at least notoriety—at her fingertips, Pearl did something really stupid: "I decided I was going to be a radical risk-taker and not to put the Clash and the Blockheads names on the album." Frustrated with its burgeoning star's foibles, Warner Brothers dropped her.

Instead of rushing back to the States with her tail between her fabulous legs, Pearl met and married her dreamboat wealthy rocker husband, Paul Simonon. "He was lovely, but all the fucking groupies backstage just zoomed in on him straight away. It was very difficult." Pearl calmed her jealousies by making rockabilly music and by tarting up their love nest.

Every Friday and Saturday—"no matter how hungover or knackered"—Pearl would drag herself down Portobello Road and shop till she dropped, filling her Notting Hill Gate rock pad with mounds of dirt-cheap, postwar ephemera and kitsch.

During the 1980s Pearl had plenty of dough with which to fund her interior decorating passions. Her husband was raking it in and she had suddenly become huge in Japan. "I got signed to Island Records and went to Japan with the Clash. I recorded an album with these Japanese rockabillys. So cute!" The locals adored her but they had a hard time saying her name, "They called me Par Habah." Pearl saw how truly unconditional her acceptance was when she played a concert in Hiroshima. "I thought people were going to make a big stink because of my name but nobody said a word. They're funny that way."

Around 1986 the Clash broke up and Pearl's husband decided he wanted to be "a freewheeling kind of biker dude." By the end of the decade, Pearl was divorced and back—with all her kitsch in storage—in the City by the Bay. Pearl continued playing all through the 1990s, putting out an album called *Here Comes Trouble*. Though things were groovy on the musical front, Pearl started to feel uneasy. "It was the invasion of the dot-comers. The old San Francisco that I knew and loved was gone." Pearl threw her Portobello *trouvés* in a U-Haul and headed for Hollywood.

Pearl is stuck to her couch again. She nips into the bathroom and emerges with a towel for us both to sit on. Her gloriously sleazy Hollywood lair is a long way from the army bases in Germany where she grew up. "I was born in Monterey, California, but moved when I was six months old to Germany—Frankfurt, Munich and Heidelberg—'cuz my dad was in the army. Me mum's Filipino, so she's a great housekeeper—and a great mom of course."

I ask Pearl about the life of an army brat and its role in the evolution of her wackiness. "I learned early on how to be brave and not to be a wallflower and to talk to new kids. The entertainer in me came out because the best way to make friends is to make people laugh." By age twelve, Pearl was doing more than making people laugh. She was a rip-roaring hedonist: "I was a hard-core smoker and drinker because in Germany, if you could pick up the bottle and you had the money, you could buy it. And me, I did like me schnapps. Same with cigarettes. That was back when doctors would be smoking in their offices while they examined you. Now you're a murderer if you smoke cigarettes, especially in California."

Nicotine was the least of hard-livin' Pearl's vices. Frustrated by the unmitigated dreariness of the army-base teen club, Pearl decided that a hit of LSD, scored in downtown Heidelberg, might add a *je ne sais quoi* to her otherwise naff evenings. "It was fun—I saw green worms coming out of me eyeballs."

When an already tripping Pearl announced to her dad that she needed a ride, her dad balked, saying, "We're going to the races and you have to make the sandwiches." Pearl went to the kitchen and started frantically buttering bread. The surrealism of her circumstances sank in and a telltale giggle-fit convulsed her body. Enter perspicacious Dad. "He started yelling at me about the evils of drugs," recalls Pearl with a shudder. "He could have waited till the next day or something. D'you know what I mean?"

Mrs. Gates finished making the ramparts of sandwiches needed to feed Pearl's four growing brothers while Pearl was sent to her room. Her bad trip quickly deteriorated, thanks to her décor. "That was a good room actually," recalls Pearl as she trips down memory lane. "It was tiny and I covered the walls with tinfoil. I didn't know about Andy Warhol, or the Factory. I wasn't that clever. I just did it because I knew that it made the room look like the inside of a refrigerator and also where it crinkled it made shapes which looked like faces and landscapes, which was really horrible if you were 'aving a bad trip but lovely the rest of the time." Pearl's creative tinfoil teen pad was an augur of the majesty with which we are currently surrounded in her sticky L.A. digs.

Miss Harbour's current lair is a deceptively anonymous, bijoux bungalow with a wrought-iron fence. It looks exactly like the other housettes on this Raymond Chandler–ish South Hollywood street. The interior, however, is anything but anonymous. Once inside, the visitor is confronted by a raging, swollen river of eclectica, layer upon layer of collections and accumulations, each with a story to tell about Pearl's wacky past.

The living room in which we have been sitting on those hot-pink-vinyl couches looks like a cross between a retro knickknack retail store and what's known in English vernacular as a "knocking shop"—i.e., a brothel. The theme is glamour, albeit of the *fromage*iest variety. Rickety, splayed-leg Formica coffee tables with plastic laminate tops are juxtaposed with two separate arrangements of vinyl-covered 1960s TV furniture, all of which looks as if it was bought with Green stamps by a Jayne Mansfield wanna-be in about 1963.

Arrangements of well-dusted souvenirs, knickknacks and piles of 1950s glamour-girl paperbacks adorn every easy-care horizontal surface. Magazines with articles about wife swapping, Vegas sleaze parties and the hot-rod lifestyle are neatly stacked, suggesting that we might be in a dentist's waiting room—or a clap clinic—specializing in the care of bikers and strippers.

A good 60 percent of the wall surface is covered in original and, one would imagine, highly collectible 1950s burlesque posters. Pearl randomly reads some of her favorite copy lines: "Luscious Cheyenne, burlesque's most beautiful thrill dancer, the red-hot redhead. Ooooooh! And over here Lili St. Cyr . . . she was the most graceful, beautiful, sexy but not trashy at all. She's me favorite burlesque star."

I ask Pearl if she has any feminist misgivings about the exploitative side of stripping and tassel twirling. Like many wacky chicks, Pearl relates easily to the empowered-but-marginalized, Salome-ish ideal of the exotic dancer. She takes a deep breath and gives me her pragmatic, semi-autobiographical perspective: "There is a certain type of woman—God bless her. She doesn't have a good education and her body just happens to look a certain way, so she does what she can to make a living and feed her kids."

I tell Pearl her pad looks like that of a professional stripper. Her expression changes to one of deep satisfaction; she looks like she just won an Academy Award. She whispers a grateful, "Thank you. Mission accomplished."

The wall space around the fireplace has an entirely different, nonsleaze theme. Pearl calls it her "black art." Countless stylized African tribal heads adorn the entire wall; they are hand-sized plaster reliefs of women and men with jet-black skin and red lips. I recognize the genre: they were most often seen hanging on the walls of white working-class English homes. "I got them all down the Bella when I lived in London," says Pearl, using the local slang for Portobello Road. "They were made in the 1950s, when Britain invited the people from Jamaica and Trinidad and Tobago to come help rebuild the country, to make them feel welcomed." Though she adores these heads and has now owned some of them for more than twenty years, she eschews the Aunt Jemima knickknackery of her country of origin: "I hate American black stuff because it's all really Sambo racist and goofy with huge lips and huge eyes. My heads show blacks at their most beautiful."

As we make our way toward the dining room, Pearl pauses to show me her vintage guitar. "It's from the 1940s. I'm not very good at it. It sort of cramps my style because onstage it covers up half of me outfit." On a tacky little table next to the guitar I spy a brochure for Dollywood, Dolly Parton's Tennessee country-and-western theme park. "I'm going in September—I can't wait. I just remember being a little girl and loving her so much"—Pearl flings open the door to the dining room and continues her Dolly diatribe—"because she had the bleached blonde hair and the big boobs and lots of makeup and lots of great clothes and yet she was really cute and sweet and not a slut at all."

We are now in the cowboy-themed dining room. The walls are covered in paint-by-numbers posters and wall hangings depicting bucking broncos and American Indian chiefs. Yellowing vintage "boy's room" cowboy-print fabric curtains cast a 1940s amber light into the room and onto Pearl, who makes a surprising confession: "I always wanted to marry a cowboy but cowboys are like rockabillys. They're really cute, they dress great, but in reality, they're mostly racist, rednecked assholes." Pearl sweeps me, along with her refreshingly un-p.c. generalizations, through into the next room.

This kitchen shows no signs of culinary activity. Every shelf is filled with vintage appliances in their original boxes: a Betty Furness meat thermostat rubs shoulders with ancient tins of Domino sugar, Pillsbury flour and Maxwell House coffee. I ask Pearl if she is ever tempted to ditch the ephemera and memorabilia and become a raging minimalist. "Never!" replies Pearl, gesturing theatrically toward her bedroom.

Pearl's boudoir is her pièce de wacky résistance: Every inch of wall space is meticulously covered with neat rows of vintage purses. "Some of these bags I've had since I was dropping acid in Heidelberg," says Pearl with pride as she contemplates what looks like an art installation: vinyl structured bags, novelty bags, a French flag bag, a surfboard bag, commemorative resort purses—Vegas, Niagara Falls—raffia bags ("probably from the Philippines . . . going back to me roots"), a stuffed bird trapped under vinyl from Hawaii, a lovely black fringe number, a chamois bag, tarty red leather with gold coins, etc., etc. The intensity of Pearl's bags-as-wallpaper installation totally upstages the rest of the room, including the startling life-sized, psychedelic 1970s art nouveau revival butterfly lady who is printed onto Pearl's bedroom curtain and presides over Pearl's leopard-print bed.

Pearl's monumental bag collection, though totally extraordinary, is by no means as wacky as some of the collections I encountered during the preparation of this book. My girls have a special penchant for *objets bizarres* and they accumulate them with panting enthusiasm. Carrie Fisher of Beverly Hills collects thrift-shop oil portraits of other people's ugly children. Hattie Griffin of London collects Peruvian llama fetuses; she swears by their magical properties and begs Machu Picchu–bound chums to bring one or two back instead of the usual duty-free fags and booze.

Such collections are designed to simultaneously appall and delight any visitors. They send a strong nonverbal message about the mistress of the house and her idiosyncratic antibourgeois worldview. "If you don't geddit, you won't get me," they seem to say.

Jocelyn Meinster of California has started a collection of Chihuahua skeletons: the first, belonging to a recently departed, apple-headed, teacup named Tuesday (after Tuesday

Weld), adorns a console in her living room. At night, with the aid of flashlight, Jocelyn entertains friends with dramatic shadow plays on the wall, animating tiny Tuesday's remains into a toweringly ominous Godzilla skeleton.

Joan Seifter of New York has a collection of oiled and be-jeweled* tortoises, which wander around her bibelot-filled Central Park apartment. "I've had Josef for thirty years: he's a box turtle. Valentino is a red-footed tortoise, and Jemima, she's a pancake tortoise, very recherché," says the avant-garde fashion devotee who substitutes Valentino's jewels for a ban-dana when she takes him for a walk in Central Park so that she can spot him in tall grass. Regarding hygiene, Mrs. Seifter is admirably casual: "Valentino has a ramp which he uses to get out on the terrace. But frankly, at my age I don't give a damn about 'accidents' as long as I'm not having them."

Tchotchke-aholic *Paper* magazine editor Kim Hastreiter, also of New York City, has various collections: artifacts pro-duced by the mentally disturbed artists of the San Fran-cisco–based Creative Growth Collective. "I own fifty-three drawings by a Creative Growth artist named William Tyler, sixteen of which show the back of his head while watching different shows on TV." Miss Hastreiter also collects "de-mented Jewish housewife art from the fifties," chairs made out of soda cans by a seventy-something artist from Harlem and lousy oil portraits of American presidents.

After the intoxicating overstimulation of Pearl's purse collec-tion, the bathroom is a veritable lemon sorbet. Again the

---

*If you want to try this, then, do as Mrs. Seifter does—adhere those jewels with non-toxic surgical glue.

walls are covered in surreal repetition; this time, the theme is hair. Row upon row of vintage packaging for hair nets, hairpins and marcel clips are stapled to the wall. A maquillage shrine is the centerpiece: the vintage lashes, mascara and pancake are all in their original packages. "I got most of this stuff from my drag queen friend Doris Fish. I took care of her until she passed away. She taught me everything I know about makeup—which is a lot—and how to safety-pin wigs on top of each other to make a big beehive."

In a slightly somber mood Pearl leads me into the last room, her spare bedroom, where she houses her 350-plus pairs of shoes and her 200-plus costumes and mountains of day clothes. As previously stated, many of my girls have pathologically overextensive closets, but none can compete with Pearl.

This meticulously stuffed boutiquelike room now provides Pearl with her main source of income. "I'm with an agency called Dragon Talent. They started out being a drag queen agency. They get me extra work on music videos." Once booked, Pearl can costume herself, according to the director's vision, from her own vast warehouse: "I can do anything from a twenties-thirties flapper girl to an eighties perfect new wave girl to a seventies perfect hippie or seventies really funky hotpants-and-suede chick." Her more noteworthy appearances include a cameo on Cher's "Strong Enough" and Madonna's "What It's Like for a Girl." Though Pearl finds this work fairly unfulfilling, she invariably auditions well and gets regular bookings: "All the other girls who show up are called Heather or Michelle and they all have fake boobs—me, I'm naturally busty, thank you very much—and they all look the bloody same. People remember me." The extra work keeps the wolf from the door while Pearl puts together her next musical venture: "a sixties soul band—very Rufus Thomas—very danceable but with nasty lyrics."

As I prepare to leave optimistic, happy Pearl in her kitschy pad, I cannot help but reflect upon the joys of bad taste, and the miseries of good taste. Pearl's décor is, after all, the cheery lowbrow style of postwar upbeat consumerism. The bright colors and synthetic surfaces are so much more mood-elevating than the Armaniesque greiges and chambeiges that have become the signifiers of good taste at the beginning of the twenty-first century. Pearl's décor is therefore an unwitting testament to the utter pointlessness of good taste.

Like many wacky chicks I spoke to, Pearl spends untold amounts of time putzing around her playful, unorthodox home. "Why go out? It's festive, colorful, it's comfy—sort of—and upbeat. There are lots of cool books to look at, there are lots of records and I can dress however I want. It's my favorite place to be."

Miss Harbour's home—and that of every wacky chick—is more than just a creative romper room. It is also a therapeutic retreat from the exhausting vicissitudes that are part and parcel of *la vie wackee,* a place to recharge and refluff their Energizer bunny. Pearl's personal style, which she expresses full-throttle in her interior décor, can bring unwanted attention once she is outside the safety of her bungalow. "Before I leave the house I shimmy and shake it in front of the mirror to put myself in a good mood and to prepare myself because I know some fucking creep might get the wrong idea and think I'm slutty."

Given their emotional and creative commitment to their respective cribs, it's not surprising that my wacky chicks are fiercely protective of their spaces. I ask Pearl what would happen if a burglar broke into her pad and encountered her Aladdin's cave of kitsch. "They would probably turn right around and leave, unless they were a drag queen." And how about if they had a stall at the flea market? "If they took my stuff and tried to flog it, then I'd come and find them and break their legs."

CHAPTER 5

WORK

Chicks with Shticks

I'm going to Carnaby Street to get a flat and a modeling job and I'll be back in half an hour," screams a thick-thighed Lynn Redgrave—somewhat optimistically—in a 1967 movie called *Smashing Time*. A pastiche of the swinging sixties, *Smashing Time* might just be the silliest wacky-chick flick ever made. Written by U.K. wacky bloke George Melly, the basic plot revolves around the arrival in London of two adorably common, working-class w.c.'s named Yvonne (Lynn Redgrave) and Brenda (Rita Tushingham). The publicity campaign, which lured me to this movie at the age of fifteen, used the slogan "Two girls go stark mod!"

As the opening credits roll, mousy Brenda and brash Yvonne barrel into St. Pancras Station, having left the dreariness of industrial Bradford behind them. The only bit of hipness in their hometown, we gather from their chitchat, was a boutique called Bits and Pieces where the flashily attired Yvonne bought all her trendy traveling clothes. Starved of grooviness, they have come to London in search of the "in set," the mythical people who, Yvonne claims, sleep "in six-

123

foot-circular beds with black satin sheets" and whose every move is documented in *Minitrend,* Yvonne's favorite magazine. Their quest provides much hilarity, but most of the chuckles in the movie are derived from the girls' catastrophic attempts to secure regular employment.

At one point Brenda snags a job in an overpriced but insanely trendy vintage clothing and object store called, appropriately, Too Much. Meanwhile, Yvonne, after an abortive attempt at modeling/hostessing, lands a job as a waitress in a trendy ye Olde Worlde pie restaurant called Sweeney Todd's, where she is obliged to dress like an eighteenth-century street bawd. Before she even has time to find out what a street bawd is, she gets fired for hurling clotted cream and fruit pies at customers.

Despite the madcap farcical genre, most of the footage, at least from the average wacky chick's point of view, is pure cinema verité. For a wacky chick who has scythed her way through the job market, watching Brenda and Yvonne's antics is like watching a deadpan documentary of her own volcanic work history. *Smashing Time* is testimony to the fact that wacky chicks like Brenda and Yvonne are fundamentally unemployable.

Wacky chicks in the workplace are like bright little comets: they rocket through offices and factories leaving a trail of hilarity and thigh-slapping anecdotes upon which their shell-shocked and less scintillating colleagues will dine out for years.

Most wacky chicks will not last long enough in one job to make it to the company picnic or the holiday party. If they do, watch out! The constipated dynamic of such corporate events brings out the uninhibited side of a wacky chick—one look at all that constipation and she will embrace the (metaphorical) role of stool softener with excessive verve. Don't be surprised if she starts goosing the CEO, cartwheeling with no knickers on or teaching profanity-laced English rugby songs to the attending youngsters.

Fortunately—or unfortunately—for most companies, wacky chicks rarely make it through the job-selection process. They often don't even get an interview. This is attributable to the fact that, when filling out application forms, they always feel compelled to inject oodles of off-putting pizzazz and catchy phrases like "you bet your sweet bippy, I can" into their responses.

In the event that a wacky chick secures a job interview, it will probably be cut short. She can tuck her cerise-colored hair under a jaunty hat, or wear sensible shoes, but there seems to be no way of stopping a wacky chick from blurting out some interview-terminating gaffe or other: e.g., "My brother is in the Krishnas—do you have a job for him? He smells a bit, but he's got a heart of gold" or "I won't need any sick days—I'm very healthy—except for the occasional bout of cystitis, which only happens in the summer, when I ride my bicycle."

If a wacky chick gets hired, her survival rate will vary, depending on the type of job. Repetitive tasks, for example, are a disaster: that unfettered creativity impels her to add flourishes to simple manual tasks. I saw this firsthand at the Huntley & Palmers biscuit factory in my hometown. A nascent wacky chick of my acquaintance had the less than fabulously creative job of taking packets of freshly baked biscuits off a conveyor belt and putting them neatly into waiting cardboard boxes. At the end of her second week she picked up a packet and, staring into the middle distance like a woman possessed, she crushed them, concertina-style, with her bare hands. She was carted off to Human Resources, staring ahead and smiling as if she had just heard the Music of the Spheres, and repeating the phrase, "I crrrrrrrruuuusssshhhhhhed them."

Anything involving detailed boring paperwork is just as fraught with potential disaster. Remember when Auntie Mame hits the skids and is forced to go work in Macy's? She sells everything C.O.D. because she can't deal with writing it up the regular way.

The basic problem is that wacky chicks don't take direction well: their tendency is to wildly free-associate or, going to the other extreme, to be insanely literal. A wacky-chick artist friend—new to New York—was hired as a waitress in a trendy restaurant and was told by the manager, "I want you to really push the desserts. I mean, *really push* them!" My friend arrived at the restaurant on her first night, threw on her uniform, grabbed the dessert trolley and just started pushing the cart maniacally round the restaurant at about sixty miles per hour, oblivious of the fact that customers had yet to order their appetizers.

With their reliance on cheeky endearments and outré attire, wacky chicks make a mockery of every fascistic H.R. guideline. Their laissez-faire attitude toward rules and regulations and their healthy disregard for office protocol always gets them into trouble. No amount of "sensitivity training" seminars can stop a wacky chick from inserting terms like "pussy-whipped" into her interoffice communications.

Firing a wacky chick can often present human resources executives with some unusual challenges. I recall a wacky chick at Barneys who knew she was about to get the chop. She charged into H.R. and made a preemptive strike. "I know you are firing me but I'm too busy—can we do it some other time?" she asked rhetorically, and strode out.

Once in a while a wacky chick finds the right niche in an organization and sticks around until pension time. When I worked in a local department store during my youth, there was a wacky chick who had been relegated to Foundation Garments many years before. Her jovial Dickensian personality, snaggle teeth and irreverence were perfectly suited to the diffusion of the embarrassing situations that are wont to arise during the sale of long-line girdles and the like.

Her patter was appropriately diverting, but her fitting techniques were less than orthodox. She kept a large pair of shears in the fitting room with which she would, with a dramatic flourish, snip, snip, snip her clients from the laced confines of their worn-out corsets. Once a new girdle had been selected she would pull out an ultramodern pair of plastic salad servers with which she would coax the flesh of these loyal clients into their new corsets. No customer left her department without an uplifting *bon mot* and an encouraging slap on the back.

Corset lady, with her many years of service, was emblematic of a certain type of twentieth-century wacky chick. These ribald coquettes instinctively channeled their wackiness and cheekiness into their jobs. Not only did they not get fired, they made a bloody fortune in tips. Remember those bawdy, funny coffee shop waitresses with outlandish corsages who took your order at Denny's? They would goose you, insult you and make you feel like a million bucks, all the while helping you select a salad dressing. Where the hell did they go? Why did we let p.c. lunatics put the kibosh on their fabulous inappropriateness? Remember that wacky dental receptionist who cracked you up with her Phyllis Diller jokes when you were terrified of getting your teeth pulled? Where is she now?

Wacky-chick charm is no longer a prerequisite of such jobs. Computer skills, efficiency and a politically correct vocabulary are. *Quel drag!*

Eventually corporate America will see the error of its ways and recognize the benefits of wacky-chickery in the workplace. For the moment wacky chicks are, with rare exceptions, persona non grata.

Girls! The good news is that you no longer need to give a rat's ass. The days when a wacky, or even a demi-wacky, chick needed to camouflage and inhibit her wackiness in order to find a place in a conventional workplace and make a living are long gone. Who cares if corporate America can't handle your fabulous ebullience! Let them all Enron one another to death! Because you, as a card-carrying w.c., are now the mistress of your own destiny.

There has never been a better time for you to shake off the shackles of conventional employment and do your own thing. Don't spend your days slogging your repressed guts out in job after conventional job alongside a bunch of drears. Start your own business! After all, the wacky-chick traits—belligerence, resilience, a lack of inhibitions, naughtiness, creativity and hilarity—are the same qualities touted as those necessary for entrepreneurial success.

Madonna, Leona Helmsley, Mrs. Fields . . . those girls have alchemized their wacky-chickery into gold. Why should kooks like Mary Kay and Martha Stewart have all the limelight, especially when there's raw talent like you lurking in the wings? Why hide your light under a bushel when you could be out there grabbing the low-hanging fruit along with the rest of the girls. (Mixed metaphors are a big part of wacky-chick-speak.) So gird up your loins and put yourself out there: life is too short to spend it suppressing your B.R.U.N.C.H.!

Grab that pink follow-spot and point it where it belongs—*on you*! And let Isabel Garrett and Amy Sedaris be your role models. Let the throbbing strobe of their idiosyncratic careers guide you as you grope to find your own unique niche.

ISABEL GARRETT—THE SPANDEX EVANGELIST

Isabel Garrett operates her business from a nudist colony, and she sells her wares at swinger and biker conventions. She has taken her wackiness and, with astounding verve and commitment, channeled it into a $200,000-a-year business. O.K., so she's not exactly a household name, but at least she has an original concept. Log onto www.bodywebs.com and try to remain blasé. I dare you.

I first learned the name Isabel Garrett when, in 2001, she

experienced a flurry of publicity regarding the alleged plagiarism of her "look" by Christian Dior superstar designer John Galliano. The storm-in-a-trailer controversy centers around a must-have swimsuit, designed by Mr. Galliano for the house of Dior (see the cover of May 2001's *Vogue*) and bearing more than a striking resemblance to the signature spiderwebs that are the heart and soul of the Garrett *oeuvre*.

In an affable open letter to Mr. Galliano, care of the house of Dior, written that May, Ms. Garrett concedes she was not the first to slash and weave spandex—"just the most outrageous." Her letter concludes: "If you're doing more sliced spandex why not just hire me—I'm experienced!" This is a monumental understatement, as I quickly found out when I grilled her about her varied and fascinating work history.

The nerve center of Body Webs, the slashed-and-sexy-spandex business that Ms. Garrett has operated since the early 1990s, is—*quelle surprise*—her motor home. It was from this traveling *atelier* that the divinely insane Isabel unfurled the torridly fascinating story of her idiosyncratic career. "I'm parked at the Cypress Cove Nudist Resort in Kissimmee," says Isabel with an educated growl. With a *faux* petulance, she further clarifies, "It's not a colony—it's a park, a camp or a resort. Colony is"—sardonic groan—"un-p.c."

In answer to questions about her age, the cheeky Isabel, whose angular good looks recall wacky thespian Anne Bancroft, says, "Let's just say . . . Cher." In the crazy collage of Isabel's life, her Bronx childhood is one of the less sizzling chapters, and she thoughtfully flits through it in kicky sound bites. "Very middle-class Jewish. There was one gentile family on our block, and they actually had a dog. I touched it. When I was a teenager and visited Manhattan, I got to touch a cat too." Isabel, an only child, adored her mother, but with a caveat or two. "She wouldn't play board games when I wanted to, which was all the time. Everyone should switch mothers with somebody else when they hit twenty-five, because that's when everyone starts to think everybody else's mother is so cute." Her father, Max, was "a famous garment-center embroidery designer who made all my mother's glamour-puss clothes."

Sassy Isabel was an early developer, both physically and humorwise. "A ten-year-old doesn't really need boobs but there they were straining the seams of my bathing suit along with all the other new curves that had arrived in time for summer." Ma Garrett confronted the problem head-on and whisked her racky gorgeous brunette daughter off to buy brassieres: "She's out of training," said the sales clerk, pulling out the 34Bs. Isabel was initially pleased with her precocious mammaries and so were the boys. It was not long before she was fending off the advances of her playmates "and their dads too for chrissakes!" Her bustline forced her to find a way to "keep them liking me but stop them wanting me." At an early age she learned the defense capabilities of humor. Thus, her developing bustline directly paralleled the development of an even more potent asset, her Eve Arden–ish wit.

Despite her dad's ties to Seventh Avenue, it would be many years before smart-mouthed Isabel donned the garmento mantle herself. "In the 1960s, I studied fine arts at the City College of New York. I supported myself by dancing topless five nights a week at, among other places, the 49er. Remember *The Odd Couple*? Their apartment overlooked the 49er." Just when you think Isabel's life is reaching an apotheosis of kookiness, the needle in the wacky-meter starts quivering again. "Then I became an objectivist." A what? "An objectivist," explains Isabel patiently, "is a follower of Ayn Rand—you know, *The Fountainhead*? We believed in capitalism and, you know, all that barbaric rational-self-interest stuff."

During the course of my Margaret Mead–like quest to understand the wacky chick, the name Ayn Rand cropped up repeatedly. I did not, at first glance, see the connection. Ms. Rand's philosophy of rational self-interest with its worship of masculinity and avocation of "pure uncontrolled, unregulated laissez-faire capitalism" seems wacky but not very wacky-chick, if you know what I mean, and I think by now you do.

Closer study of Rand's less than hilarious writings revealed to me only one thing: that I'm not very intelligent. Most of the time I couldn't tell what the hell she was screeding on about. Only on the subject of happiness did she reveal an accessible wacky-chick-relevant point of view: "The right to the pursuit of happiness means man's right to live for himself, to choose what constitutes his own private, personal, individual happiness and to work for its achievement so long as he respects the rights of others." Illuminating though this was, it still did not explain why so many wacky chicks thought A.R. was so hot.

All was revealed when, eventually, I found a telling photograph of grim-faced Ayn. Taken in the 1930s, this photo showed the great philosopher smoking a fag in the concrete backyard of the all-steel futuristic Richard Neutra house—with reed-filled moat—that she had purchased from Josef von Sternberg. The camply futuristic spaceship of a house was the perfect accessory for the otherworldly Ayn. Now I understood perfectly: Ayn, like Brenda and Yvonne, was stark raving mod!

Brooding in this sardine can in some godforsaken L.A. suburb, she must surely have been the wackiest chick in the hood. With her googly eyes and severe Hitlerish haircut, I'm sure she scared the hell out of her neighbors when she leaned over the aluminum fence to borrow a cup of sugar.

Back to Miss Garrett. In the 1970s, with capitalism, rational self-interest and creativity burning in her veins, Isabel's career took a sharp left. She joined the toy and game industry and created the legendary Whoopsie Doll. The Whoopsie was a simple enough concept: You squeezed her tummy and her pigtails shot up in the air. "I designed it for Ideal," recalls Ms. Garrett. "They sold over 400,000." Other Garrett triumphs in the toy world include Magic Hair Crissy and, in the 1980s, the VCR interactive game Clue. Despite Clue's success—"it was voted game of the year in 1984 and I was cooking with the big guys"—Isabel's toy career was not destined to propel her into the 1990s.

A stint as a freelance toy designer produced tons of brilliant ideas and no sales. "I was forty-two, looked thirty-two, had car, awesome bod, nude beach tan, danced great and knew how to handle rowdies," recalls Isabel with film noir insouciance. But with no firm job prospects, Isabel felt increasingly out of place in New York. By day she hondled for jobs, by night she drew caricatures and delivered strip-o-grams. She almost snagged the job of art director at the Muppet Mansion, but the world of kinky couture was beckoning.

In 1989, Isabel—who professes to have "always been a vacation nudist"—found herself in need of a slutty outfit to wear to a costume party at the Paradise Lakes Nudist Resort near Tampa. "It's the fantasy-nightlife place," explains Isabel helpfully. The resourceful Ms. Garrett pulled out her nail scissors and, in a Norman Bateslike frenzy, attacked her spandex unitard. The swingers at the party went batshit over the attacked-by-a-thousand-moths-with-scalpels-instead-of-wings look of her ensemble. It was a total *fashiphany*.

Permit me to explain. Apocalyptic, epiphanous moments of creative innovation are, contrary to what PR flacks would have you believe, really quite rare in the world of fashion. These eruptions of transcendental creativity—or fashiphanies, as I like to call them—are milestones for us fashion professionals. Only once in a blue moon does one encounter that mind-blowing persona and/or garment, the stratospherically high style-quotient of which renders obsolete everything else on the fashion landscape.

Examples of fashiphanies of yore: the Courrèges space-age look, the YSL safari look, Bowie and glam rock, Vivienne Westwood's bondage trousers, Jean Paul Gaultier's cone bras and Versace's early 1990s streetwalker/gladiator looks. Appalling, beautiful, ingenious and utterly logical all at the same time, Isabel's designs are the *ne plus ultra* of fashiphanous fromage.

Endearingly, Isabel gives more credit to her medium than

her own creativity. When she talks about her beloved spandex, her wacky-chick passions erupt, and she gets positively haikuish: "It was a miracle. It held without hardware. I slashed it and the edges rolled and healed. It smoothes and cinches and brings out the latent diva in the lady next door." On that historic night at Paradise Lakes, slasher Isabel got the thumbs-up on her next career and, *voilà*, Body Webs were born.

By the early nineties, Miss Garrett and her stretchy, kinky wares were a fixture at the various national swinger conventions—e.g., the Lifestyle Convention in Las Vegas and Dressing for Pleasure in New York. Isabel's go-with-the-flow, soft-core entrepreneurship is typical of all wacky chicks. Though they lack the kind of ruthless strategy that might make them fabulously wealthy or incredibly famous, they have the ability to recognize and seize wackily stimulating opportunities.

One day, a well-meaning swinger sidled up to her booth at Dressing for Pleasure and commented, "Bikers would like them things." Not knowing Sonny Barger from Sonny Bono, Isabel called *Outlaw Biker* magazine. In no time, she had strategically plugged herself into the fun-luvin' hogs-and-heifers scene—and with it, an important new source of Body Webs revenue. With her preference for what she calls "open-minded alternative lifestyles," Ms. Garrett slotted seamlessly into the unpretentious, boob-flaunting biker milieu.

Nude! Nude! Nude! Isabel is not the only one. The clothing-optional lifestyle, of which Isabel was an early proponent, has now become an unstoppable trend that is gripping America from coast to coast. The avalanche of post-9/11 and non-ironic sincerity has done nothing to reduce the amount of exposed flesh currently being proffered as middle-class entertainment on TV. Without the deployment of cumbersome and expensive medical equipment, it is hard to imagine that the new episodes of *Sex and the City* could expose any more human organs.

Wacky chicks like director-stylist L'Wren Scott are madly pro-nakedness: "Nudity is always chic, and it's the ultimate couture. I mean, you're never going to run into another person wearing your skin."

I myself am more cautiously enthusiastic: the sight of grown people in various states of physical fitness frying their genitalia on public beaches can really put one off one's pasta salad. I must, however, confess to being a huge fan of nude volleyball (spectatorship): rivetingly Monty Pythonesque, this earnest, wacky team sport is the very essence of hilariously hearty, old-fashioned, nonsexual naturism.

Here are a couple of tips for first-time nudies: Make a conscious effort not to ogle your fellow nudesters. Pervy gawking is frowned upon in the clothing-optional community, especially if you have elected to remain clothed. Don't linger, but rather flit—like thistledown—quickly through the fleshy masses and marvel at Dame Nature's jiggly diversity. And communicate: regular nudists, many of whom are tattooed and pierced, are garrulous folk who walk around chatting compulsively, as if they are enjoying the sidewalk afterglow of an Alcoholics Anonymous meeting. Finally, careful with your dogs! I had to put my Liberace on his leash on a Saint Bart's beach after he surprised a couple of clothing-optional funsters with vigorous licks to their various areas, lending new meaning to the term *amuse bouche.*

Now back to Izzy, who, as it happens, was nude during many of our telephone interviews.

Reluctantly putting Body Webs aside for a moment, I cautiously approach the subject of Isabel's personal life. I brace myself, unnecessarily as it turns out, for the inevitable uninhibited Pandora's box of hideous hetero disclosures. Despite her louche lifestyle and her stripperish fashion niche, Isabel apparently prefers more old-fashioned sex. "I like swingers," she explained. "They are the only people who will proposition you and, if you say no, they will still have breakfast with you the next morning. But you won't find me third buttock from the end in a love pile. I don't like having sex with strangers. But I do reserve the right to cut one out of the herd occasionally." Her current status? An ex named Archie is a close friend, but Isabel describes herself as follows: "Very available. Likes brilliant men. Someone as interesting as me."

Until this peer materializes, Isabel is content to crisscross the country, prophetlike, spreading her empowering philosophy. Despite the totally revealing nature of what she calls her "street- and beach-legal" designs, Isabel uses Body Webs as "a way to get the bitches to stop loathing their own bodies." She hands out her very own evangelical tract, "Ten Ways to Stop Hating Your Body," which contains much nurturing hilarity— e.g., "Try hating your cat because she got older and gained weight." Yes, the former proponent of barbaric self-interest has become a do-gooder. What gives? "I like undoing all the self-loathing that keeps women from strutting," she said, with Billy Graham–ish zeal. "Fashion model is a job, not a value judgment. The only guys who really prefer painfully thin mannequins are rock stars and insecure corporate executives. The rest of us get to have curves and bellies and soft spots that guys love to snuggle."

Though wildly confident about the value of her philosophy, Isabel is convinced that she is "short on the trappings, mystique and business savvy that might make me quote-unquote important. I'm shark meat and I know it." The hardcore objectivism is long gone; for guidance Isabel now looks to a number of wackily right-on sisters, including Guru Ma Jaya Sati Bhagavati, "a true holy woman who founded World Tibet Day and teaches compassion and service to others as a way to God. She's my mother now." Auspiciously, Guru Ma named Isabel "Jaya Gita," which means "song of victory."

Though Isabel's spiritual side is blooming, her ability to concentrate is not. "I'm a total poster child for ADD," confesses Ms. Garrett with borderline pride. When I ask her if she's tried Ritalin, she replies, "Honey, as Nietzsche once said, 'You must have chaos within to give birth to a dancing star.'"

Aahh!

And she has. Nietzsche notwithstanding, Isabel has combined her wacky-chickery with an entrepreneurial spirit and created an original product. Yes, she has all the headaches of running a small business. But she also has all the freedom and the creative satisfaction (that's the dancing-star part).

Isabel's story of self-invention and creativity is truly inspirational. She has all of Yvonne's wacky Carnaby Street optimism and more. However, for the wacky chick looking to give birth to her own dancing star, but who is less than enthusiastic about spending her days hanging out with society's clothing-optional outlaws, it's important to remember that there is more than one way to skin a cat.

AMY SEDARIS—VERMIN AND CHEESEBALLS

Amy Sedaris created a product too, just like Isabel. Only hers lives inside her head and it's called Piglet.

"I live on the corner of cocksucker and faggot," says Amy Sedaris sweetly and breezily when I call to set up our interview time and location, adding a rhetorical, "Don't you just love the word 'faggot'! I do." Her brother is the famous faggot writer David Sedaris, a fact that seems only to have increased Miss Sedaris's love affair with the incendiary f word.

Not everyone shares her opinion. When Amy was shooting her Comedy Central series *Strangers with Candy*, for which she was co-writer, co-director, co-editor and star, her commitment to the f word made the producer very nervous. "For some reason 'pussy' was fine, but they made me wait until the fourth episode before I could say 'faggot.' I still don't get it," recalls Amy with an uncomprehending frown that recalls the permanently creased mien of Jerri Blank, her *Strangers with Candy* character.

Jerri is a poignant and highly original concoction, recalling Gilda Radner, Phyllis Diller and Erma Bombeck with just a top note of John Wayne Gacy. The real Amy is just as strange, albeit in a wackily genteel kind of way. When we meet at the Original Espresso Bar on Christopher (cocksucker) and Bleecker (faggot), she greets the lesbian waitress and faggot waiters with a Mrs. Butterworth's sweetness. She then hands me a box of Lilac chocolate-covered pretzels as a nice-to-meet-you gift. She's almost dainty.

Petite, gamine, slightly disheveled but definitely clean, Amy is not only well mannered, she is attractive. She resembles a younger, cuter, blonder version of celeb felon Robert Blake. If the Beach Boys had had a cute little androgynous faggoty brother, Amy could play the part in the made for TV movie, minus the apron. Yes, apron. Today she wears a tie-in-the-back dark plaid apron with improbable Mexican embroidery across the front shoulder yoke, capri pants* and a nice pair of burgundy suede high heels. She dresses as if she were the owner of a folksy but successful bakery. "I love baking. That's my look. Aprons—I have thirty of them—with high heels. I did a play with Sarah Jessica Parker—she's such a lady. I look at her doing stuff and think, 'Oh that's what a lady does.' Anyway, she got me into wearing high heels. Manolo Blahniks. I bought a pair with the $500 I got for going on David Letterman, and I wore them the next time I went on. Every time I go on I think I'll buy another pair." In the sum-

---

*In the capri, the ladies trouser has found its most perfect expression. The slouchy *palazzo* pant has, much to my consternation, gained popularity of late. Even more disturbingly, so has the flared, butt-crack-exposing jean. Soon everyone will realize that the capri is the norm to which we must all return. P.S.: Do not—whatever you do—try to authenticate your pronunciation. It's Capreeeeeeee!

mer, when Amy goes Blahnik shopping she usually wears her True Value Hardware tool apron: "I don't like to carry a purse when it's hot."

Her uninhibited stream of consciousness is peppered with apologies for the fact that we can't meet at her apartment. With any other celeb I would have chalked this up to a healthy paranoia about not letting strangers—with or without candy—into your own home. With wacky Sedaris I sensed there was a more interesting explanation. I was right: she cannot receive visitors at the moment because her apartment is a mess because she is having wall-to-wall carpeting installed . . . for Tattle-tail, her eight-year-old pet rabbit. "It's not really carpet. It's green-produce-department flooring, sort of like AstroTurf but softer."

Miss Sedaris dotes on Tattle-tail. "The whole place is designed around her. Everything is painted with rustic woodgrain. I have a liquor cabinet that's carved out of tree trunk, and the walls are painted with Benjamin Moore green—cream of asparagus. There are woodland creatures, ceramic mushrooms and taxidermied squirrels."

(What is it—you are no doubt wondering by now—about wacky chicks and animals? Why does every w.c. seem to have an iguana or a ferret in her purse?

W.c.'s are just as susceptible to the unconditional loving licks of animals as the rest of us. W.c.'s are keen animal rescuers—it appeals to their swashbuckling sensibilities. And let's not forget the addictively tranquilizing feelings that accompany the fondling and petting of all animals, even unrewarding and smelly ones like parrots and potbellied pigs.

But my girls have a far more direct connection to animals than the rest of us. They resonate with animals because they recognize so much of themselves—because animals are wacky too!

Animal behavior is nothing if not B.R.U.N.C.H.: at the drop of a hat, cats or dogs will avidly lick their genitalia, even in front of deeply religious, uptight visiting relatives. How wacky is that? When the local priest stops in for a cuppa, FiFi the poodle will celebrate his arrival by dragging her butt back and forward across the kilims, with nary a backward glance. Animals, like wacky chicks, will do whatever it takes to break the ice.)

Amy has a complex menagerie that extends way beyond Tattle-tail's soothingly familiar tail—way beyond: "I had a plague of mice because there is always so much food everywhere— baked goods and rabbit food," explains Amy. She has struggled to rectify this problem, but when she got rid of the mice, the roach population exploded. She concluded—correctly, but nonetheless disgustingly—that the mice were eating the roaches. Amy has allowed the mice population to increase again, creating a more desirable residential eco-equilibrium. "Today I found a mouse's nest in my closet," says the young thespian, getting a bit dewey-eyed. "Ten little babies the size of Cheetos."

Before we get down to the nitty-gritty of Amy's career, I ask about her non-rodent family. Her brother's hilarious scribblings have made the Sedaris family public property, and I'm dying for an update. "Dad is the same. Last week his Great Dane knocked him down and hauled him down the street and left this huge nasty-looking mark on his leg," says Amy with a wince. "He went over to my brother Paul's house for dinner. There was a lady there who had just been bereaved and was in that fragile needy state. My dad drops his trousers and shows everyone his bloody mark. Yes, Dad's doin' great. Thanks for asking."

Amy's mother has been dead for many years, but is fondly remembered: "She was a real mom. Her philosophy was do whatever makes you happy because everything works itself out in the end. She wanted me to be a policeman and frost my hair. I recently started highlighting my hair. I go to Rena down on Orchard Street. I always think of Mom when I'm under the dryer."

I ask Amy if the other members of the Sedaris family are creative. "*Sure!* My brother Paul has his own floor-sanding business and he's doing really well. Lisa's an eternal student. Gretchen loves flowers—she works in a nursery—and my sister Tiffany works at an Italian bakery decorating pastries and cakes."

Amy's childhood was happy, give or take a gnarly incident or two. At elementary school she slammed into one Bobby Marshall, "an unfortunate kid with a water head." After she banged into her hydrocephalitic playmate, the teacher forced Amy to kiss him to make it feel better. "I was repulsed. It was my first kiss—and then when I did it, it wasn't so bad. He's probably passed on. Isn't that sad?" recalls Amy mistily.

Romance aside, a wholesome and almost Partridge Family-esque commitment to singing and performing enlivened the Raleigh, North Carolina, Sedaris family home. "I was a huge

Streisand fan. I could imitate her and make myself look like her. It stopped after *Butterfly*," chirrups Amy, sounding a bit like an old-school faggot. "Whatever we did, we had to have an audience. When we baked cakes, David and I pretended we were on a cooking show. Counting pocket money? It's more fun if you pretend you're a busy accountant. I still do that."

Other miscellaneous portents of the show-biz career to come included spontaneous entertaining at airports: "I used to sing country songs to entertain people as they came off planes." She also played a rooster in a production of *Charlotte's Web*, and, "when my yaya was in a convalescent home," recalls Amy, using the Greek word for granny, "David and I used to put on shows to cheer everyone up. 'Knock 'em dead,' we would say before every show."

A beneficent theatricality was emerging, but so was another more ominous side: a fascistic love of order and uniforms. "When I was a senior in high school I was still a Girl Scout. I loved the camping and baking Girl Scout cookies, and, of course, cheeseballs and muffins. I used to wear my Girl Scout uniform everywhere. I fell in love with uniforms." From her Brownie uniform and her Winn-Dixie, Amy has accumulated a spectacular uniform collection, each reflecting a different period of her life. She is meticulous about the cleaning, ironing and accessorizing of these beloved garments. On first arriving in New York, she took a food-service job at Gourmet Garage: "They wanted me to wear a baseball cap and I wanted to wear a hair net. They said, 'No way,' so I gave two weeks' notice."

Uniform-lovin' Amy showed no desire to go to college.

The only subject that interested her was criminology. She toyed with getting a job at the local prison. "Just because you like crime doesn't mean you have to go work at the prison— just read about crime," said brother David, giving her a copy of what must surely be one of the most horrid crime books of all time, *The Basement*, by feminist writer Kate Millett. This grisly account of the actions of torturer/murderer Gertrude Baniszewski only served to fuel Amy's dark fascinations.

Amy, it must be pointed out, is not unusual in this regard. Many w.c.'s with whom I spoke had watched and cringed their way through the Jeffrey Dahmer trial on Court TV, though most prefer lighter fare: an evening spent watching *COPS* or *America's Most Wanted*, or a film noir classic with a malevolent heroine like Phyllis in Billy Wilder's *Double Indemnity*. While generally law-abiding, w.c.'s enjoy the comforting frisson which comes from reading about gruesome crimes that didn't happen to them, or about anybody who is clearly more appalling than they could ever be accused of being.

When she wasn't inhaling facts about serial killers and the like, Amy was working as a cocktail waitress, and loving it. "I learned so much. I learned that it's better to say 'how 'bout a gin and tonic?'—rather than 'how 'bout *another* gin and tonic?' You can't make people feel like they're alcoholic even if they are. It makes them uneasy." Amy continued to hone her professional waitressing skills until she was twenty-five. Brother David returned from Chicago one weekend and laid it on the line: "You can't spend the rest of your life doing this." Amy followed him back to Chicago, where she enrolled for improv acting classes at the legendary Second City workshop.

The year was 1985. Once reunited in the Windy City, the two young Sedari rekindled their childhood silliness. They started writing and performing plays, and dubbed themselves the Talent Family. Their readings at a place called the Lower Links soon developed a cult following.

By 1993 the Talent Family had both moved to New York, and were mounting plays, the first being *Jamboree,* a dramatization of David's *Barrel Fever* stories. Their growing reputation was based on their hokey hilarity. "We don't take ourselves too seriously, but we took the plays and casting very seriously. Uptight actors didn't get it. Put it this way, nobody can work with us unless they've had a dick in their mouth," says Amy with the straightforward earnestness of a neighbor exchanging a cheeseball recipe with another neighbor. "Our approach is infantile, it's 'Let's put on a show!'"

I ask Amy about the Talent Family's sources of inspiration. "I never get any ideas from comedies. Tragedies are more inspiring. I look at things and try to see what could be funny about that. Remember when that poor retarded girl got raped by those five boys with a broomstick. Horrible! It gave me the idea for a play where five retarded girls rape some jock up the butt with a broom. Tragedy is where you get all the best ideas for comedy.

"That's why I love country songs—all that emotion," continues Amy, getting kind of dramatic herself, "that's why I am fascinated with dramatic acting—I love Helen Mirren. So dramatic and stern in *Gosford Park*! I can't do that." Amy pauses briefly to respond to a couple of Jerri Blank fans and then continues, self-deprecatingly, "I'm one of those actresses who always plays the same part."

I challenge Amy on this last point. I insist that she has range. She doesn't just play one part. Isn't it more like two? And they have names. They are Miss Lexington and Piglet.

"Miss Lexington" is how David and Amy refer to the earnest, sincere part of Amy's *oeuvre*. When Amy becomes Miss Lexington she dons a very pained expression: the lower jaw is yanked down and back, the tendons on Amy's neck throb and twist. The resulting mega-overbite causes the occasional dermatological problem: "Sometimes my teeth give me a rash on my chin." Her forehead, meanwhile, is marked by a furious frown. Her eyes get suppressed and slanted by the contraction of her face muscles. She looks like she's really really concerned, but that it might be about something as simple as having dropped her kitchen-witch into a bucket of soapy water. Eager and sad, but never unkind, Miss Lexington is poignant and angelic.

Piglet, on the other hand, is the devil. "She's the part of me that loves to cuss and cuss until the words just don't mean anything anymore," chuckles Amy slipping into white-trash* Piglet mode and pulling up her nose to make a snout. "I don't give a fuckidy fuck who the fuck you fuck—you ain't getting a shit-smeared nickel outta me. Nobody was protecting my ass when I lost half the nerve endings in my pussy," trills Amy effortlessly to illustrate her point. Amy says that this character is a female version of her floor-sanding brother Paul, and feels strongly that her creation is a very sympathetic character, "Shucks, everyone knows a Piglet!"

---

*Don't even think of reproaching Amy for making fun of the underprivileged: like all wacky chicks, she is democratically classist, skewering the foibles of people from every strata.

Combining the farce of Joe Orton with the edgy idiocy of *Mad TV*, the Talent Family plays were the petri dish for the development of these two characters. Though the plays were a collaboration, the dada plots offer a disturbing view into Amy's mind. Many, incidentally, carry the theme of successful self-employment:

Stump the Host: Jocelyn Hershey-Guest (Amy Sedaris), a children's book author lives in her son's head. She moves out and they become roommates and she helps him with his writing. She has an animal foot. The other cast members also have animal parts.

Stitches: A woman called Brittany gets in a terrible boating accident and ends up horribly disfigured, in hospital, rooming with an acting teacher/drug dealer named Victoria Swaggs (Amy Sedaris). Victoria is in a wheelchair with mysterious "gang-related injuries." She teaches Brittany how to act, and she lands a sit-com called *Stitches* (her character's name). Stitches becomes hugely popular and everyone wants to be like her, so they scarify their faces and inflict disfiguring deformities on themselves. Piglet (Amy Sedaris) plays Brittany's irate, foulmouthed, jealous sister.

One Woman Shoe: A bunch of welfare recipients are told that they won't get any more money until they each put on "one woman shows." A misprint turns "one woman show" into "one woman shoe" with hilarious results. Amy plays two parts: a golfer named Bobbie Sheridan, and Tula Saccas, a terrifying monkey-owning, bikini-wearing pig of a woman who many believe was Amy's finest creation.

The Book of Liz: This play is set in the Cluster Haven Squeamish community. The Squeamish are similar to the Amish. The sales of Elizabeth Dunderstock's legendary cheeseballs are the economic foundation of this contented religious group. A Squeamish follower named Nathaniel Brightby (played by writer/thespian David Rakoff) takes over the manufacture of the cheeseballs, sending an unhappy Elizabeth off on her own odyssey. The cheeseballs no longer sell well. They are missing a secret ingredient that turns out to be Elizabeth's own sweat.

Bon appetit!

Miss Lexington and Piglet's most high-profile incarnation occurred in the thirty legendary episodes of her nasty cult Comedy Central TV series, *Strangers with Candy*. The premise is as follows: Jerri Blank, a guileless semiretarded individual, misspent her youth in full trick-turning, drug-ingesting Piglet mode. We now find her rehabbed and Lexingtoned and middle-aged and back at high school, where she has been given a chance to finish her education. The humor in the show comes as appalling vestiges of the previous Pigletesque Jerri leak out via the new earnest, burned-out Jerri. Nothing can stem her flow of inappropriate redneck commentary: "I'm adopted and I'm not Indian. It's just a coincidence that I have a love of gambling and booze and a knack for catching syphilis." By taking the most horrifyingly unacceptable bigotries, combining

them with smut and channeling them through the now be-
nign Jerri, Amy and her collaborators created what must
surely be one of the wackiest chicks ever to hit the TV screen.

After *Strangers with Candy*, Amy developed a huge cult following: Hollywood started calling and it made her nervous: "I
get the feeling I'm in witches' territory when I'm in L.A.—you
can't believe anything anyone is saying to you." When lucrative jobs started coming her way, she interviewed tons of
agents until she found one who would agree never to call her.
Like many talented wacky chicks, her goals relate more to creative fulfillment than material success. When I ask her what
she considers to be her best achievement, she replies, "I can
take care of myself. I don't get lonely or bored. I'm content."

Miss Lexington and Piglet are more than just a source of artis-
tic satisfaction for Amy. They are a therapeutic outlet for the
full mania of her own wacky-chickery. The manageable
residue she deals with, without the help of a psychotherapist.
"A shrink? Oh no, that's not me. But I do love listening to people's problems." Or a boyfriend. Though Amy has had several
long-term relationships, "at the moment it's just me and Tattle-tail." Her friends find it hard to set her up because guys are
scared of dating Jerri Blank. But Amy remains optimistic: "I
like guys who can do things with their hands. I'll probably
meet Mr. Right in a hardware store."

Busy Amy is not waiting around for Mr. Butch to complete
her life: apart from baking, she enjoys pilates, and she rocks.
"It's my addiction," explains Ms. Sedaris and lays down on the
floor of the Original Espresso in order to demonstrate. First

she makes her already tight little body into the shape of a miniature croissant, and then, much to the concern of an adjacent faggot, she starts agitating herself from side to side like a frenzied fetus. "David did it for years—He stopped when he went to college and got a roommate. He taught me. I set the alarm so that I can wake up early and do some extra rocking. That's when I do all my thinking."

Amy made her break with the conventional workforce in her twenties. She was content being a waitress but only because she had yet to experience the joys of marrying her wackiness with her métier. And she never got cold feet.

Amy and Isabel are living proof that it's never too late, or too early, to do your own thing: Got a penchant for dressing up in costume and belting out show tunes? Start a candygram service in your town. Got a knack for fixing things? Start a company called AAA Repair Service: you might not make a fortune but you'll be at the front of the phone book and you're bound to meet loads of interesting people. Love collecting tchotchkes but lack knowledge of history and provenance? Open a pawn shop. Compulsively nosey and gossippy? Start a private investigation bureau. Make a career out of your shortcomings and eccentricities! Start today!

Toward the end of *Smashing Time*, things take an optimistic turn. Yvonne wins money on a humiliating *Candid Camera*–type show called *You Can't Help Laughing* and plows it all into a career as a pop singer. She has a hit single entitled "I Can't Sing but I'm Young." Meanwhile Brenda, despite her lack of height, has been recognized for the exotic beauty she is and becomes a top model, snagging a contract to represent an avant-garde fragrance that is inspired by sixties political unrest called Direct Action. These two scenesters would appear to have turned their wackiness into gold.

After a disastrously trendy birthday party for Yvonne, the two old friends close ranks and dis the whole groovy scene. Clutching their return railway tickets, they head back toward the train station, leaving the superficiality of groovy London behind, but also leaving all the wacky chicks in the audience feeling totally betrayed. What, pray, are they returning to? A job at the local raincoat factory, or pulling the giblets out of chickens in a butcher's shop. If Yvonne is lucky they might hire her as an assistant manager at Bits and Pieces.

Retreating to the hinterland, clutching a return train ticket is so totally un-wacky-chick! When things plateaued for Isabel, she didn't hide at the nudist colony: she followed the Harleys down Route 66 and found new customers. When roaches invaded Amy's pad, she didn't go running home to Raleigh, she aligned herself with a bunch of rodents and vanquished the pests herself.

A real wacky chick never surrenders.

CHAPTER 6

MATING HABITS

Men cluster to me like moths around a flame
And if their wings burn, I know I'm not to blame
Falling in love again . . .

So sang the sultry Marlene Dietrich, a Teutonic wacky chick who starred in camp movies like *The Devil Is a Woman* and *The Blue Angel*. The mythical, cinematic Marlene spent her days dragging languidly on Turkish cigarettes while casting heavy-lidded, all-knowing gazes at the world through a black spotted fascinator (eye-veil).

The real-life Marlene was far busier than her nicotine-wreathed screen persona. Men clustered round her like the proverbial moths, but so did women, hermaphrodites and almost anything that was breathing. When she wasn't lensing a movie, Miss Dietrich typically spent her days entertaining, calming down or fending off her assorted enthusiasts. Like many wacky chicks, this freaky *fraulein*'s flaming allure attracted hordes of ardent admirers.

Some lights, like Miss Dietrich, burn brighter than others: Mae West, Shelley Winters, Eartha Kitt and L'il Kim, these superfreaky soubrettes might have had a rough time with the censors, but they are/were irresistible flypaper to their fevered fan base. The attractions speak for themselves: as one devotee explained to me, "Why would you eat Spam when there were crepes suzettes flambées on the menu."

Though blasts of societal antipathy confront the average wacky chick on a daily basis, there is, paradoxically, no shortage of gushing admiration coming from various other directions, and it's got nothing to do with good looks. There is a powerful force field that sizzles and crackles around every wacky chick—regardless of how high her checkbones are—attracting a varied and fascinating collage of suitors, acolytes and moths: old men, young bucks, other chicks, puppies, members of the transgender community, butterflies, lint, children, pygmies and nuns. In all my wacky-chick research, I never once heard a wacky chick say, "I wish I had more friends." And "Nobody wants to shag me" is so much rarer than it is among non-wackies. In fact, the w.c. faces the opposite challenge—i.e., how to carve out a little quiet time for herself and repair the ravages of all that fan worship.

I call these rabid fans "wacky chickolytes"—or "wackolytes" for short—and number myself among their happy ranks. To say we enjoy the company of a w.c. is a raging understatement: the fact is, we wackolytes can barely function without it. B.R.U.N.C.H. is our favorite meal. Our mental metabolisms rely on regular transfusions of the infectious reckless *joie de vivre* that only the w.c. can provide.

We wackolytes are not necessarily interested in copulating with our idols. This honor goes to another subspecies known here at the W.C. Research Headquarters as the "wacky-chick chaser." When a wacky chick turns on her love light, there seems to be no shortage of folk whose elastic predilections send them rushing toward it to give their wings a good old-fashioned singeing.

Who are these wacky-chick chasers? And why are they so impelled to mingle it up with these B.R.U.N.C.H.-y broads? I wanted to get inside their heads and find out what makes them tick. I started by calling Terence Sydney Doonan, life partner to Northern Ireland's wackiest chick, my mother.

First, a word or two about Terry Doonan, also known as Mike. (When he went to work for the BBC in the news-monitoring service, there already was another Terry. So, just as if he were in a hair salon, the new arrival was forced to adopt an arbitrary new moniker.) Seventy-six-year-old Terry, who has all of his marbles and many of his teeth, has had an unconventional life: he left home at age fifteen and enlisted as an aircraft apprentice in the Royal Air Force. Most of his service was spent learning the trade of wireless operator and mechanic. For the last months of the war, he was based in India from whence he and his young cohorts made regular flights over the Bay of Bengal, off the coast of Burma. Terry recalls those missions with a lack of emotion: "We were looking for Japanese targets, and did sink some defenseless coastal craft. We were hepped up and excited to be doing our job. We weren't smart enough to be scared."

Like many wacky-chick chasers, Terry has always been a snappy dresser. Photos from this particular period show he was into a crumpled khaki look: bush shirt and shorts (cleaned daily), wool ankle socks with *chaplis* (Indian sandals), pipe, side-tilted forage cap—i.e., very late-eighties Banana Republic. He has always been an odd David Niven–ish combo of the effete and the butch—e.g., he rode a motorbike but wore an ascot. I would like to think I have inherited a modicum of his sartorial snap.

During my childhood, handsome, spiffy Terry worked for the British Broadcasting Corporation listening to foreign broadcasts, most often from the USSR and Eastern Europe during the Cold War. He made it into the papers as the first to report the Kennedy assassination in the U.K. During this period, he sported a 1950s *Look Back in Anger* groovy-schoolteacher look—white shirt with knitted tie, battered tweed sport coat with suede elbow patches, flat-front slacks and Hush Puppies. Very nifty.

Gentlemanly Terry readily admits that, when he encountered Betty Gordon, he was quite naïve in the relationship/love department. "I hadn't met many women, only the old slags who hung around pubs. The only woman I knew well was my mother, who was a different kettle of fish. She was not feminine. She was more of a neuter, in fact."

The location of his first encounter with Betty was hardly auspicious. Sandes Home, an Air Force welfare canteen in Northern Ireland, was a grim place where well-meaning civilians served cupcakes, sandwiches and hot snacks to the war weary. But when Betty swept in the door, Terry almost choked on his fish fingers. "I noticed her because she was attractive and modish. She wore an expensive green New Look coat." Like all w.c.'s, attention-magnet Betty was an expert at entrance-making. As my dad describes the first sighting of his future wife in that fit 'n' flare garment, I instantly recall it—the coat, that is—not on my mother, but on me.

Betty's coat had a high-rolling collar and was scalpel-cut

into a million panels that cinched at the waist and then flared dramatically to a circular midcalf hem. My best friend James Biddlecombe—he would later go on to become one of Europe's premiere cross-dressing cabaret entertainers—and I used to take turns trying it on and twirling in our attic. Speaking at my mother's memorial, the multitalented James, a.k.a. Biddie, paid tribute to Betty's singular maquillage and style: he magnanimously credited her with informing the glamorous sensibility of his own extensive repertoire.

Aside from that gala coat, Terry also recalls noticing Betty's fetching upswept hairdo and, most important, her tomato-hued suede platform shoes. "She always had stylish shoes even if they had cardboard in them," said Terry, recalling that austere time when even a clunky pair of platforms might wear thin. Betty, like so many pixie-sized charmers, was a lifelong devotee of the platform shoe: I vividly remember her triumphant euphoria when, in the early 1970s, 1940s platforms came stomping back into fashion. In her wacky contrarian view, the return of the platform was a sign that common sense had finally prevailed in the world of footwear.

Though fantastic on his recall of Betty's outré style, Terry had a hard time articulating recollections of her wackiness. When asked to describe what it was like to live with a wacky chick on a day-to-day basis, he replied, "Very nice. We had a lot in common. She had a great Air Force sense of humor."

Though the wackolytes openly exalt in the wackiness of their chicks, many of the chasers I spoke to shared Terry's disinclination to characterize their chicks as wacky at all. They are poignantly loyal and reluctant to label their women in any way that could possibly be construed as negative. "I had no prospects," admitted Terry, sounding a bit Dickensian. "The wackiest thing Betty ever did was to take up with me."

The magnetism of Betty's wacky allure reached way beyond good-natured Terry. When Betty ate her lunch at the BBC canteen (canteens are a Doonan leitmotif), co-workers would fight to sit within earshot of her witty repartee. Specific examples of her hilarity are unavailable: like most w.c.'s, mater didn't tell jokes. She was a raconteur.

Over the years Betty had perfected brilliant ways of keeping her audience in the palm of her hand. She had a knack for cataloguing the incompetencies and foibles of friends, colleagues and family, and then flinging them back at them with great panache at the specific moment when it might most suit her purpose—e.g., "for somebody who can't mend a bicycle, you're pretty free with other people's afterdinner mints."

Her skimpy education did not prevent her from throwing Franglais around like a man with four arms. She figured out that French was an innately camp language long before Miss Piggy came along with her *mois* and *magnifiques*. Every conversational gambit seemed to contain if not an *au courant*, then at least a *de rigueur* or a *bête noire*. Going on the assumption that they all meant "fabulous," Betty would happily swap you a *dernier cri* for an *éminence gris*. If she was really bonkers about something—be it a pair of shoes or a dessert topping—it was always "very *entre deux mers*."

The banter and fan worship would continue in the evening when lodgers and friends bearing cheap wine and ciggies would ensconce themselves at Betty's dining room table to enjoy hours of contentious rants and challenging badinage.

When Betty died two years ago, she left a big New Look–shaped hole in many lives, most especially Terry's. "I think about her every day and especially now when marching season is here," says Terry referring to the incendiary July 12 Orange Marches that occur throughout Northern Ireland. Betty was indeed an out-and-proud Northern Ireland Protestant. "She was very aware of her background. Her people were tough. They farmed and survived on the inhospitable Antrim Hills, surrounded by myriad hostilities."

At the close of our interview, I give Terry one last opportunity to dredge up some wacky recollections. I remind him of several of Betty's more extreme habits—e.g., throwing the entire contents of the linen cupboard out of a top window to let off steam. His reply was touchingly simple. He stared at her saucy, high-heeled, lace-up leather ankle boots, which he keeps on the mantelpiece as a reminder of their former occupant, and replied, "We took pleasure in each other's company." Terry and Betty shared an unconventional worldview.

"Neither of us were very sensible," admitted Terry at the end of our chat. "We both wanted to get away from the milieu of our childhood. And we were both determined to be different." A wacky chick like Betty is never short of company. However, if she wants to find a successful long-term relationship, clearly she must team up with a wacky bloke à la Terry.

Similar Betty-and-Terry scenarios prevailed among the other chasers and chicks with whom I spoke. Spider Fawke was insistent that Alan, her collection-officer boyfriend, had out-wackied her from the get-go.

For their first date, B.R.U.N.C.H.-y Alan took her to see the movie *Sphere* at the Westlake Shopping Centre, chauffeuring her in his 1986 Cadillac Brougham. "Twenty feet long, a real pimpmobile. I nearly wet my knickers when I saw it pulling up the street the first time!" recalls Spider, who realized instantly that Alan was a kindred spirit. The wacky rapport—which had them chuckling through the absurdities of the movie—culminated in a post-movie parking lot shag. "A great car for a bunk-up," muses Spider, "but sadly it died last year, so I kept the hood ornament as a memento."

Conclusion: The significant others of wacky chicks—those who form long-lasting relationships with these women—are invariably folks who share the wacky worldview. As Alan put it to me, "We have fun because we take the piss out of each other and out of the world around us."

Other miscellaneous camp followers and wackolytes—though not necessarily in for the long haul—play an equally important role. They are the fan club/extended family/Greek chorus of the wacky chick. Their mission in life is to goad and encourage their mistress to new heights of B.R.U.N.C.H.-y excess in the hopes that one day she may offer them a teaspoonful of her royal jelly.

AUDREY "GOLIGHTLY" SMALTZ—JUST GIVE HER $50 FOR THE POWDER ROOM

Managing all this glorious attention requires a veritable Cirque du Soleil of interpersonal juggling and contortionist skills, not to mention a heapin' dollop of diplomatic savoir faire. Of all the chicks I met, nobody handles the exigencies of her position better than wackily empowered Audrey Smaltz. And nobody gets more attention, or jewelry. She's been riding the Love Train—and the Soul Train—for as long as she can remember, and she has always occupied the driver's seat.

"I was born, bred, toasted, buttered, jammed and honeyed in Harlem!" intones the gorgeously magnificent fashion diva and self-described "minor celebrity in the African-American community" known as Audrey Smaltz, adding, "I'm sick of that line, but it works. No matter where I am in the world, they love it."

"They" is Audrey's adoring public. For her entire life, Audrey has been on display, in front of an audience, a camera or a panel of beauty-contest judges. Men have clustered to her like moths to a flame, and for the most part, their wings have been only benefited from the experience, give or take a slight singeing here or there.

Life-enhancing Audrey, who looks about forty-nine, recently celebrated her sixty-fifth birthday. "A total surprise, honey! It was at the Friars Club. Sixty-five of my friends and ex-lovers," recalls Audrey, brimming with birthday afterglow. "Incredible. Oooh! I was crying, honey!" Admirers flew in from around the globe—so many that Audrey was barely able to say hi to them all. And ex-bandleader Lionel Hampton came too. "Yess! That was one of mine," says Audrey using the impersonal article and thereby sounding a bit like a female Alfie,* "for fourteen and a half years that one lived with me. Do you mind if I smoke?"

---

*Re Alfie: see the 1966 eponymous movie starring Michael Caine, a sexist bloke who refers to girlfriends as "it"—e.g., "It's going to start crying any moment."

I ask Audrey to nail down what exactly has made her such a draw to men and women. Is it her wacky essence? "There is something about me. I don't know what it is, but my lovers are always with me. If they haven't dropped dead, they're still with me. And I tithe. Do you know what that means? Ten percent of my income. Yeah, it's in the Bible. When you give you receive."

Before Audrey embarks on her life story, she avails herself of a little nicotine. The sportily attired Miss Smaltz stretches her magnificent physique and reaches into a little birdhouse that contains her cigarettes and dangles from a giant umbrella on the wraparound terrace of the Fifth Avenue penthouse she calls home. "I like to be chic and discreet with myself," she offers, by way of explanation.

Her hair is currently clipped into a boyishly chic and discreet afro. She wears Dolce & Gabbana ocelot-print shoes, Levi's made-to-order jeans and a navy-and-white-striped sailor top from the Gap. The latter form-fitting garment was, so Audrey tells me, donned for my benefit: "I just wanted you to see, at sixty-five, these titties are still up there." After giving her magnificent boobs an affable jiggle, she closes the birdhouse door, elegantly drags on a Marlboro Ultra Light and returns to the subject of her birthday party and gifts.

From where we are sitting I can see the giant pile of birthday loot that is artfully displayed in Audrey's living room: a director's chair emblazoned with the words "Fashion Diva," a fuchsia cashmere stole from Donna Karan herself, a checkered Burberry golf bag, magnums of Veuve Clicquot and various items of gold jewelry. Wacky chicks like Miss Smaltz are not greedy or materialistic; they do, however, have the ability to inspire reckless generosity in others. As Audrey talks me through her gifts, I cannot take my eyes off the massive gold-coin choker that twinkles and glints an inch below her voice box. I ask her about its origins. "Years ago Lionel gave me about twenty fabulous coins," recalls Audrey with cat-who-got-the-cream eyes as she caresses the heavy gold chain. "This one is a 1901 Prince Albert of Monaco. I took it to Mr. Luigi in Florence—do you know him? He made it into a pendant. For twenty-five years this coin has been around my neck."

I take a deep breath and ask Audrey if she was ever a prostitute. "Hell no!" she replies with an amused shriek. "The men in my life gave me money because I asked for it, not for sex. I just asked them for it, and, believe me, honey, I asked for plenty." I encourage Audrey to elaborate on these transactions. Did she, for example, demand money for a purse or a particular frock? "No! *No!* I asked for *CASSSH!* I could go buy my own frock—thank you very much!" Suddenly, before my very eyes, Audrey Smaltz morphs into Audrey Hepburn, asking her men for fifty dollars to visit the powder room in *Breakfast at Tiffany's* and I realize I'm looking at Holly Golightly's uptown sister. "One time I wanted to go to Carnival in Trinidad," continues Miss A. "I had no money and it was cold in New York. I told three men I needed money. I paid my rent, paid my bills, went to Carnival, bought everyone a gift and came home." *Moon River, wider than a mile . . . I'm crossing you in style. . . .*

I'm swept along by Audrey's Golightlyesque skip-along attitude toward men and compliment her on her prefeminist sense of entitlement and her aggressive tactics. "Today, women don't know how to ask men for money. They give the cherry for *nothing!*" responds Audrey, sounding morally outraged, "I *never* did *that!*"

By way of explanation, Audrey shows me some pictures of herself in her youth. To say she is beautiful is a ghastly understatement: she makes Naomi Campbell look like Buddy Hackett. Though clearly African-American, the young Miss Smaltz, with her heavy eyebrows, dark eyes and prominent cheekbones, recalls Miss Hepburn in her prime—and I don't mean Katharine. Miss Smaltz is flattered by the comparison, and tells me that she once crossed paths with the late Miss Hepburn: "I told her, 'Honey, I'm the Technicolor Audrey Hepburn'—she laughed."

Her staggering gorgeousness explains the moth-flame ardor of her suitors but it does not explain her confidence. I ask Audrey about the origins of her monumental moxie. "I am tall and brown and I'm different. I got a last name Smaltz. It wasn't Johnson, Brown or Williams—those are colored names. I didn't have a colored name, I had an unusual name. A-u-d-r-e-y S-m-a-l-t-z. I went from A to Z. I was the Alpha and the Omega." Audrey, like many happy well-adjusted wacky chicks, has built her self-esteem using her idiosyncrasies and her points of difference as a foundation.

Imagining a vast spectrum of enthusiastic suitors with varying degrees of gentility, I ask Audrey if she was ever involved with abusive guys. Audrey is utterly horrified at the idea. Her beautiful brown eyes widen to three times their size, her mouth opens in operatic shock, she sucks in an enormous gasp of mock outrage, does a triple neck roll, splays her lovely jewel-encrusted hand across her upper chest and answers, "*Never!!* Why would any girl do *that*! When I finally gave up the cherry, I was twenty-one and that was very old. Those girls were going to bed with those young boys—not me! I went to bed with a Mr. John T. Patterson Jr." According to Audrey, J.P. was a successful investment banker who had become aware of Audrey when she started winning beauty contests in the 1950s. Miss Smaltz's fiercely independent spirit did not preclude the receipt of a little cosseting from J.P.: one of the best things about being a wacky chick is that you get to rewrite the rules while keeping your own best interests on the front burner. In return for "the cherry" Audrey got stocks and furs. "I had a chinchilla shrug. I had a silver fox stole that was made to order. It was six feet long either side, it had to be as tall as I was. Yes, I was always with nice guys."

In the mid-1960s, looking very mod in a Twiggyish mini with a matching oversized starched babushka, Audrey married an attentive and adoring bloke named Dr. Stanley Hughes and moved to Chicago. When the cosseting abated, Audrey moved back to New York. The marriage had lasted eighteen months. "After he got what he wanted, he didn't bother wanting it anymore—but we're still good friends. I'm Auntie Mame to his wife and children."

After only a few minutes with the captivating and hilarious Audrey, I am desperate to know what kind of hothouse could possibly have produced this alluring and idiosyncratic Capoteesque bloom. "I was born a princess," says Audrey with a coquettish and perfectly choreographed pursing of the lips, a lowering of the chin and a batting of the eyelids over up-slant-ing, almond-shaped brown eyes. "I grew up in the Harlem River Houses," continues Audrey with pride and emphasis, "the very first government housing ever in the U.S. at 151st Street through 153rd Street from Seventh Avenue to the East River." According to Audrey, this was no laundry-draped tene-ment. "We didn't even know we were in the ghetto, honey! It was like a country club! We had tennis courts, basketball courts. I learned how to paint and play the piano. We could play checkers and chess and my parents played bridge. It was beeeeeeeyond chichi! And the rent was seven dollars a week *cash!*"

By now I realize that Audrey's favorite word is "cash" and she says it with such infectious gusto that I find myself want-ing to rush to the nearest bank teller just to fill up my wallet. "I love *cash!*" admits Audrey, as if her passion were exotic and unique. "In my neighborhood, growing up you needed cash for when the boosters came around." The boosters? "They sold hot clothes—I'm talkin' about shoplifters, honey! They didn't take no credit cards—just casssssssh!" The boosters would drop by unannounced, so Audrey wisely made sure she always had enough extra cash in her purse to snag the good stuff. She got to know these fashion Robin Hoods and they got to know her sassy predilections. "I loved pearlized leather coats with full skirts. I had them in every color."

Unlike Holly Golightly, Audrey grew up in a sartorially so-phisticated household. Her father, Raymond Smaltz, was a clerk at the post office. "He went to work dressed to kill—the best posture—very spiffy. That's how I learned how to dress."

Audrey recalls how Mr. Smaltz would buy a yard of linen on Orchard Street from which he would cut and hand-roll hand-kerchiefs for himself and for Audrey.

Her mother, Dodie ("her real name was Dora, but she never used it because there was a cartoon at the time called Dumb Dora"), was a housewife who made money playing illegal numbers on horse races. Audrey explains, "She used to sit down and figure out what was going to be the first digit every day of her life . . . the second digit, the third digit and then she would play the whole number. She was winning all the time and she loved cash too." Along with a love of dollar bills, Audrey also inherited her mom's innate style: "She rode a bicycle. A man's bike. A Schwinn. She had short hair, but always over one eye, like Veronica Lake. She would wear my father's pants and a bad belt and a beautiful blouse and a Persian lamb coat on the bike, honey!"

I ask Audrey if it was hard being so szhooshy in the middle of gritty 1950s Harlem. "There were bad girls. They were lesbians. We called them studs. I had to fight the studs off all the time because they didn't like that I was always dressed up looking pretty and fresh." Audrey looks back on her chicly clean childhood with pride: "We didn't have roaches. We were fresh and clean, like we just took a scrub bath. We looked fresh all the time. That was important, to look fresh and clean all the time."

Freshness combined with style is a huge part of Audrey's allure, and of her m.o. As Audrey unfolds her diverse and celeb-filled life for me, I am also struck by her ability to ground every reminiscence with a fevered description of what she was wearing at that particular moment. In Shelley Winters's autobiographies *Shelley I* and *II*, wacky-chick Winters does the same thing, only with food. Whether with celery sticks or jelly doughnuts, each incident in her life, no matter how catastrophic, is grounded with a detailed culinary recollection. In 1960, after John F. Kennedy won the presidential nomination, rabid supporter Shelley "ate two tuna-fish sandwiches, drank three chocolate milk-shakes and took two sleeping pills." With Audrey it's clothes.

Her stand-out attire played a significant role in propelling the young, inexperienced Audrey out of the Harlem River Houses and into the glittering sociopolitical epicenter of 1960s New York life. "I met Shelley Winters at Harry Belafonte's. She slept with Martin Luther King and she was proud of it. She was very political, and I was very political too," says Miss Smaltz fervently, adding, "I raised money, I knew them all. Malcolm X, Martin Luther King, Bayard Rustin—he organized the March on Washington. I was there on August 28, 1963. I had on a peach dress. I'll never forget that dress." Martin Luther King made the "I have a dream" speech, Mahalia Jackson sang and a glamorous ingenue Audrey—out of 250,000 people—got her picture in the *Washington News* on the following day. She still has the clipping from which she reads me the caption with a professional orator's modulation: "'*She said she knew over a month ago that she wanted to take part in the march and then had arranged to take a day off of work to fly down*'—I wasn't going on the bus, honey! Lester Gribetz, a fabulous guy, he gave me the money for the plane ticket—'*She was present as an individual but she said she had met many friends on*

the planes . . . changing from medium heels to a pair of flats she car-
ried in her purse, the sleekly quaffed Miss Smaltz said, 'We're not
asking too much, we need to be completely free.'"

Alluring Audrey soon found out that not everyone in the
world was going to fall in love with her, or her chinchilla
shrugs. While on vacation in Miami Beach, she had her first
Rosa Parks moment. "I was once at the Atlantic Hotel. We
were at that counter and the waitress said, 'I'm not going to
serve those niggers.' We just sat there. So I got arrested. I was
wearing a sleeveless yellow cotton pant suit—with capri pants.
They were normal pants—but capri on me 'cuz I'm so tall."

Fashionably attired Audrey was at the epicenter of 1960s
tumult. "I attended Martin Luther King's funeral dressed to
the nines. Mrs. Kennedy—Ethel—she was sweating and I had
my nice handkerchiefs. I gave her one. I had my fan too. I still
have a fan everywhere I go. People say, 'You're so Karl Lagerfeld.' I say, 'I'm older than Karl and I've been using a fan
longer than Karl!!'"

Audrey's stylishness, like her freedom, was acquired with
a Golightlyish diligence. "When I was thirteen, I used to take
the bus down to Tiffany's just so I could learn about diamonds and see how they would set their tables. They taught
me everything." The trips to Fifth Avenue fueled Audrey's
passion for luxury goods and fancy clothes. As a result, Audrey began to channel oodles of creative energy into her appearance. Every spare moment was spent in endless fittings at
dressmakers in Harlem and the Bronx. Despite her rail-thin
physique Audrey started wearing foundation garments: "Playtex all in one. I was fourteen. Rubber Playtex! You could

sweat, honey!" Though Audrey was prepared to go to great lengths to look fabulous, she was not a proponent of skin bleaching. "That was for women who were very dark. I wasn't dark. I wasn't high yellow either. I'm honey brown."

Her hair required far more maintenance than her skin. "It took forevaaah! Because it was pressed and curled. Which means, you'd shampoo it and then it would be very kinky, then they would take this hot comb with stuff called Dixie Peach—which was just a fancy name for grease—and make it straight like a white lady's, and then curl it."

With this growing investment in time and cash, it wasn't long before Audrey decided it was time to deploy some of her God-given and store-bought assets to generate an income of her own. Following a stint at the Laura Dell School of Charm, where a young Diahann Carroll was the receptionist, Audrey joined the Grace del Marco Modeling Agency and immediately started to get bookings. I ask Audrey if she modeled for white companies. "Hell no! We used to picket the big model agencies. Eileen Ford had me thrown out of her office. We picketed *Harper's Bazaar* too. They didn't start letting black girls model for mainstream companies until the late fifties."

On the subject of contemporary models, Audrey becomes uncharacteristically irate: "Iman and Beverly Johnson broke through in the 1970s—but now we are back where we started. Black girls are hardly ever on the covers or on the runway, which makes me crazy because *white girls can't walk!!!!!!!!!*" Audrey jumps out of her chair and does a brilliant imitation of a graceless, gangly white girl clomping down the runway, and then, by way of contrast, she executes her own perfect swanlike glide, complete with superelegant, glove-removing hand gestures.

Modeling led to beauty contests at which Audrey regularly wiped the floor with the other girls. She won loads of awards, including Miss Transit, 1954. Her proudest moment did not arrive until almost a decade later, when she became the first black chick to enter the Miss New York City contest, a prelim to the Miss America contest. "The press were saying 'you have to let a black in,' so a lot of us showed up and I was the one selected. I'll never forget that swimsuit, I paid fifty dollars. It was all white. A Roxanne swimsuit. Fabulous."

Though Audrey was only a runner-up, her appearance brought the house down and she had made history. "The press went crrrazy! That was 'sixty-two, and so, Vanessa Williams, that was 'eighty-three, 'eighty-four. Honey, I did a lot of firsts, what can I tell you?"

Audrey was the first black female registered representative authorized to sell mutual funds at Basche and Co. She became the second black executive at Bloomingdale's—a first of sorts. "I got my nephew in there and he became the third. Doris Salinger—you may have heard of her brother, Mr. J.D.?—she hired me. I told her, 'I want to be a fashion coordinator. I don't know what that is, I just know I want to be it.'" Audrey was acquiring new skills and jettisoning old habits: when she got her job at Bloomingdale's she magnanimously deserted the boosters and never wore hot clothes again.

Over the next few years Miss Smaltz—unlike Miss Golightly—developed a sterling work ethic. During her long and varied career, she has done everything from graphic design to traveling sales. "I worked for Lena Horne Beauty Products," recalls Audrey, who effortlessly translated her wacky allure into record-breaking salesmanship. "I went all over—and, ooh! I had the best luggage."

Her most triumphant gig—and the one for which she is best known—came along when she was in her thirties. "From 1970 to 1977, I was fashion editor and fashion coordinator and fashion commentator—and I sold advertising—for the Ebony Fashion Fair," recalls Audrey, adding humbly, "and I became a minor celebrity in the black community." The killer fashion shows that Audrey brought to every nook and cranny of America were an innovative piece of marketing. The concept was simple: Audrey and her entourage of models and camp followers, traveling by Greyhound bus, staged fashion shows for snappily dressed middle-class African-American style lovers. Attendees happily purchased tickets for these modish spectacles; cunningly included in the price of each ticket was an *Ebony* subscription.

Audrey's raucously wacky charisma guaranteed that everybody got his or her money's worth at her invariably sold-out appearances. Wearing a culotte,* a riding boot, an oversized

---

*Save valuable time by languidly referring to the contents of your wardrobe in the singular, e.g., a Manolo, a pantie, a Galliano, a fishnet, etc. I picked this habit up from busy L.A. director/stylist L'Wren Scott, who regularly decompresses her breakneck schedule with this timesaving device—e.g., "I'm wearing an Ossie with a hoop and a Perry." Trans.: a vintage Ossie Clark dress with a pair of hoop earrings and pointy boots by Michel Perry. Wacky L'Wren claims that referring to everything in the singular has "given me a whole new lease on life. Nothing would get me back to plurals except maybe if I had to dress a celeb who was missing a limb. 'You need a croc Manolo' might sound a bit shady to someone with one leg."

In addition to the L'Wren Scott method, I also recommend the following time-savers: always abbreviate "naturally, I would love to" to the infinitely more economical "natch," and instead of "I totally agree with you," simply say "tote," as in bag.

hoop earring and an afro, she habitually whipped her adoring audiences into such a fierce fashion frenzy that possessed audience members would often leap onto the stage and engage in bouts of impassioned, spontaneous modeling. If these attention junkies refused to leave the stage, m.c. Audrey would sternly stop the music and turn her back on them until they did, sending them on their way with a tough "Don't you mess with my show, baby!"

The Ebony gig taught culotte-clad Audrey how to take her electric one-on-one mojo and use it to work a crowd, wowing up to five thousand people at a time with her looks and her engaging patter. Her best show ever? "We were in Hartford, Connecticut, during a snowstorm, with less than ten people in the audience. I invited our bus driver to fill the place up, and all of a sudden this bus driver starts asking questions: 'Tell me about that dress!' and 'Where the hell would you wear that?' Can you imagine? By the time we finished he was a fashion expert."

I ask Audrey if she ever had to protect her models from sleazy dudes. "We didn't have sleazy dudes," replies Audrey with agile mimicry, but sounding more proud than indignant. "We had the tippy-top, crème de la crème—doctors and lawyers and even Indian chiefs." Was Miss Smaltz ever cast in the role of procureuse? "Of course, honey! But I'm much too chic and discreet to name names!"

After seven years on the bus, and approximately one thousand shows under her Elsa Peretti for Tiffany belt, Audrey turned forty and decided to hang up her culottes. Like many a wacky chick, she had tired of the constraints of employment and was ready to start her own business. With w.c. vision and entrepreneurship, she kick-started fashion's first professional backstage support organization, calling it the Ground Crew. Historically, fashion designers had relied on friends and family to perform the backstage functions, particularly dressing. Audrey brought her experience and savoir faire to this previously chaotic fashion moment. "We have tailors and seamstresses but it's mostly dressing. I got that name—the Ground Crew—from Martin Luther King."

One Sunday, back in 1965, Audrey had wandered into the Convent Avenue Baptist Church in Harlem. Martin Luther King was the preacher. "It was just about the time they introduced the big jumbo 747 planes. He spoke about what it took to get this big machine up in the air—all the people who were behind the scenes but just as important as the pilot or the plane. He called them the ground crew." This metaphor stuck in Audrey's memory and gave her the name for the company, which she operates to this day.

Her remarkable career never prevented her from juggling millions of friendships and a varied romantic life. "I have an apartment in Paris. Girl! I knew who to sleep with when I was young and tender and I still have that apartment in Paris." I ask her about the ratio of suitors, white to black. "I never went to bed with a white man—I just played with them. I'd dance with them and lead them on but, honey, they weren't giving up any casssh so forget it."

I ask Audrey about her current status and am totally unprepared for her reply. "I have a partner now. Her name is Gail.

She's forty-seven years old—a financial manager at Merrill Lynch! All of my friends accepted her and my pastor accepted her." It was Gail who organized the party at the Friars Club. Audrey has done something Holly Golightly never managed to do: she has snagged her Rusty Trawler.

Not surprisingly Gail is getting a hard-core fashion education from her new spousette. "I gave it to her straight, I said, 'I want you in Giorgio Armani suits. Go to Saks Fifth Avenue and ask for Beau'—that's my guy, who takes care of me." After making over Gail, Audrey speculates that her next mission might be to save gay women from their antifashion doldrums: "These girls are working my last fashion nerves. Why do they have to look so damn rugged 24/7? They need finesse."

Unrugged Audrey toys with a bundle of old snaps while she muses on her own life-long attractiveness. "I am fun, and I don't gossip. I used to, but no more. I haven't gossiped in years. The only gossip I know is what's in *Women's Wear Daily* and I . . ."

Miss Smaltz comes to a picture of herself and gasps mid-sentence. "Wait a minute . . . this coat was made to order, by John Weston. A yellow mohair coat, princess-style, three-quarter-length sleeves, a winter coat, it had great buttons, side-seam pockets and a scarf that just wrapped and wrapped and wrapped. Look at my wicked eyebrows. Oooh, and a black fox muff, honey! Muffs were *very* important."

When Mother Nature—a wacky chick if ever there was one—selected be-muffed Audrey for wacky ordination, she gave her a special gift, but she also placed huge demands on her chosen one. Noblesse oblige! The keys to wacky-chickdom gave Audrey access to a fabulously spotlit privileged life, but those keys came with a whole macramé of complex obligations and pressures, every bit as complicated as those faced by Miss Holly Golightly herself.

Undaunted, even at sixty-five, Audrey girds up her chichi loins every day and hits the streets. If any overenthusiastic wackolytes or chick-chasers get out of hand, she puts them in their place with a strict but caring, "Don't you mess with my show, baby!"

CHAPTER 7

FAITH

Squeezing Your Inner Shaman

Not every wacky chick is a full-blown, hippie-dippy, rune-casting, crystal-gazing, primal screaming, toe-ring-wearing, crop-circle-visiting, Joni-lovin', aura-cleansing, toxin-releasing, earth-shoe-sporting, tempeh-broiling, chakra-opening, sage-burning freak. However, honesty compels me to admit that many of my girls have what might be described as "new age leanings."

The typical wacky chick is far more likely to embrace random, kooky, alternative ideologies than the average broad. Scratch a wacky chick and you invariably find ad hoc spirituality of some description lurking near the surface. And why not? Today's emerging wacky chick is a curious, outgoing sort of a gal: she feels duty-bound to inspect new cultish ideas or road-test any exotic new fads.

Wacky chicks crave spiritual sustenance as much as the rest of us, but they have always had a hard time with organized religion, and vice versa. Most religions are overly focused on constraining any B.R.U.N.C.H.-y behaviors in their female devotees. Be it with a wig, a burkha or a wimple, the faiths of the world also seem hell-bent on forcing chicks into decidedly unfetching garb. Small wonder wacky chicks seek out—and find—more wacky-friendly gurus and shamans.

New Mexico is the unofficial H.Q. and breeding ground for much of this random and mostly innocuous hocus-pocus. It is not uncommon to attend a dinner party in Santa Fe and find oneself seated next to a "walk in"—a chick who has been "occupied" by a space alien. Or even a "breathairian," one of those gals who believes we can survive by ingesting air. And let's not forget the dear old "crusties," those aging hippie dreadlocked mamas (and papas) who don't bathe as often as the rest of us and arrive for cocktails looking biblical and stoned with a pet donkey in tow. Not all of these freaks are wacky chicks, but there is an undeniable overlap with this patchouli-drenched, guru-infested world.

JESSICA PORTER—HIP HYPNOSIS AND ZEN COMEDY

Jessica Porter, a celebrity hypnotist of Portland, Maine, is one such idiosyncratic chick. Canadian-born Jess has a fascinatingly schizo history—radio host/actress/manicurist/macro guru—that has largely been driven by a not altogether unhealthy desire to evolve, or rather devolve, from being an overachieving type A personality to a laissez-faire type B.

Her journey has resulted in, amongst other things, a lasting commitment to the macrobiotic teachings of Michio Kushi. Miss Porter, an inveterate show-off, has done much to improve the image of the macrobiotic milieu, a world all too often dismissed as a dreary and tasteless hellhole of Japanese stoicism. She is, for example, generally acknowledged to be the first woman to write and produce macrobiotic dinner theater and stand-up comedy.

But Michio Kushi was by no means her first guru. That honor goes to Carole Jackson. Yes, I'm talking about Carole *Color Me Beautiful* Jackson.

There is nothing so powerful as a self-help book whose time has come, and so it was with *Color Me Beautiful*. Author Carole Jackson exploded onto best-seller lists in the early 1980s, mesmerizing the women of America, not to mention color-confused Canadians like Jessica.

The 1970s, as you recall, were all about *beige*. Fawn, ecru, parchment, taupe, call it what you will, beige was king—or queen (if ships are female, then so—as far as I'm concerned—are colors). Beige was not just a color during that decade, she was an evocative style-signifier with a whole macramé of multiple associations. See Faye Dunaway in *Network*, anything Halston, early Armani, late LeSportsac. Love her or hate her, she was easy to wear and she always connoted sophistication—even if it was the aspirant sophistication of the Members Only masses. And then, all of sudden, she didn't.

The style pendulum swung and jewel tones erupted onto the 1980s fashion landscape—electric blue, hot pink, and cerise—blasting beige into irrelevance. In no time the trend for bright color filtered down: women at all style strata were now free to indulge in Nancy Reagan red or Christina Ferrari fuchsia. But freedom carries its own oppression, and the good women of the 1980s found that certain colors worked on some broads while simultaneously giving others a corpselike, pukey pallor. Confusion reigned. Enter—on a white horse— Carole Jackson and the cult of *Color Me Beautiful.*

The basic premise of Ms. Jackson's style bible is that chicks can be divided into two groups: gals with warm skin tones and gals with cool ones. These two groups can then— based on eye and hair color—be further subdivided into four "seasons": autumn and spring (warm skin tones); winter and summer (cool skin tones). The differences between the four seasons can be a bit nuanced, so the easiest way to understand the whole idea is to use contemporary celebrity examples. Nicole Kidman, Faith Hill, Matt Damon and Jude Law are all springs; Charlize Theron, Elizabeth Hurley, Cameron Diaz, Justin Timberlake and Steven Spielberg are all summers; Hilary Swank, Julia Roberts, Russell Crowe and Penelope Cruz are all autumns; Ben Affleck, Catherine Zeta-Jones, Christina Ricci and Keanu Reeves are all winters.

Color-me-Carole spawned millions of followers and apostles. In swanky living rooms and tawdry trailer parks across the nation, Color Me Beautiful consultants courageously attempted to cut the cackle out of clothing consumption. They did it with a system of color swatches that were matched to the season and specific skin tone of the devotee in question. Cult members like Jessica call this cult ritual "having your colors done."

This simple process provided the color-confused 1980s shopper with the tools with which to cobble together a coordinated wardrobe for herself. People took it all very seriously: deviating from "your colors" was seen as fashion suicide.

Devotees wouldn't even buy a pot holder without cross-referencing their swatches and making sure it complimented their season; some terminally ill devotees even swatched the linings of their own caskets.

Getting slightly dewy-eyed, tall, striking, high-cheekboned Jessica Porter recalls her first Color-me encounter. "My mother initiated me. It was in the early 1980s; I was only fourteen at the time," says Jessica with a Kathleen Turner–ish toss of her auburn mane. "I was taken to a Colors salon in Toronto." As Jessica and her mother trudged through the permafrost to the Colors salon on that fateful day, they had no idea their lives were about to change, forever. "A fat lady put a big swatch of pink fabric on my chest," remembers Jess with a nervous chuckle, "and my cheeks looked sallow, like I was going to puke, proving that I was, indeed, a low-contrast autumn."

For poised, patricianly Waspy Jessica, this meant that she could wear any color as long as it is based in orange, as opposed to pink, and has a little earthiness to it. "We autumns move through life like a dried leaf, spiraling and encircling you with a naturalness and nonchalance," says Jessica, sounding a little deranged. "We are the earth, the sand, the mud. You will find us in a brick, a pumpkin or an apple going bad."

After her life-changing consultation, earthy Jessica happily embraced her allotted 25 percent of the color spectrum. "I bought the autumnal Color Me Beautiful makeup, and that's what I used for years. I even took my colors [bag of swatches] with me to Brown University." A class of '88 member recalls Ms. Porter as "a swatch-crazed but well-coordinated autumn."

To this day she remains an unapologetic devotee. "Carole Jackson is correct. I look best in earthy tones and I always will," she said. "It was a positive experience, a mother-daughter thing, like est. It stays with you. My mother—she's an autumn too—just recently redid her house in muted autumn tones."

Jessica feels positive about her experience but admits that, as with any cult, there is a Jim Jones–ish side to the story: "Not every Colors consultant was as idealistic and skilled as Carole Jackson. I heard a lot of horror stories." Jessica is referring to the reckless treatment meted out to some of Carole's followers, innocent believers who were bamboozled by over-confident inexpert color consultants into kamikaze decisions, like wearing bright orange lipstick or getting married in teal. Misdiagnosis by these unskilled Colors consultants was common, wreaking havoc on the lives of many followers. Some women, after hasty consultations, threw out rails of quality garments, only to find they had been assigned the wrong season. They rushed back to the Goodwill to reclaim their castoffs, only to be confronted with droves of poor and needy folk spewing into the parking lot wearing—and looking just as fabulous in—those erroneously discarded duds.

A well-documented example of C.M.B. misdiagnosis occurs in Michael Moore's documentary *Roger & Me*. Janet, a bouncy Amway gal and Color Me Beautiful consultant from Flint, Michigan, insists on being refilmed so she can let the world know that she is not, as stated in earlier footage, an autumn, but rather a spring.

Though autumnal Jessica believes Carole's ideology still

has a place in her life, she no longer worships at the temple of La Mode. "I used to be obsessed, but then I turned my back on fashion. It's my defense against people who have their shit together in the clothing department. I fear them. They are what I call 'shoe people,' which means they actually look down at other people's shoes and evaluate them during the course of a conversation."

Jessica believes that there are two types of people in the world, spiritually bankrupt "shoe people" and gorgeously-empathetic-but-not-so-stylish "non-shoe people." The former care about footwear, even to the point of worshipping specific shoe designers and collecting their *oeuvre*, while the latter go "for the supercomfortable pair of Mephisto's every two years."

As a child Jessica had all the earmarks of a Blahnik-collecting shoe person in the making. By the time trendy, camply precocious Jessica was nine, she was already hawking Wella Balsam to herself in the bathroom mirror with a deep husky "Hello, I'm Farrah Fawcett."

At around this time, thanks to her father, Miss Porter had a life-changing encounter with rock royalty. Daddy Porter was well connected and spent two years as president of the Canadian National Exhibition, "our little annual urban Disney World." Big names from around the world would come to play concerts for all the Canucks. "The Osmonds . . . I met the fucking Osmonds! They all wore leather suits à la Elvis with little tiny mirrors on them," recalls Jessica breathlessly, "and I almost died. Donny was about eighteen and at the height of his swoonerishness. Jimmy was sort of pudgy, being just a kid, and Marie—who was not yet a star—had her hair in curlers." Jessica shook Donny's hand and realized, at that moment, "that life didn't suck," even in Toronto. This encounter put little starry-eyed Jess on the show-biz fast track.

By age fourteen Miss Porter landed a gig as a radio host for a national kids' show. "I got to interview a lot of great people like Jim Henson and Joan Jett." Jessica is conscious of her good fortune: "the years between fourteen and sixteen, so easily a shit-pile for most teens, were really stellar for me." The burgeoning type A media maven drew a weekly paycheck, was interviewed by the press, met a million people and even got fan mail.

She went on to study theater at Brown and NYU, and seemed destined to follow in the footsteps of fellow Canadian mega-talents Jim Carrey and Mike Myers. Jessica attributes her precocious theatricality, and that of Mr. Myers and Mr. Carrey, to growing up in Toronto. "It's no accident that my hometown is the seat of so much theatrical wackiness. The freakishly evil weather made us a little skittish. You can't go out much. You spend a bit too much time in front of the TV on the couch, thinking weird thoughts and eating Tang crystals."

The sizzle of show biz started to fizzle when Jessica woke up one morning and realized that she "did not have a self." How was she supposed to inhabit other people's identities when she didn't have one herself? "I had just spent the summer in Rome painting my nails and wishing I could fly into the life of another woman," recalls an increasingly woo-woo-sounding Jessica. "I had thirty shades of polish. Having smoked pot every day for the previous two years, my brain was raw and romantic, hesitating to make the leap into its own job of sorting out my future." Every night she painted her nails a different color, "concentrating all of my world onto each little pad of dried protein." Though her nails looked great, Jessica had lost her identity and was clearly on the verge of losing her mind.

Miss Porter pulled herself back from her acetone-infused brink and, with the open-minded enthusiasm for new philosophies that characterizes many a wacky chick, headed to the Kushi Institute in the Berkshires "to study the phenomenon of total transformation via the pressure cooker"—i.e., she became a devotee of macrobiotics and its leading proponent, the aforementioned Michio Kushi.

Childlike exuberance enlivens Jessica's face when she talks about her guru: "Michio has taken the teachings of Georges Ohsawa, a guy who cured himself of tuberculosis, and disseminated them throughout America for the last fifty years." The beneficent Michio is, according to Jessica, "the father of the health food industry in this country, being one of the first to import miso, tempeh and tofu into America." The evangelist that seems to lurk inside every wacky chick has jack-in-the-boxed out of Jessica. Miss Porter catches me midsmirk over her soy-derived enthusiasms and counters my derision by adding, "Hey! The Smithsonian recently honored him and created an archive of his teachings."

Despite being immersed in hijiki and adzuki beans, the spotlight-loving performer in Jessica began to rear her low-contrast autumnal head once again. "I served as m.c. on talent nights and other big gatherings of macrobiotic people, and I put together a one-woman show called *Zen Comedy*." Cheeky Jessica even managed to persuade the reserved Mr. Kushi to don Mickey Mouse ears and do a little dance while she led two hundred people in singing "M-I-C-H-I-O K-U-S-H-I" (à la *Mickey Mouse Club*) at a macrobiotic conference.

In this wholesome cultish environment Jessica found herself, and somebody else. She fell in love. Jessica and her new macro-beau embarked on a whole-grain odyssey. "We traveled the world as private chefs, spreading the word. We cooked for sick people, rich people, poor people, deeply religious people, crazy people, famous people." Her celeb clients included Pink Floyd's Roger Waters, and she even cooked lunch for JonBenet Ramsey's mother, Patsy: "Putting aside the whole question of whether she murdered her own daughter, I must say, I liked her. She had a very open mind and asked intuitive questions," recalls Jessica magnanimously.

The macro lifestyle was, for sincerely committed Jessica, far more than an excuse to hobnob with notorious celebs. She remains a serious, dedicated Kushi disciple and will proselytize to anyone within earshot. "The quality of food in our bodies is the only real, structural defense we have against the disintegration that is taking place around us on all levels. The continual nourishment of the human organism with whole foods is everything. The people who wake up in the morning and make good-quality food for themselves and others are keeping the threads in our collective tapestry strong."

I myself plunged down the well of tofu some twenty years ago and remain a strong believer. Over the years, horrified friends have tried to discourage me, but to no avail. Why? Because, shockingly, I actually like the way it tastes. Compared to the school dinners and gray overcooked vegetables of my country of origin, every macro-meal is a gourmet explosion. Like Jessica, I am also a low-contrast autumn; this may or not be a factor in my willingness to tolerate tempeh.

After several years in the macro-milieu, Jessica discovered that some of the threads of this tapestry were more compliant than others. Not everybody's idea of a lip-smackin' gourmet freak-out consists of sucking on a bitter umeboshi plum or scarfing down bowls of natto—a fermented soy delicacy with the smell and texture of cat poo. Jessica saw that many people—even the chronically sick—needed help if they were going to go macro. "Diabetes, arthritis, even cancer—macro food has the potential to save lives, but only if the patient can adhere to the diet." To facilitate this process, Jessica became the high priestess of hypnotherapy.

"I interned with a guy called Gerry Kein—like so many great hypnotists, he hails from New Jersey," recalls fast-learning Miss Porter, who, before she knew it, was approved by the National Guild of Hypnotists and had set up her own practice. She spread the word by taking out a series of inexpensive local TV ads, to which she added her theatrical aplomb. Her sultry voice and the fact that her contact number was 773-EASY attracted many pervy callers, and she eventually ceased advertising. Fortunately by this time Jessica had built a solid client base.

Though most of her work focuses on smoking cessation and hypno-birthing ("Helping people to have really mellow,

happy babies by teaching them hypnosis during pregnancy"),
Jess will take a crack at anything from nail biting to sexual
dysfunction. She has found that working directly with people's subconscious minds is much more satisfying than working with their stomachs: "material that it might be very hard
to access from a normal waking state is present and available
to the client. During hypnosis, the self-love which is at the
core of all living beings is released and allowed to flow. Emotions and belief systems pop out of nowhere. We can aim the
imagination in a sustained and effective way to help the client
design their future."

The experience is intense for both hypnotizer and hypno-
tee. When conducting a session, Jessica's subconscious mind
goes to work, and she enters the trance with her patients: "It's
insanely draining because I am actually doing hypnosis from a
state of hypnosis myself."

She is incredibly well suited to this profession. With her
theatrically trained baritone and her improv ability to shoot
from the hip, she has found a métier that fits her like a glove.
Successes are commonplace and screwups are few and far between; she recently found herself calling a client Bill multiple
times until his eyes popped open angrily and he said, "My
name is *Wayne!*"

Jessica operates with an expanded definition of the word
"hypnosis." She believes that positive and negative hypnosis
is part of daily life. "Howard Stern makes me laugh, but I
think his daily hypnosis is probably doing serious damage to
the country, in terms of lowering our collective consciousness
into the sewer." She feels that Dr. Laura Schlessinger is worse:

"Being a macro chick of long standing, my liver is too clean to actually feel hate, but she really bugs the shit out of me. Dr. Laura espouses ideological teachings and hypnotizes from the high ground, which is a total mind-fuck. Her vibe is totally toxic. At least Howard admits he's in the sewer. I hope her poor, poor son turns out to be homosexual, and then she will spontaneously combust."

Jessica also believes that the media can, with a power similar to that of an organized religion, collectively hypnotize us all into unquestioning belief or deep denial. Her current wacky *bête noire* is the British royal family. "Prince Harry is the complete and utter doppelganger of James Hewitt—that guy Diana had the affair with. He is a motherless bastard living in the royal family. I feel for him, being a redhead and all, but I just can't believe that we don't talk about that every day, or that Prince Charles doesn't kick him out or that Harry doesn't freak out and run home to Dad. This obsesses me." Miss Porter convincingly adds, "Think about it: What if Prince William dies in a tragic plane crash? Or decides to marry Britney Spears, who—we all know—is not a virgin, thereby having to abdicate the throne out of his love for her, à la Wallis Simpson? It just blows my mind that this precious, snooty, glistening royal lineage is being jeopardized by the collective unwillingness to admit that Diana was a wee bit naughty."

Miss P. also believes we have been collectively hypnotized by Madonna. "I admire her guts. She moves forward in her life, like a shark, publicly, and without shame. But if stars are balls of fire that burn, giving off light and energy around them, she definitely qualifies."

Detecting the tiniest tinge of envy, I ask Jessica if she's jealous of Madonna's success? "I think it's the other way round. I hear she turned macro and sent her sister to the Kushi Institute," replies Jessica triumphantly. "Macro food is transformational. It will be very interesting to see who she is in five years." Madonna's developmental path, according to a gleeful Miss P., is pulling the mega-star songstress in a more self-aware direction: "One of my greatest satisfactions in my hypnotism work is showing type A people that being a type B can actually make you more effective at life. Madonna is learning this lesson—she's not stupid. She knows we're all going to end up dead and there are no Manolo Blahniks on the other side." Jessica reveals to me that the working title for the macro self-help manifesto she is currently writing is *Madonna, Gwyneth and Me*.

Busy Jessica has a patient waiting and politely encourages me to depart. I decide to leave her on a bracingly superficial note, by asking her if there are any spiritual components to her beauty routine. Though the pathological nail-worship is a thing of the past, Jessica does admit to "staining my face labia." Her most valuable cosmic beauty secret? Seaweed. "A plateful of hijiki or arame a couple of times a week keeps my skin really nice looking. It's also amazing for keeping my hair shiny, thick and strong. By the way, how dare you call my beauty routine!!!" concludes Jessica, like the stand-up macro comic she is.

KAZUKO—CRYSTAL-PACKIN' MAMA

Kazuko is a tiny, doll-like, white-clad Japanese lady who seems devoid of hang-ups about her lack of height.

This adorable, unstoppable, pocket-sized jewelry designer has led an artsy, complicated sort of life. Every sentence out of her mouth is fascinatingly cross-referenced with at least six degrees of cross-cultural name-dropping. And we're not, as we were with Jessica, talking about the likes of Joan Jett and Donny Osmond. The titans of twentieth-century culture, no less, are drawn to Kazuko and vice versa by a powerful magnetism that she enigmatically describes as "a preordained psychic storm." Though most of her associations have been classy and arty, her highly idiosyncratic, celeb-peppered résumé does include the totally haunting fact that she once understudied for *Fantasy Island* midget Herve Villechaize.

Every time her cell phone jangles, which it does several times during our cosy green tea tête-a-tête, the ensuing chitchat is littered with famous names like Holly Solomon, Gloria Vanderbilt and Mitsuko Uchida. It seems as if her life story is the product of a mystical circuit diagram created by cinematic, fateful encounters with these influential bohemians. "When certain people walk into my brain range, I get a psychic message from them and I have to respond." These high-profile folk are also devotees of Kazuko's crystal jewelry—which she calls "one-of-one healing sculptures"—and will attest to its magical properties at the drop of a name.

Ironically, in 1993 Kazuko made a cameo appearance in the movie version of John Guare's play *Six Degrees of Separation*. "I knew the couple on whom the story is based. They had already bought my first big crystal bracelet. Stockard Channing was married to Paul Schmidt, who introduced me to Peter Sellars," continues Kazuko, losing and confusing me almost completely, "I met Paul because of Bob Wilson, who was a close friend of my boyfriend who was a . . ."

Kazuko's intense focus on the overachieving bohemians of her generation is, despite her woo-woo ideas about "psychic storms," insanely logical. Why would you schlepp all the way from Japan—remember, it takes five hours just to get to the airport from Tokyo center—and hang out with a bunch of losers? Wouldn't you expect to meet Bianca Jagger right away?

Kazuko is, it should be pointed out, not in the least superficial. She is a serious artist and a psychic who communicates with humans and animals. Beauty, art and geology are the cornerstones of her religion. While Jessica Porter was eating crystals, Kazuko was starting to incorporate them into healing fashion accessories. And, like many of my girls, her life has been a creative and often tortured struggle to overcome parental disapproval.

By Japanese standards Kazuko is a very bad daughter indeed. In 1968, she did the unthinkable for a chick of her generation: she flew the coop—on a Fulbright scholarship, no less—and moved to New York. Kazuko vividly recalls the day the sushi hit the fan: "When I was under the dryer at my weekly beauty parlor visit, a call came from mother, who opened my letter and found acceptance from Fulbright fellowship, which is big prestige, so, family, being establishment, could not deny me from leaving."

For her traveling outfit, Kazuko commissioned a dress from her great-aunt, Countess Umeko Hijikata, who had studied under the bias-cutting Parisian curmudgeon Madeleine Vionnet. "I would design with her some outrageous outfits, and then I would go to school in amazing concept clothes not so prevalent in Tokyo in those days." For Kazuko's trip, the Countess made her a discreet Mary Quant–ish dress, white daisy print with a border of olive green. The perky departure frock transformed Kazuko into an urban Western chick, but did nothing to soothe her tormented parents. "Poor mother and poor Father, totally at a loss. They never spoke about me till they died, except to the chauffeur and then only once."

As Kazuko recounts the story of her epic departure, she smiles sweetly and cajoles and adjusts her complex loose-fitting, multilayered costume around her tween-sized body into the form of a little nest. "I am obsessed not to be too tight in dressing. Restricted energy—like kimono and obi—it is to be avoided. Clothes were always a symbol of freedom to me. Freedom, floatingness, looseness with gauzy textures, chiffons, organzas, silk veils. Even thin gold wires. I believe in things not spelled out . . . things that are invisible . . . things that are like shadows."

Kazuko disentangles her long silky hair from her wire and crystal necklace and gives her white nest one final fluff. Her clothing is fully integrated into her spiritual life: she has, she whispers, special reasons for wearing white. The switch from black to white was made a number of years ago after her Chinese acupuncturist, while peering at her eyeballs, announced that she had developed "nun's symptoms in the iris" and that "wearing all black from lingerie to outerwear for fifteen years had weakened my inner organs." Kazuko took him at his word and changed her entire wardrobe to white.

Her clothes might be monochromatic but her style is bohemian and diverse. She prefers natural fibers and ethnic styles. Her faves? "Tibetans have formulated the most sophisticated way of dressing. I love Kashmiri men's wear."

As un-Japanese and wacky as Kazuko has become, she has retained the Japanese passion for designer labels. "I'm loving Yeohlee, Gaultier, Chanel, Dolce & Gabbana, Gucci, Prada, Issey Miyake and of course Giorgio Di Sant'Angelo. For suits of course it has to be white Giorgio Armani with Lyn Revson scarves and Daniela Morera's special Tibetan cashmere scarves woven by monks."

Despite her designer addictions, Kazuko lives mostly in a nonmaterial world of chakras, auras and psychic energy. Cynics might dismiss her ideas as the ramblings of a barely functional lunatic, but nobody can accuse sweet-natured Kazuko of jumping on the new age bandwagon. She's been at it for years.

Paranormal powers emerged during childhood. "I had no idea I was psychic person. One day I told Mother that Mrs. S. was going to have another baby—being devoted Catholic, she was already mother of five. Mother is scolding me; I am a little child, not knowing anything. Three months later, Mother apologized as she just found out Mrs. S. was indeed expecting the sixth child."

It soon became apparent to Kazuko that these psychic powers extended beyond these neighboring followers of Rome and into other species. "Every day when Father—whose nickname in the family was Tormented Japanese Hamlet—came home from Finance Ministry, a rabbit, which was called Mr. White, squeaked to welcome Father coming and made Daddy very happy. I spoke with Mr. White and he knew what he had to do."

Kazuko's father often needed cheering up because he suffered badly from malaria. His gorgeous resourceful wife was concerned about the lack of wholesome food for her ailing husband in postwar Tokyo, so, according to Kazuko, "she became a Swiss milkmaid and is bringing home a goat to our residential neighborhood and soon learned to milk this goat." Finding food for the goat in the bombed-out desolation of Tokyo was no mean feat. "Mother, beautifully dressed, took us children and the goat on a rope around the neighborhood, looking for wild weeds, and goat finds them because he know he has an important job."

The most amusing psychic communication occurred with a gender-dystopic, flatulent cat called Paris. "He was born when Father was in Paris and although he was a boy cat, I knew through psychic communication he thought he was a she cat." Paris's favorite occupation was eliciting admiration: "for a long time he sat still feeling absolutely like a beautiful woman. I understood him. All the ladies who came to visit Mother during the day for tea watched Paris on the top of the big table. I knew he/she was asking everyone to give her a rave review. Before tea was served he lifted his long tail in a tiny motion . . . and farted."

Fortunately not all of Kazuko's animals have been as gassy and narcissistic as Paris. In 1987 a ratty little one-legged sparrow flew into her twentieth-floor Manhattan apartment and, uninvited, took up residence in an old antique birdcage. Kazuko named him Bobi Bird: she cleaned him up and discovered that he was a canary. From August 1, 1987, until his death on December 4, 1992, he twittered and warbled, filling Kazuko's apartment with song. "He danced, he sung, and he was my companion while I worked, sometimes helping me by carrying beads and threads." Empathetic Bobi would always know if Kazuko was having a bad day. "If I was going to throw up, he would follow me into the bathroom." Like a demanding adoring husband, Bobi would even point to dresses he wanted Kazuko to wear.

"Healing tapes" were made of Bobi's uplifting warblings and distributed to illustrious friends, who played them as ambient music. Soon Bobi became a legend. "Before he died, he was in *Vanity Fair,* in the article of one of his godmothers, the pianist Mitsuko Uchida . . . and he became the first canary to have his name fact-checked."

Kazuko's attitude toward Bobi's death and death in general is not typically Japanese. "For many people, life is something which is easy to give up because Japanese Buddhism promises you a better world, and suicide becomes glorified." Kazuko was exposed to the concept of poetic suicide at an early age: "We lived next to a famous figure of Meiji. He became such a pessimist, he wrote a famous farewell poem, and committed suicide by jumping to his death in the most beautiful waterfall in Nikko."

On a separate occasion Kazuko saw a casket being carried out of the house of another neighbor. "This handsome young

man died who used to come over to the house and play piano
all the time and I learned the whole phrase of *Moonlight Sonata*
from listening to him. I thought he was bitten by a dog, and
had contracted rare disease and died. Everyone, including
Mother, lined up and we watch the sad procession resulting
from this mad dog bite."

Years later, Kazuko's mother gave her the real story: enrap-
tured by her gorgeousness, the young man had asked
Kazuko's mother to leave her father. "He was totally infatu-
ated. She was a kind of Japanese Sophia Loren or Gina Lollo-
brigida—very passionate—nicknamed Japanese Scarlett
O'Hara. Her great grandfathers had contributed to Meiji—the
beginning of modern and international Japan. When denied,
this boy jumped in front of a train and committed suicide. She
was terrified, as this was the third man who had killed himself
for her. Before she married my father, two young men who
were friends of her brother fell in love with her and when denied, took their lives. There were also some who were sent to
mental institutions—with nervous breakdowns. So my life in
postwar Tokyo was adventures after adventures of death.
There was so much death I fell into thinking it was normal."

Her girlhood was not all suicides and farting cats. Like many
high-society young ladies of her generation, Kazuko was regularly sent to studio portrait photographers. Her favorite trick
was to undertake a sitting right after a ski trip. "Every young
women would prepare with skin care and beautiful coiffure.
Imagine the shock of a photographer, when I stare at the lens
like a chipmunk, or Tanuki, you know the Japanese creature?"

This sweet, chipmunkish wackiness made Kazuko the darling of the Tokyo postwar arty set. "I became an attractive pet-like person who was so mysterious and fun, and yet totally a society girl dressed also properly but with adventure in my mind." When Kazuko left the house on the weekends, her family thought their well-brought-up daughter was at the museums studying "the authorized masterpieces." Instead Kazuko would go to watch the first Japanese avant-garde action painter, Ushio Shinohara, who had "a bucket full of paint and was using his Mohican haircut as a paintbrush."

Egged on by her bohemian clique, she secretly applied for various scholarships. "The Fullbright started my new life. A chance to be me, not a daughter and then a wife, which would have caused miseries."

Kazuko arrived in New York in 1968 and began graduate study in theoretical drama at NYU. With the help of her "psychic storm," she lost no time in getting hooked up with influential and groovy people. "I became a girlfriend of Paul Ronder, an eccentric professor of film at Columbia." Unlike many wacky chicks, Kazuko is less than enthusiastic about talking about her love life. Though forthcoming about her free-form paranormal ideas, she has a geisha girl's respect for intimate emotional matters. She does however acknowledge that she was once married to the poet Abram Maguire: "In 1975 in Mobile, Alabama, and we divorced in 1982. It was a happening, avant-garde event. Just two of us, and we never told anyone till about six months later." As for Mr. Ronder, "he died young at the age of thirty-seven, in 1977 after the opening night of the New York Film Festival, from mixing drinks with longevity pills he was taking as part of a Rumanian health treatment."

Upon graduation Kazuko went to the legendary La MaMa Theatre and began work on a review called *Mink Marie*. "It was a play with a Warholesque transvestite image. I was the assistant director and assistant producer for Shuji Terayama, the most prolific Japanese avant-garde writer, poet and filmmaker, who advocated, 'Young people, throw away books, and leave home.'"

Herve Villechaize had a nonspeaking but critical role in *Mink Marie*. With a subtle little smile Kazuko recalls the memorable occasion when the little guy threw a giant hissy fit. "One day he walked out because he was not liking just being a mute tableau." The director told Kazuko to go home and come back with a Japanese kimono. Kazuko soon found herself improvising the part of a madwoman and "setting fires as revenge of lost love, dancing to the strobe." She can still remember the shocked faces of the Japanese friends who came to the show "not knowing that I was suddenly taking place of Herve Villechaize, the midget, and was a madwoman." Mr. Villechaize returned but Kazuko continued to play the part of a madwoman.

Mink Marie had a short run but her next producer gig, *The Golden Bat* at Sheridan Square Playhouse, was the summertime sensation of 1970, attracting everyone, "even Ed Sullivan with heavy pancake makeup." But after six months Kazuko was burned-out: "I went silent and took up photography."

Staying in the theatrical milieu, Kazuko shot posters for Andrei Serban and Robert Wilson. "Bob asked me to do his poster for a twelve-hour-long play called *Time and Life of Joseph Stalin*, a play before *Einstein on the Beach*." Kazuko has many happy, Dada memories of hanging out backstage at these avante garde productions "wearing layers of vintage silks and velvets and watching goats and other animals waiting for the cue."

The photography career came screeching to halt when Kazuko found out she was allergic to the developing fluids. In December 1979, chemically sensitive Kazuko, undaunted, created a series of multimedia video happenings, beginning with *Symbols Disrupted II,* using donated equipment from Polaroid and Sony. "My point was to predict the coming age of video that will change the world. I was predicting too early—no Blockbuster yet. I was told by Robert Frank, photographer and filmmaker, to do something simple and make me happy."

The quest for happiness drew Kazuko to her beloved rocks. She was no stranger to the enigmas and fascinations of semiprecious stones, having previously been a member of the geology club. "I traveled around Japan with the senior members and saw the crystals in the caves and realized that the cavemen must have felt the energy of the stones," recalls the endearingly woo-woo Miss K. without the slightest twinkle of self-consciousness. According to Kazuko's theory, these nelly Neanderthals then created the first fashion accessories: "They broke off the shining clear quartz and wrapped them with the skin of animals and wore them and they were protected by their beauty."

Inspired by her vision of glamorously accessorized cavemen, Kazuko started to create "healing scarves": stole-sized pieces of exquisite vintage fabric to which she attached crystals and beads. Selling at Robert Lee Morris and later at Barneys, Kazuko developed a cult following among rich bohemians. Her work reached a wider audience when, in 1984, she covered a white silk veil in 1930s mercury/silver glass rice beads for Madonna's "Like a Virgin" video.

She and her burgeoning high-profile clientele became more and more focused on the mystical power of the stones, which she attached to her scarves. Kazuko, who is almost psychotically generous, would dole out the stones to friends and strangers in need. "Why don't you make it so that we can wear them?" chirruped one loyal patroness, who was tired of carrying them around in her purse.

Aping the jewelers of the ancient world, Kazuko started to wrap and cage her crystals and stones with wire. "I never soldered, so no chemicals or bad energy, everything primitive. I became obsessed with making metal and stones—which are hard and solid objects—into soft and tender looking jewelry." Using shiny gold wires, she caged the raw crystals into bangles, pendants, bracelets and earrings, each unique in its design. The result is bold, funky, primitive and, according to Kazuko, quite un-Japanese: "Perhaps the reason I like to wrap stones with thin to medium-thin gold wires rather than have them set is because I don't want perfection like origami. No one is perfect except God."

The healing quotient, claims Kazuko, comes not just from the intrinsic beauty of the stones, but also from her ability to imbue her pieces "with positive energy." She creates every piece of jewelry "from my hands and heart so I must be positive. Any thoughts negative—such as anger, hatred, jealousy, greed, competition—is making the work a disaster, and a failure. Once I begin to create, it's pure joy and the wires move freely."

Kazuko is very knowledgeable about the specific powers of each stone. This information she has gleaned from the vast array of often conflicting literature on the subject. To navigate this wacky world Kazuko prefers Scott Cunningham's *Encyclopedia of Crystal, Gem and Metal Magic* and *Love Is in the Earth: A Kaleidoscope of Crystals,* by a lady named Melody. With more than fifteen years' experience under her belt, Kazuko has started to formulate her own ideas. "I believe the strongest stone still is the most available, clear quartz—it's historical and eternal. Diamonds have been corrupted by their value, which defeats their natural energy. Diamonds have to be cut— crystals are faceted by nature—diamonds are cut to resemble crystals. My jewelry is opposite of Harry Winston that one would wear at Academy Awards."

Kazuko is—it should be noted—rabidly democratic in her solicitous crystal healing and frequently doles out free pieces to people experiencing difficulties. When a cancer-afflicted Barneys alteration seamstress received a rose quartz heart from Kazuko, her family said "her life was extended few more years because of my jewelry."

Two cinematic stories from Kazuko's childhood might explain her obsessive desire to reconfigure and reunite chunks and fragments of crystal into a complete whole.

At the age of seven Kazuko borrowed her mother's Chinese jade ring. "I tripped and hit a rock. Somehow it broke into half. Mother kindly said, it was a glass, so protecting me from being upset, but the green jade is in my memory and a very sad moment of my childhood."

Later when she was learning to wash dishes "in a proper manner because I was being prepared for the *omiai* market— arranged marriage—I wash this most beautiful and perhaps the thickest cut glass salad bowl I had ever seen at the sink." The anxious bride-to-be had no idea about the nature of glass. She filled the magnificent vessel with hot water, and then cold, "and of course the bowl split with terrible crackling sound. I cried and cried and Mother said don't worry, it's just a glass. She wanted to make sure I understood material possessions were not important, but I know I never saw such a beautiful thick bowl again."

Half a century later, crystal is playing a crucial role in Kazuko's life. At the time of our meeting Kazuko is in the fourth year of her battle with toxic mold. "I was almost expiring. The mold spores mate and expand at nighttime. I am certain huge amount of the spores were trying to enter my body through my nostrils. But I sneeze, cough and my crystals— which I sleep with—are falling to the floor and waking me up. So I breathe at the window and so I am protected."

Kazuko's rocks have now become her guardian angels. "My turquoise becomes whiter when health is in danger. I know now my health is improving, as my old Tibetan turquoise suddenly shines immediately as I put it against my body, my skin." By way of a demonstration she proudly shows me her shiny blue nugget.

With the help of her crystals, Kazuko has also managed to stave off the Japanese melancholy that dogged many of the suicide-prone youth of her generation. A flying varmint was also involved.

"I became positive thinker after I was attacked by a bat and got very sick." Kazuko claims her attacker brought her a message: "Because of this bat and my crystals, I kicked the habit of negative thinking." Kazuko's new if-God-gives-you-lemons-then-make-lemonade attitude did not go unnoticed by her family. "My mother told me that positive people are called stupid in the Buddhist scriptures. They are the dragon-flies—Gokuraku Tombo— which look happy but are so silly."

With her positive attitude, Kazuko lost her fascination with dying a beautiful death and is now happily focused on survival: "I am proud to have survived toxic mold. I won't tell my age, but I will tell you that this is my personal battle." Her experience has turned her into something of a mold crusader: "Now I share the knowledge of toxic mold and all the danger of spores, pesticides and bacteria warfare."

It was a while before Kazuko fully understood her mother's challenging, borderline-insulting remarks; she was not quite sure what the Japanese Scarlett O'Hara had meant about those dragonflies. "Then one day I see a great movie, the Kurosawa epic called *Ran*. The royal court jester is dressed as a dragonfly—very happy and positive—and I decide I am happy to be a silly dragonfly."

Though Kazuko has managed to craft a full life for herself, her bad-daughter guilt still nips at her heels. She illustrates her situation with a haunting anecdote from her seemingly endless repertoire. When Kazuko's well-provenanced mother was hospitalized in Tokyo in the early 1990s, she shared a room with a stranger, whom Kazuko describes as "the grande dame of the local seaweed company." Kazuko's daily visits to the hospital allowed her to develop a passing acquaintance with this "important seaweed lady."

Kazuko's father was also in the hospital, albeit in another location—a fact that limited the amount of time she could spend with her mother. Kazuko's curtailed visits did not go unnoticed by the always attended seaweed lady: "Her daughters came morning, noon and evening. Though we talked cordially and she would generously share her daughter's hand-made lunches, she stared at me critically for not being a good daughter in the Japanese style."

The day came for Kazuko to bid her mother farewell and return to New York. When she said her good-byes to the important seaweed lady, said lady handed her a special gift. It was a box of seaweed in a shopping bag, the side of which was emblazoned with mysterious Japanese calligraphy. Kazuko thanked the lady and left to catch the train to her father's hospital. Exhausted from the stress of hospital visiting, the departing daughter dozed off.

When she awoke she idly scrutinized the side of the shopping bag: as she deciphered the brushstrokes, sleepy Kazuko turned ice cold with horror and shame. The inscription read, "Those who betray and do not take care of parents will be punished for not knowing the virtue of filial piety." "Can you imagine?" recalls Kazuko with whisper and a horrified look, more No theater than Kabuki. "While I am on the train, every Japanese can read the inscription of this shopping bag and I was an advertisement of being a bad daughter."

* * *

Kazuko is not the only dragonfly on the pond. Ever curious, wacky chicks tend not to follow any one ideology exclusively. Rather they buzz and flit, joyfully sampling and nibbling at various spiritual lily pads. They create their own little lotus blossom; they then add to and reconfigure the petals to match the ever-changing iridescence of their own frantically beating wigs. As a result, the spiritual life of every wacky chick is as unique as her fingerprint, or at least her belly button.

CHAPTER 8

THE FUTURE

The Wacky Chicklettes

There's no denying that the girls profiled thus far have all been at or around that mood swings 'n' mustaches stage. None of them will ever spit on thirty-five again. But, as you will recall if you've been paying attention, most of my girls were wacky way before their hormones started to erupt and gurgle.

If further proof were needed that wacky-chickness is not menopausally determined, you need look no farther than your local college campus or shopping mall, where a fomenting plethora of fresh young wacky chicks fills the streets and sidewalk cafés with their shrieks and protestations.

This new generation is every bit as B.R.U.N.C.H. as their elders and far more plentiful. For every Spider there are thousands of spiderettes awaiting their turn to spin that gossamer web of alluring wackiness which entrances and entraps we lesser mortals. The startling and exciting truth of the matter is that the vast majority of today's American wacky chicks are in their early twenties. They are the wacky chicklettes.

I have privileged middle-aged wacky chicks over their precocious *dauphines* simply because, with their additional mileage and experience, the older w.c.'s invariably offer more entertainingly rich life lessons than the wacky chicklettes. The latter group does not yet possess the wisdom, the wealth of anecdotes or the scars of experience that distinguish my girls. They are, however, the future of the wacky-chick movement and, as such, they deserve a chapter.

Having come of age in the turmoil of 1990s bohemia, the wacky chicklettes were raised on grunge and techno. They formulated their ideas about life while watching their elder sisters dive headlong into the mosh pit of the Riot Grrrl movement.* Their rights of passage included tongue piercing, a hit of ecstasy, a one-way ticket to the Burning Man Festival and starting a 'zine.

How do you spot a wacky chicklette? As with their w.c. elders, species identification is far from straightforward: a wacky chicklette might be dressed like a tart or a preppie, or even a cheerleader. She could be ranting about Trotsky or toxic shock. One thing is for sure, she will probably be reading somebody the riot act. Or she might even be reading *Pussy*.

P5—THE EDITOR IN CHIEF

Her name is P5 and she started her own magazine and named it *Pussy*.

Pussy's unique combo of sass and alternative detritus

---

*Riot Grrrls: this highly fecund, early 1990s girl-quake, said to have originated in punk, found expression in bands like Bikini Kill and Bratmobile, as well as in a plethora of 'zines—*Girl Germs, Satan Wears a Bra* and *Quit Whining,* to name but a few. Eradicating sexism and inequality were the primary goals. The term "Riot Grrrl" was soon corrupted and applied to any chick who snarled a lot and wore too much lipstick.

caused one reviewer to label the editor in chief "a female John Waters editing *Cosmo*." P5 found the analogy deliciously flattering, but more for the *Cosmo* part than the John Waters part. "I am very much inspired by Helen Gurley Brown," says P5. "I love her sassy style of writing. *Having It All* is my favorite book of all time. Now *Cosmo* sucks. There's plenty of sex, but it's not trashy in the right way. I miss Helen. She wanted women to use their pussy power."

Though P5 is the editor in chief of *Pussy*, she has never attended the Paris prêt-à-porter presentations. You won't find her front-row at the Christian Dior show gossiping with Andre Leon Talley or breaking bread at the Four Seasons with Oscar de la Renta. She gets no designer discounts or holiday graft from Karl Lagerfeld, and you won't see her gliding through Midtown in the back of a town car on her way to Frederic Fekkai for a quick between-appointments blowout. She's much too busy paginating *Pussy*.

Twenty-nine-year-old Pelin Morawski lives in Williamsburg, wears pastel glitter Cleopatra eye maquillage and prefers to be called P5. "It's my graffiti tag. I was into that whole graffiti scene in the 1990s until I got arrested. But I still use the name." After being "scared straight" by a gnarly prison experience, she elected to keep her tag but leave the rest of the graffiti world behind. "I went to jail for two days," explains P5 as we chat amicably in her graffiti-covered one-bedroom apartment. "I was surrounded by crackhead women throwing up. Going to the bathroom in front of forty other chicks really sucks."

The post-graffiti P5 filled me in on her background. The name Pelin, which means "seedling," was given to her by her

Turkish-born mother. From her Polish dad P5 got her Eastern European strapping good looks, and the surname Morawski. With her pale skin and boyish bleached-blonde haircut, P5 looks like a funky, glam-rock, slutty Dusty Springfield. Her unicorn-emblazoned T-shirt sports a fringe of large garish luster beads at the shoulders and hips, which rattle festively as she bops around her pad. Her T-shirt is teamed with low-slung sexy pink corduroy jeans and combat boots. This sleazily dégagé outfit, home-bleached hair, showgirl makeup ("I use stuff called Cookie Puss liquid sparkle") and garishly painted chipped nails ("Skyscraper by L'Oreal") give the general impression that P5 might be an early 1970s carnival stripper, as opposed to the editor in chief and publisher of a fashion magazine.

Technically, *Pussy* is a 'zine rather than a magazine. In P5's artsy, alternative milieu, 'zines with names like *Spit, Happyland* or *Dreemykreem* are far more common than *Elle* or *Marie Claire* or *Vogue*. Like many wacky chicklettes, P5 could never wrap her head around the regular offerings from Condé Nast and Hearst publications. "I like flashy glamour—Thierry Mugler and Versace and Alexander McQueen—but most of that Calvin Klein and Donna Karan stuff bores the shit out of me." Neither the fashions nor the lifestyles depicted in mainstream magazines ever resonated with P5's stripperish sensibility. "*Vogue* is too uptight. I was always looking for a more funky approach—not just rich people, not just society people. I mean, if I was a socialite I would dress like L'il Kim."

Cheeky, antifashion *Pussy* got started when P5 saw copies of the homemade comic book that her punky boyfriend-at-the-time was producing. "The minute I saw it, I realized that doing a 'zine would be a cool way to express myself. *Pussy* would reflect my taste."

Producing *Pussy* was more complex than P5 could have imagined: "I cut and paste the whole thing with glue sticks. No computer. One time I spilled a huge cup of soda all over it. That was a real bummer." Printing *Pussy* was equally challenging: in the early years a lot of P5's energies went into trying to meet people who had regular jobs and who could be coerced into allowing her to sneak into their place of employment and hijack the Xerox room for the evening. Despite the endless obstacles encountered by its editor/publisher, *Pussy* has just celebrated its fifth birthday. At the time of our interview, issue 10 had just hit the newsstands, and subscriptions—four issues for twenty dollars—are now available.

The cacophonous, collaged, scrappy pages of *Pussy* #10 are strewn with fiction, beauty tips, amateur cartoons and provocative vintage photos of busty babes. P5, the proud owner of an alluringly voluptuous figure herself, adores 1960s pinups like Jayne Mansfield and Betty Page: "She was an independent chick. I appreciate a woman who knows how to carry herself."

P5's powerful vixens do not preclude the inclusion of a few political rants. Like many of the wacky chicklettes I encountered, P5 is a them-and-us conspiracy theorist and proud of it. "It's easy for them to keep us in the dark," she says, becoming wackily somber. "They knew 9/11 was going to happen. It was a distraction, which they needed. I don't buy into what they spoon-feed us."

With the intention of getting P5 back onto more familiar turf—wacky chicks and chicklettes tend to engage with politics on a brayingly emotional rather a quietly analytical level—I ask her why, with her passion for La Mode, she chose magazine publishing and editing over fashion design. "I dreamed of being a fashion designer, so I went to F.I.T. [Fashion Institute of Technology]. I thought it would be this groovy creative environment but the whole scene was fake and full of shit. Everyone wanted to find the formula to be the next Calvin Klein."

P5 quit and did what any enterprising, cash-poor, wacky chicklette would have done in early 1990s New York: she became one of the now infamous club kids. "I had my own guest list at Disco 2000 at the Limelight. I got fifty bucks just to hand out flyers." The club kids were the followers of the notorious nocturnal pied piper Michael Alig, an enterprising young junkie who glued blue dots on his face and embellished and exposed his genitalia.

Allow me to explain: according to my disco-sociology research files, it all started in the early eighties, when trendy New York clubs became huge and numerous (the Palladium, the Tunnel, etc.) and there were not enough groovy people to fill them. So club owner Peter Gatien employed rent-a-freak—a.k.a. the club kids. He plied them with cash, free drink tickets and flyers and sent them out to bring hordes of wanna-be groovers to his clubs. Michael Alig was mother superior to this group of guerrilla promoters—or Charles Manson, depending on how you look at it.

Alig's world was, for a while, a fabulously safe haven for

wacky chicklettes. The club kids, male and female, were distinguished by their commitment to dada attire. No wacky chicklette could ever be reprimanded for excess in this deranged, topsy-turvy environment. Alig's disco light became a beacon to unconventional youngsters; he lured them into his hedonistic web by his screechingly high level of creative, entrepreneurial moxie. Alig gave fashion direction to the club kids with a Vreelandesque hauteur, and they took it.

P5 recalls those halcyon days: "The club kids were what I thought I would see when I went to F.I.T. They would wear anything—a toaster strapped to the head . . . pants with a butt flap. Everything was kooky, innovative, really cartoony and refreshing." There was no such thing as going too far: one wacky chicklette named Ida is fondly remembered as the daredevil who inserted a battery pack up her rectum so that she could walk around nude covered in Christmas lights. To the club kids, who frequently ran around with extension cords looking for a power outlet to plug in their outfits, Ida's mysterious power source caused far more comment than her nudity.

Faced with competition from these wacksters who thought nothing of wearing galvanized metal buckets on their feet instead of shoes, P5 felt almost like a plain Jane. "I did my best. I liked to dress silly, so I would do a Hawaiian thing or a go-go sixties thing. I would take looks that already existed and twist them to make them funny."

The chuckles stopped when many of the club kids became dope fiends, resulting in a massive increase in generalized piggy behavior. The latter was for the most part produced by the widespread addiction to ketamine hydrochloride—special

K, the animal tranquilizer and funster drug. Former club kid James St. James documented his descent into an almost permanent K-hole with great verve in his book *Disco Bloodbath*. "For almost nine months in 1990," recalls Saint James, "I wore a bloody wedding gown and glued flies to my face."

P5 was not into special K. "I tried it but I didn't like being in a K-hole. I used to drop acid instead. It really opened my mind and I have had some totally religious experiences on it."

While P5 was tripping her brains out, Michael Alig was going to the devil. On March 17, 1996, Alig and an accomplice named Freeze murdered fellow club kid Angel Melendez with a hammer and some Drano and then cut his legs off. Fortunately they put his severed bits into a cork-lined box, which floated and was found. The ghastly murder put a damper on P5's nocturnal *joie de vivre*. "I don't know what to think. I saw Michael all the time and I always thought he was nice and cute. I thought all he cared about was having a good time. I was shocked but strangely fascinated."

P5 emerged from her club kid years relatively unscathed and has constructed a creative rewarding life for herself. Like many wacky chicklettes, she is insanely multitalented or at least multiprofessioned. For starters, she plays drums in a band called Miss Pacman: "It's punk-rock but we mostly sing silly songs about our cats and about barnyard animals." She also manages a café in Williamsburg called Supercore, where her duties include curating the art and musical performances: "I love it. Occasionally we have uninvited performers. A weird white guy with afro hair kept coming in and break-dancing during lunch, which was annoying but O.K. until he puked in the bathroom with the door open in front of customers. He said he ate a bad piece of lettuce."

Miss Morawski seems very content with her life in Williamsburg. "Shit happens to me but I try not to let it destroy me. I don't have possessions but I have a sense of purpose." I ask P5 if she has any regrets about her lifelong commitment to exhibitionist fashion. "Once I tried the goth thing. I had friends who were goths. I dyed my hair black, and wore black lipstick with white makeup and listened to the Cure. I suddenly realized how goofy and played out and totally eighties it was. When I look at my goth photos, I feel like such a total idiot."

As I flipped through *Pussy* on the way home, a collaged snippet catches my eye: "A psychological study in 1995 found that three minutes spent looking at a fashion magazine caused 70 percent of women to feel depressed, guilty and shameful." Not if they're reading *Pussy*, they don't.

MARY CHRISTMAS—THE RADICAL CHEERLEADER

RIOT DON'T DIET
GET UP GET OUT AND TRY IT
RIOT DON'T DIET
GET UP GET OUT AND TRY IT
hey girl [clap clap clap]
get yer face out of that magazine
you are more than a beauty machine
you've got anger soul and more

take to the street and let it roar
RIOT DON'T DIET
GET UP GET OUT AND TRY IT
RIOT DON'T DIET
GET UP GET OUT AND TRY IT
ugh! UGH! [clap clap clap]
If Cosmo makes you sick and pale
You know what you need to do
MOLOTOV COCKTAIL!
Liberate the beauty queen
Burn the bibles of the fashion scene
LET'S [CLAP] GET [CLAP] MEAN!!!!!!!

Mary Christmas, whose real name is Emily O'Hara, recently got a call from a friend who, while watching TV in Brazil, had seen a group of Radical Cheerleaders in Quebec chanting "Riot Don't Diet," the fat-positive cheer that Mary had brilliantly penned herself in spring 2000. "Riot Don't Diet" has, much to Mary's delight, become part of the international Radical Cheerleader repertoire.

Miss Christmas herself is a shoo-in for any cheerleading squad, whether radical or otherwise. She possesses the critical combo of attributes without which great cheerleading *n'existe pas.* Being long of limb, graceful and beautiful—all of which she is—is simply not enough. Great cheerleading can occur only when the cheerleader in question possesses the ability to get insanely raucous and wild . . . on cue. Mary has that magical gift.

In her downtime Mary is—as I quickly ascertain when I

meet her at her Brooklyn apartment—almost perversely genteel and well mannered. Her anarcha-wackiness is all the
more fascinating because of its serenely stylish package. Today
she is wearing flip-flops, a knee-length denim skirt illicitly
yanked from a Salvation Army drop-off and a tank top ("I
don't call them wife-beaters—it's classist stereotyping"). As
she fills me in on her role in the Radical Cheerleaders, she re-
minds me of that smolderingly wacky thespian Sean Young.
Her vivid red hair is recovering from a recent peroxide attack.
"I went blonde recently. I got obsessed with sorority girls,"
explains Mary with a perverse giggle, "so I went for the
stereotypical cheerleader look—tennis bracelet, tan lines, etc.
Then I woke up and went ugh!"

The Radical Cheerleaders, Mary informs me, were started
in 1996 by a group of young feminists in their late teens and
early twenties who had become "tired of activism being boring and male dominated." The first Radical Cheerleader was
instigated at an anarcha-feminist gathering called Sister Sub-
verter, by the Jennings sisters, Aimee and Cara and Colleen,
and a woman named Bracken Firecracker. Mary met Bracken
at an East Village bookstore called Blackout Books. "I was
working there. I was fascinated by her because she was wearing bloody tampons strung up in her hair—she is totally out
there." Bracken, Mary tells me, has written many of the anti-
tampon cheers, hence the unorthodox hair decoration.

Issue-oriented Mary took to Radical Cheerleading like a
duck to water. Part performance, part protest, Radical Cheerleading is a spontaneous form of demonstration that can be
staged in any context. You don't need pom-poms or goofy uni-

forms. There are no costs. You just have to be irate about something.

Aficionados quickly discovered that screaming one's lungs out was, if not always effective, then at least wildly therapeutic and ragingly infectious. It spread like wildfire. In March 2001, Radical Cheerleaders from all over North America gathered in Ottawa for the first Radical Cheerleading Convention.

The goals of the movement have broadened out beyond the original feminist issues. A popular Canadian website lists them: "to eliminate patriarchy, capitalism, inequality and poverty and to live happily ever after."

There is a *joie de vivre* to this neofeminist movement, which adds hugely to its appeal. The naughty, hilarious belligerent chants that roar forth whenever Radical Cheerleaders congregate are the very essence of wacky-chickery. As is its spontaneity: a squad can be formed and trained and ready to roar in a matter of minutes. "I've started a few myself," recalls Mary with a flash of pride. "We younger girls like it because it's feminist *and* funny, which is so rare as to be thought of as a contradiction."

> *Throw those arms up in the air*
> *Let me see that armpit hair*
> *We don't shave or use that Nair*
> *Sleek and chic, we do not care.*

The not-especially-hairy Mary is one of thousands of wacky chicklettes currently residing in the various *faubourgs* of Brooklyn, New York. Skyrocketing Manhattan rents have forced thousands of chicks like Mary and P5 to colonize all kinds of improbable neighborhoods. As we chat under a peach tree in the yard behind her apartment, she gives me the anthropological dish on her hood: "This is Park Slope, which is very lesbian, which is fine with me since I'm queer identified." Does that mean Mary is gay? "I've dated women, men and transgender people, which was quite dramatic," adds Mary with an enigmatic chuckle.

Much to my disappointment, Mary is reluctant to elaborate on her trannie dalliances. She is, however, happy to talk about her nonsexual passions, of which there are many. Her proud mother, Sunny Chapman—the ex–mead wench in chapter 2, from whom Mary clearly received a fiery baptism in activism and feminism—had previously described her progeny to me as "a musician, collage artist, film/video maker, vegetarian anarcha-feminist." Mary hoots with laughter when I tell her this, but acknowledges that she does indeed have her finger in many pies. "But I'm narrowing my focus. I'm writing more now—that's why I changed my name. It was Mary Xmas. But I figure if I want to get stuff in *Ms.* magazine and the *Nation*, I should change it. So I go by Mary Christmas now. It's more formal."

Though magazine journalism is Mary's official métier, most of her time is dedicated to "grassroots political work." Miss Christmas's activism exploded at the age of fourteen when she became a model at the Next agency, and then changed her mind. "I chucked it all when I realized how sexist and exploitative the modeling thing was." I ask Mary to clarify. Was it the tortuous go-sees with leering corporate execs that skeezed her out? Her reply bespeaks a thoughtful, altruistic young mind: "Everyone wanted me to shave my armpits and be image-focused and be this girly thing. I realized that modeling is a type of sex work. But it's the most destructive, and I couldn't live with the guilt." Guilt? "Think about it," replies Mary, rallying to her topic. "It's more destructive than prostitution or exotic dancing because you become this example which is then printed in millions of fashion magazines and negatively affects other people's lives."

Fashion mags, however, are not Mary's current *bête noire*. That honor goes to street harassment. "Every day I scream at a guy who checks me out or says something. I get way too much shit on the street." Mary was part of a group called the Street Harassment Project. "It was going well until some antifeminist idiots got into our website and replaced it with a fake website called the Street Embarrassment Project—signed the Men." Despite the heinous hackers, Mary continues to do whatever it takes to make the streets of Brooklyn safe for her sisters. "I threw a beer bottle at a guy who was following me. I'm not afraid to act crazy to scare someone off."

I ask her to explain exactly what it is about being ogled and verbally harassed on the street that she finds so totally unacceptable. As a gay man, I have frequently envied those chicks who possess the mystical power to set off a torrent of admiring whistles and catcalls simply by wiggling down the Spanish Steps in a well-tailored frock and black patent slingbacks. When Raquel Welch, wearing only a crochet mini and a lion's mane bouffant, danced on the gun turret of a battleship in front of ten thousand panting G.I.'s during the Vietnam

War, guess who I was identifying with. What could be more validating to a woman—or, as in my case, a middle-aged homosexual who has seen too many 1960s Italian movies—than a roar of blue-collar adulation?

"I can tell the difference between a compliment and harassment," clarifies the catcall-worthy Mary. "It all depends on the guy's attitude. I object when the harasser has no concept that I have boundaries. He thinks that I am not a person in the way he is, so he thinks he can say whatever he wants. In other words you are just there to amuse him. He thinks he owns you."

Mary's is a raging old-school feminism—this is her particular brand of wacky-chicklettery. She is sincerely and committed to restoring the luster and credibility to the f word and the feminist movement in general. "Some girls in my neighborhood think being a feminist means reading *Jane* magazine and buying cool underwear. And they don't know their herstory at all." To Mary the early feminist lingo is precious. "I want to reclaim it." Her motivation is good old-fashioned respect. "It's a way of showing gratitude to the women who fought in the past. We wouldn't have rape crisis centers if it weren't for the original feminists. Artists like Cindy Sherman wouldn't be doing their thing if it wasn't for the Judy Chicagos of the 1970s."

Mary's feminist commitment is wackily all-embracing. "I love the S.C.U.M. Manifesto," she says, referring to the man-hating bible written by Valerie Solanas, the deranged chick who started the Society for Cutting Up Men and gained immortality when she shot a defenseless Andy Warhol at point-blank range. "Valerie was funny. I think a lot of people didn't see her humor. Andy Warhol seems like he was cool. But the other people in the Factory were mean to her."

One of Mary's equally improbable heroines is Aileen Wuornos, the raunchy Florida hooker who gained cult notoriety when, in the early 1990s, she was arrested, tried and convicted for murdering her johns, mid-hanky-panky. Prior to Miss Wuornos's 2002 execution Mary rooted for her in the best way she knew how, with a radical cheer:

> FREE [clap clap—clap clap]
> AILEEN [clap clap—clap clap]
> FREE [clap clap—clap clap]
> AILEEN [clap clap—clap clap]
> Aileen Wuornos is her name and she don't take no shit
> When some men tried to rape her, well she shot them in the
>   dick
> Now she's on death row they wanna give her the chair
> What do we say? We say GET HER OUTTA THERE!
> FREE [clap clap—clap clap]
> AILEEN [clap clap—clap clap]
> FREE [clap clap—clap clap]
> AILEEN [clap clap—clap clap]

"I don't see myself murdering anyone," says Mary, much to my relief, "but I am inspired by women like Phoolan Devi." Mary regales me with the story of the Indian woman who was gang-raped by a group of upper-caste males. She subsequently started her own gang and eventually killed every one of her rapists. "I honor this trinity of holy angry goddesses—Aileen,

Phoolan and Valerie—as cultural icons. It's a real struggle to not snap in a world that hates feminists."

Mary leaves me with a snippet from a cheer, which she has just penned:

> *We're sexy, we're cute*
> *We're feminist to boot*
> *We're angry, we're tough*
> *And we have had enough*
> *We're butchy, we're fem*
> *We're transgender girls and men*
> *We spank it [bend over] we roar*
> *We support our local whore*
> *We're here we're queer*
> *And we slept with Britney Spears*
> *Hate us 'cuz we're sex-positive*
> *Well we don't like you neither*
> *We're queer leaders!!!!!!!!!*

Brace yourself for the impact of this approaching tsunami Radical Cheerleaders and 'zine queens. Raised by the counter-culture taboo-busters of the sixties and early seventies, their biggest fear in life is, naturally, being labeled namby-pamby or prrrrrissy by their own mothers. These roaring wacklettes give every indication that they will at least outnumber if not outwacky the Sunnys and Spiders of yore. They are looking for ways to rebel and they are finding them in art and, surprisingly, in a nouvelle feminism.

Though slightly formulaic, the wackiness of grrrls like P5

and Mary Christmas is nonetheless sincere. In fact, the most fabulous aspect of the wacklette movement is the ardent commitment to making the world a better place. These post–Me Generation grrrls are altrrrruistic. How grrreat is that?

Support your local wacky chicklette. After all, they are a vaste improvement on the 1980s Gen X-ers, whose materialistic ambitions revolved around selling screenplays and, in the 1990s, generating financing for pathetically pointless dot-com ventures.

They are deeply disdainful of the pseudo-feminists amongst them, the Spice Girl bimbos who buy cheap, made in China, crochet tops at H & M to wear to a world trade demo to protest the making of cheap crochet halter tops in China. They are justifiably irate that Baby, Posh and Ginger et al. hijacked and diluted the Riot Grrrl movement and the whole notion of Grrrl Power.

CHAPTER 9

THE DARK SIDE

When Wacky Goes Wack-job

I know an old lady who swallowed a spider
that wiggled and jiggled and tickled inside her.
She swallowed the spider to catch the fly.
I don't know why she swallowed the fly.
Perhaps she'll die.

Portly folksinger Burl Ives used to scare the poo out of me with this haunting little ditty every time I heard it, which was once a week without fail. Every Saturday morning in the 1950s, televisionless kids, like *petit moi*, would gather around their huge crackly Bakelite radios to hear a croaky old senior called Uncle Mac host his radio program. Uncle Mac's offering was called *Children's Favorites*, and Burl's recording of "I Know an Old Lady" was invariably among the disc selection, which also included, but was not limited to, "The Teddy Bears' Picnic," "The Runaway Train," "Nelly the Elephant" and "How Much Is that Doggie in the Window?"

Though stripped of all sexual content, these child-appropriate songs were nonetheless surreal and, dare I say it, quite wacky. I have happy memories of bopping along with all these dada recordings, but it is Burl's kooky cantata that is forever seared into my consciousness.

Something about this folk tale, or rather everything about it, sent a shiver down my scoliotic little spine. Who was this freaky old crone who spent her days ingesting—and hopefully excreting—animals as if they were bonbons and with seemingly no pain or ill effects, and, more important, how was she dressed? In ghostly, shredded raiment like Charlotte Brontë's Mrs. Rochester, or in a crisp apricot shantung dress with matching coat and hat, like Her Maj Queen Elizabeth II? Where did she live and with whom? What made Burl's bitch tick?

Her domain was undoubtedly bucolic, hence the access to various barnyard fauna. Since songwriters Rose Bonne and Alan Mills saw fit to omit all details or description of this carnivorous old trout, my mind was left to free-associate. I searched for parallel personalities in my little universe and did not have to look far. There was no shortage of crazed females in my hometown of Reading, England, many of whom regularly swallowed extraordinary things like fish fingers and shepherd's pie, which I thought was made with real shepherd until I was eight. So why not a spider?

There was that ancient, incoherent, wraithlike chick who ran the dusty old newspaper shop around the corner from our house. She wore a stained, floaty Blanche DuBois frock, and her head was adorned with a giant hennaed Mary Pickford wig trimmed with limp, faded yellow ribbons. She hadn't had a newspaper delivery, or a bath, since the Second World War and her ancient faded fashion magazines touted foxy 1940s women with poodle hairdos on their covers. Despite the lack of currency of her offerings, she opened for business every day. She would guard the door with a broom and shriek at passersby through a haze of pink gin.

This was way before Oprahization of America, so nobody tried to stage an intervention or to rehab this unfortunate hag and extract her from the jaws of madness. We locals observed and accepted her as a bit of local color. We were like passive old Burl, who watched and strummed while the old broad "popped open her throat and swallowed a goat." The very least he could have done was to get off his big butt and offer the old lady the Heimlich maneuver, or a nice cup of tea laced with DDT, the preferred insecticide of the 1950s.

There were other crazies even closer to home than pink gin lady: our horrible and sadistic spinster schoolteachers, whose sweater sets reeked of mothballs and who vented their rages on us, turning every day into a veritable S&M session. With their pendulous breasts and tobacco breath, they thought nothing of tying us to chairs with our own skipping ropes, force-feeding us gruel or fracturing our craniums with those giant wooden pegs that held up the huge black chalkboards. I'm not complaining. After all, their crusty viciousness added a much needed dollop of drama to our rain-soaked dreary schooldays and gave us the warm and memorable camaraderie that only comes with suffering under the tyranny of a common enemy.

The shenanigans of our always-irate-for-no-particular-reason teachers paled in comparison to those of an infinitely wackier chick who was lurking even closer to home; in fact, she was *in* my home. And I'm not talking about my mother— I'm talking about my poor mad gran, who resided *chez nous*— in our front parlor, to be exact.

A cook by trade, Elsie Payne had, by all accounts, been a vibrant and risk-taking young lass. Two husbands, three kids, two world wars and one lobotomy later, she wasn't in such great mental shape.

The popular conception of a lobotomee is of a zombielike person who has been left in a barely cognizant state by his/her encounter with the surgeon's knife. Liberated from his/her paranoia and hallucinations, the lobotomized patient sits staring at a wall, an empty husk sucked dry. Not my gran. For some reason her surgery produced the opposite effect.

She sang and whistled and shrieked and banged doors, and disclosed family secrets at the drop of a hat, and at the top of her lungs. She belted out hymns and beat her carpets on the front lawn, frequently before daybreak. She had an anarchic streak that caused her to do things like disrupting the local Salvation Army Yuletide Senior Talent Show. When one old geezer got up and started singing sea shanties while accompanying himself on the concertina, Gran showed her appreciation by clamping her hands over her ears and loudly begging for mercy. She was brought home by an important-looking lady in full Salvation Army drag, complete with bonnet, who lodged a formal complaint with Betty. It was around this time that I stopped calling her Gran and reversed it to the infinitely more descriptive Narg.

Regarding Betty: like many mothers-in-law, Narg was less

than approving of her son's choice in marriage. Narg being Narg, her antipathy toward her glamorous daughter-in-law manifested itself in broad brush strokes of uninhibited behavior. Emboldened by cover of darkness, Narg would stage her anti-Betty demonstrations just at the time my sister Shelagh—abbreviated to Slag by me—and I were making our nightly teeth-brushing trip to the bathroom. My dad was invariably working a night shift and my mum was engaging in loud witty repartee with our lodgers while the TV blared. Safe in the knowledge that her stealth attacks would go undetected, Narg would leap out of her room and declare, in a theatrical *sotto voce,* "Painted face. Pretty legs. Your mother's a prostitute!"

This well-rehearsed little chant did not always come out right. One night I distinctly remember hearing her sputter, "Painted legs! Pretty face!," thereby unwittingly predicting the body-painting trend of the late 1960s.

Narg's nocturnal theatrics paralleled those of Bette Davis in the classic wacky-chick vehicle *What Ever Happened to Baby Jane.* Coincidentally, this movie was released just at the same time Narg's rants were gathering momentum. It was being reviewed and discussed in every newspaper, and on the radio. One day, while listening to a Sunday afternoon show called *Movie-Go-Round,* I heard Bette Davis tell her sister, "Blanche, we've got rats in the cellar," shortly before feeding her a fried rodent. Instead of horror, I remember experiencing a distinct feeling of relief. We weren't the only family on earth with a Baby Jane in residence.

This gave me the courage to fight back. Slag and I were

crazy about our mum. She was glamorous and fun. (Who else but Betty would have repeatedly consented to remove her teeth every morning and obligingly recite the alphabet for our amusement? By the time anything-for-a-laugh Betty got to f, g and the totally unpronounceable h, we were usually totally hysterical.)

Betty had earned our loyalty the hard way—i.e., with dentureless humiliation—and we were very sensitive to any implied criticism about her fabulous personal style, her legs or her flawless professional life. We resolved to get our own back on Narg. We crafted our revenge with Baby Janesque panache. We bloomer-bombed Narg with her own bloomers.

Narg always dried her gigantic old-fashioned knickers—known as bloomers—in the attic. One wet Wednesday, we snuck up to the attic, unpinned a few pairs and, laughing maniacally, dropped them through the three-story stairwell and onto Narg's head as she milled about on the main floor of the house. Narg shrieked and then halfheartedly castigated us.

We repeated this assault tactic on a number of occasions with the same result: no matter how successful we were, Narg never really seemed very upset about having her "essentials" used as depth charges. Her reaction seemed almost phoned in, as if she was reading from a rather dull screenplay. It was almost as if, in wacky Narg world, bloomer-bombing was a common practice and an acceptable way to communicate. I noticed the same wacky laissez-faire after the Great Immolation.

The Great Immolation—or G.I., as it came to be known—occurred during one of Narg's weekly fry-ups. Every Friday night, Narg would dump a mound of sprats (horrid little fish) into a giant seething cauldron of white-hot churning pig lard. The resulting odor perfumed the entire house. On this particular Friday night Narg had—in a rare moment of gentility—closed the door to her kitchen to contain the smell. Suddenly a gigantic fireball erupted; flames licked through the cracks and crevices of Narg's closed door and into the dining room, where my sister and I were reading the local paper and ruining our appetite for dinner by eating an entire box of Jaffa Cakes. The roar of the flames was accompanied by a halfhearted, slightly bloodcurdling scream.

"Narg is no more," I remember thinking in a *schadenfreudeish* way. Eventually the door swung open and a blackened, almost sesame-crusted Narg emerged *sans* eyebrows. Her lard had caught fire, she explained between coughs, and she had stupidly thrown water on it instead of flour. Despite the magnitude of the disaster, there was an eerie sangfroid to her reaction and quick recovery. For certified lunatics like Narg, there must be something quite comforting about concrete disasters—like bloomer-bombing and lard napalm—that can be experienced by the people around you, as opposed to the infernal cacophony in your head that is yours to enjoy *toute seule.*

Narg was a Rasputin-like survivor who was destined to fry many more sprats and lived to a ripe old age. Her life force was that of an uninhibited proto–riot grrrl who seemed capable of eating, if not a goat, then at least a ferret. And she definitely had something wiggling and jiggling and tickling inside her.

As I child, I didn't have the back story on Elsie's troubled life and her unfortunate wack-job trajectory. I knew very little about her, and much more about my other relatives. I knew, for example, that my great-aunt Flo was an amateur ventriloquist, and that I had an uncle called Vyvian and a redheaded aunt called Marigold; I was aware that my shady uncle Dave had done time; I knew that the most stable member of our household was my mum's wacky and fabulous blind friend Phyllis, who uncomplainingly lived in our stuffy attic for years with her series of Seeing Eye dogs; I knew that my uncle Kenneth, the handsome swimming pool attendant who lived on the second floor of our house, was also a paranoid schizophrenic and had suffered through electric shock treatment. But I had no idea what had caused Elsie to turn into Narg. I only knew that every time she entered the house, it was as if the circus had come to town.

While preparing this book, I prevailed upon my dad to give me the lowdown on Elsie. I was anxious to know about the origins of her insanity and to verify a suspicion that she might have gone wack-job as a result of a societal pressure to repress a functional innate wackiness.

My hypothesis was based on my recollections of the women who inhabited the grim manufacturing town of my childhood. Though fortunately not every woman in 1950s Reading had had a lobotomy, there were many who seemed unable to meet the demands of living in the latter half of the twentieth century. For every functional, composed, twinset-wearing, conforming Reading housewife, there seemed to be an irate deranged witchy figure who had . . . gone strange. Is it possible that these wretches were nothing more than derailed wacky chicks? At odds with the restraints and conventions of their day, these broads had imploded or exploded.

Deprived of a "safe space" in which to blossom into fabulousness, they went doolally instead. Like many of the homosexuals (it was still illegal) of the time, they had turned in on their blessed little selves and taken to drinking crème de menthe, the wearing of elaborate coiffures and worse.

Being of that generation that isn't so hell-bent on hanging up their dirty bloomers in public, Terry, my dad, was not particularly forthcoming with the kind of provocative material that I was looking for. He did, however, provide some interesting insights.

He recalled his prelobotomy mother being an "outgoing, enterprising young woman." Elsie had escaped the Thomas Hardy–ish toil of farm life by throwing herself into "service." She started off as house drudge and clawed her way up the *Gosford Park* hierarchy and into the kitchen to become a cook.

Elsie hung up her fancy copper-bottomed saucepans when she met and married Cecil Roy Doonan, a professional astrologer from Australia. He was a playful young man who is remembered in our family as the bloke who cheekily daubed "Auntie Nelly is a skite" on the garden shed. "He cast horoscopes by mail," recalls Terry, as if it were the most normal thing in the world, "and his customers were all in the colonies—Nigeria, Ceylon, India. He took ads out in newspapers in countries where people were more superstitious, and far away. He didn't want them coming round and demanding a refund."

I asked Terry if Elsie was *au fait* with the zodiac. "She didn't believe in it—neither did he for that matter. He had a formula, which he had learnt from his auntie Nelly. He didn't tell people he was an astrologer: he said he was a mail-order trader."

With her oddly professioned husband and growing family, 1930s Elsie was a modern girl who had loads of girlfriends—other chicks she had met in service—and always extended a helping hand to the other struggling folk in their Cardiff neighborhood. To Terry she was a caring mom in a clean pinny who, though not extrovertly wacky, was happy to indulge his eccentric appetite for painstakingly prepared tomato-seed sandwiches. Despite the familial closeness, Terry was not tied to Elsie's apron strings. "Elsie let us run all over Cardiff and neighboring Splot—that's where Shirley Bassey is from—disappearing for the whole day. Our parents didn't have to worry. This was back when men had work to do. They didn't have time to become perverts even if they were so inclined."

The rambling good times ground to a halt when Roy Doonan got depressed, scarfed down a bunch of pills in a woodland glade and said good-bye to the world. Elsie was understandably blue. The war loomed. Elsie got bluer; a disappointing second marriage added to her misery. Eventually she started hearing voices and began the sad transformation into Narg.

Prelobotomy Elsie was not, as would have suited my hypothesis, a wacky chick. Her descent into madness was attributed by professional shrinks to a predisposition toward schizophrenia. But there was another obvious factor: money. A few shekels could have insulated her from the emotional and practical repercussions of her husband's suicide, single parenting in the tail end of the Depression and the imminent Armageddon of the Second World War. A posh lady, or even a middle-class lady, would have been left to wander round her garden sniffing peonies and talking to the fairies. Poor Narg had no such luck.

Despite Terry's account of his hardworking, troubled, unwacky parent, I can't help thinking that a bit of B.R.U.N.C.H. would have enabled her to externalize her pain. Women like Elsie had it rough—prefeminist ladies were constrained to don the mantle of wifely duty even in the face of personal devastation and grinding poverty. There was a very low societal tolerance for eccentricity among working women. Just like the men whom Terry said were too busy to become perverts, Elsie was too busy to cultivate a multifaceted self. These overburdened chicks would eventually start swigging the cooking sherry or, worse still, implode completely like Narg. If society had cut Elsie a bit more wacky slack, maybe Narg would never have arrived.

Though we live in a wacky-positive era, there seems to be no shortage of high-profile chicks who make the Narg-like transition from wacky to wack-job. Who would have thought fresh-faced, former lesbian thespian Anne Heche would end up dehydrated in somebody's backyard in Fresno, speaking an alien language and waiting for a spaceship to spirit her away to heaven? But she did.

A million names spring to mind from the pages of the *Na-*

tional Enquirer: Claudine Longet,* Margot Kidder, Anna Nicole Smith (the racky wacky chick) and Carnie Wilson (the snacky wacky chick). And the patron saint of celeb wacky chicks, Carrie Fisher, whose well-documented addictions and freak-outs have provided a validating beacon for a generation of wacky-to-wack-jobbers. Miss Fisher and her ilk have proven that, despite all the yoga and pilates and primal screaming, it takes effort and good luck not to lose one's gourd.

The plain truth is that being a wacky chick means walking that wacky/wack-job knife-edge. But how does a girl stay on the right side of the wacky tracks? How can she channel her obsessions and compulsions into positive endeavors?

Joan Crawford–esque obsessive-compulsive behaviors are common among wacky chicks: the trick is to do as Mommie Dearest did, and divert them into a hobby. Her particular pas-

---

*When belligerence becomes a wacky chick's dominant trait, she can become dangerously wack-job—e.g., Lizzie Grubman and Claudine Longet. For those of you not familiar with the latter, here goes: Claudine Longet has two claims to fame—her performance in the 1968 Blake Edwards film *The Party*, costarring Peter Sellers, and her 1976 snuffing-out of professional skier Spider Sabich.

Parisian Claudine Longet was a Las Vegas showgirl when bland-but-fab-in-retrospect crooner Andy Williams saw her having car trouble, pulled over and married her. Claudine and the kids became regulars on Andy's incredibly twee, early 1960s Christmas specials. A recording career followed: haunting covers of pop hits sung in a wackily, ethereal voice that gave no hint of the *horrors* to come. The piss-taking notes on her *The Very Best of Claudine Longet* CD describe her as being "among the precious few who can effectively deliver a song with near-whispers." Highly recommended, by *moi*, for wistful *après*-ski ambience.

It wasn't until after she'd left Williams, however, that Claudine really got famous. In 1976, she shot and killed champion skier Vladimir (Spider) Sabich, her longtime boyfriend. After a highly publicized murder trial, Ms. Longet was convicted of criminal negligence and sentenced to thirty days in jail; one third the jail time received by the excitable Lizzie Grubman after she mowed in reverse over sixteen people in her S.U.V.

time was cleaning. It took a while for the Oscar-winning Joan to graduate from cracking her daughter Christina over the head with Bon Ami containers to finding more functional ways to manifest her obsession with germs, but by the time she was living in New York in the 1960s she had succeeded.

"There were more objects wrapped in plastic in Joan's apartment than in an A&P meat counter," recalled her New York decorator, Carlton Varney, in his memoir. In Joan's wacky pad, furniture and lamp shades were all protected against the sooty metropolis: she covered her windowsills in removable fitted sheets of easy-to-clean white plastic laminate. Guests were asked to remove their shoes upon arrival, and Joan herself wore floor-protecting, rubber flip-flops. She always carried a box of Kleenex with her in case her pooches pooped on the floor.

Mr. Varney dismisses analytical theories about Joan's fastidiousness, claiming that she simply "enjoyed being neat, clean and tidy" and that "her mania never prevented her from living well. If you disregard the bother of having to 'break the seals' on rising from a plastic-covered couch in warm weather."

As a former compulsive hand washer (my nickname for several years was Lady Macbeth), I understand Joan's behavior and applaud her for having found a constructive outlet for her neuroses. I am a proponent of both cleanliness and the therapeutic benefits of carefully managed obsessive behaviors. When the hand washing ceases to be anxiety-reducing, that is the time to worry. That's when wacky goes wack-job.

Regarding hand washing: a psychotherapist once told me that this particular compulsion was traceable, albeit indirectly, back to my grandmother's lobotomy. He posited that being raised among mentally disturbed individuals makes a child strive to avoid "catching" the afflictions of those around him. My hand washing was apparently a gesture of psychological self-protection. It must have worked because I haven't gone bonkers . . . yet.

But hand washing alone will not keep a wacky chick out of the nuthouse. A girl needs a creative outlet: Joan had her acting, Brigid has her needlepoint, Spider has her geckoes and Pearl has her rockabilly. These all-consuming creative endeavors can mean the difference between functional wackiness and raging insanity. Trust me, I've been there.

For thirty years I have channeled my obsessions and neuroses into my window-dressing career, with only positive results. Who has time to go nuts—or become a pervert—when you have relentless weekly window changes to worry about?

The level of creativity that I have been able to exhibit in my window displays is a function of my wacky sensibility, which is in turn a function of my wacky background. The wacky background produced the compulsion to create while at the same time informing the creative sensibility and content thereof. In other words, growing up wacky was a totally groovy positive thing, one from which I have benefited enormously. That's why you won't find me—or any of my girls—uttering victimy complaints about the drawbacks of living in a dysfunctional family.

We don't do victim.

I happen to think that I was hugely enriched by growing up with both wacky chicks and wack-jobs. And my compulsive hand washing was merely a sign that I, like Joan, had discovered the joys of germ-free living.

CONCLUSION

From the fourteen wacky chicks profiled in this book (sixteen if you count Betty and Narg), few common denominators emerge. They love Howard Stern, Elvis and Ayn Rand, but not necessarily in that order. Some vote for the Democrats, some voted for Reagan and some haven't read a newspaper since—but not because—Claudine Longet shot her ski instructor.

Three out of sixteen of my wacky chicks are redheads; one third are well above average height and one fifth—Sunny, Lisa and Kazuko—believe they can communicate with birds. Bizarre correlates may well exist, but unfortunately, due to the small size of my sample, it is impossible to do anything other than celebrate the fact that, finally, they are *here*!

More than thirty years ago, a wacky Australian prophetess foretold the coming of the wacky chick. "The world will not change overnight, and liberation will not happen unless individual women agree to be outcasts, eccentrics, perverts and whatever else the powers-that-be choose to call them." Thus spoke Germaine Greer in her epoch-making, hilariously pungent feminist screed *The Female Eunuch*.

When they leapt from the margins of society and into the spotlight, my wacky chicks were all subjected to the slings and arrows of a disapproving society. They were called perverts and much worse, but they held their heads high and carried on regardless. In doing so, they paved the way for a more liberated future and for the wapidemic that is now making its impact on our culture.

Wacky chicks of all hair colors are thriving. They are blooming in the current humid climate of our postfeminist, Bobos in Paradise, anything-goes, shagging-on-television, permissive world. Now, in the louche twenty-first century, *Wackus chickimus* has the optimal conditions to hatch and stagger out into the daylight, without the kinds of struggles that Kazuko and Brigid and Sunny encountered during their formative years. Like the endangered Madagascan geckoes that Spider breeds with such care, young wacky chicks now flourish because their older sisters have fought for and established new levels of acceptance. *Bravo*, girls!

So take advantage of the good work done by the courageous broads who have poured forth their wisdom and frivolity into this book. Release the wackiness within you.

Set yourself some achievable goals. You don't have to keep a Honduran iguana in your kitchen to qualify as a wacky chick. Just because you never lived in a storage locker, or tried to throttle your boss, or demonstrated outside an abortion clinic dressed as Satan, it doesn't mean you can't join the club. If you measure yourself against Kazuko or Mary Christmas, you may never get off the ground.

Use Betty or Auntie Mame as your role models rather than

my gang of jolly extremists. They had kids and chores and mundanities to deal with. Their lives, like yours, had a totally normal framework, but within that structure they approached each quotidian task with a wacky chick's panache and originality.

You may never wear porno heels from the Pigalle, dye your hair lemon yellow or attend a swinger convention in slashed spandex. You may never experience the urge to dress like Sammy Davis or fill your apartment with jeweled tortoises. That doesn't mean you can't wacky-up your life a bit. The fact that you are not inclined to perform macrobiotic dinner theater, make art with your breasts or wear a Winn Dixie uniform in no way disentitles you from your share of the wacky pie.

To kick-start your new B.R.U.N.C.H.-y self, try the following simple exercises:

1. Give everyone in your family a roll of tinfoil and demand that they create a headdress to wear to Saturday night dinner. Offer a corny Erma Bombeck–type prize—e.g., no cleanup duties—to the creator of the best headdress.

2. Throw out all the inspirational "Successories" plaques in your office. Give everyone infantile, alliterative nicknames based on their shortcomings and have desk plates made for each name (e.g., Contentious Cora, Nicotine Norman or Long-winded Lurline).

3. Invent a new stupid game every week. Jonathan Adler (my partner) and I like to invent insulting and sadistic

games when we are on vacation. Last year I invented the best game, which was called "Soothing or Annoying?" It's quite simple: You think of the most heinously un-soothing thing you can do—e.g., grinding the mesh of a tennis racket into the end of your partner's nose. Then, while applying the tennis racket, you ask your partner, "Soothing or annoying?" They win or lose, depending on how long they can endure the pain and maintain the lie that it feels "soothing."

4. Give names to the rooms in your house. If cheesy banquet rooms in moderate hotels deserve names, why not the rooms in your lovely home (e.g., Guinevere, Lancelot or Zsa Zsa)?

5. When a family member takes a nap, utilize the opportunity to noiselessly create lurid or grotesque tableaux around the sleeper. Record your efforts on film, and embarrass the victim with the results at a carefully chosen later date. Make sure the tableaux have strong, visibly discernible themes (e.g., "Folksy Sing-along", "Medieval Religious Persecution" or "A Night in a Victorian Brothel").

Honing and developing your wackiness may take a while. Osmosis can speed things up. Therefore, go find yourself a fully actualized wacky chick, share her flights of fancy and applaud her outbursts. Becoming a wacky-chick hag will facilitate your own transformation from Nora Normal to B.R.U.N.C.H.-y broad. Surround yourself with wacky chicks, cultivate them as friends, inaugurate a w.c. salon, take one out to dinner and spoil her. Feeling special, as you have no doubt gathered by now, is extremely important to a w.c., so give her the movie star treatment. Remember that she, far more than any movie star, actually deserves it.

And if, once your own wacky-chickery emerges, you don't quite reach the apocalyptic heights of P5 or Spider, don't reproach yourself. Not every w.c. has what it takes to run off and join the circus, but there is plenty of room for all my girls under that big top.

P.S.: Re my inclination for a sex change: at the moment it seems to be fairly dormant. But if I were to get the chop, you bet your sweet bippy that I would want to be just like Isabel or Brigid or Janet, or Kazuko or Spider or Lisa or Susanne. . . .